Literacy Roots:
Nurturing Your Child's Reading Journey from Birth to Brilliance

By
Lauren Daugherty

LITERACY ROOTS NURTURING YOUR CHILD'S
READING JOURNEY FROM BIRTH TO BRILLIANCE

Copyright © 2024 by LAUREN DAUGHERTY

All rights reserved. No part of this book may be reproduced or transmitted in any form or by any means without written permission from the author.

979-8-3305-5368-6

Printed in the USA by Ingram Spark

Table of Contents

Dedication: Page 4
Author's Note: Page 5
Introduction: Page 7
Chapter 1: The Literacy Crisis: Understanding the Challenge, Page 9
Chapter 2: Parents as First Teachers: The Foundation of Literacy, Page 36
Chapter 3: The Home Literacy Environment: Setting the Stage for Success, Page 61
Chapter 4: Beyond Reading: Comprehensive Literacy Skills, Page 90
Chapter 5: School-Home Connections: Building Strong Partnerships, Page 114
Chapter 6: Navigating the Challenges: Addressing Literacy Difficulties, Page 147
Chapter 7: Cultural Literacy: Honoring Diverse Practices, Page 179
Chapter 8: Digital Literacy: Navigating the Online World, Page 201
Chapter 9: Literacy for Life: Developing 21st Century Skills, Page 236
Chapter 10: Community Matters: Leveraging Local Resources, Page 267
Chapter 11: The Future of Family Literacy: Innovations and Trends, Page 294
Chapter 12: Empowered Parents and Lifelong Readers, Page 337
Endnotes: Page 372
Index: Page 376

Dedication

To my husband, whose unwavering support and encouragement made this book possible. Your belief in me gave me the courage to share these ideas with the world.

To our children, who inspired every page of this book and taught me more about literacy, learning, and love than any research ever could. You are my greatest joys.

To my parents, who pushed me to be the best version of myself and were endearingly patient with my questions. You both shaped who I am today.

And to Matthew O'Brien, whose editorial guidance transformed this manuscript from a dream into reality. Your insight, expertise, and dedication helped clarify these pages.

Above all, to the Lord, who blessed me with the gifts and courage to write this book and surround me with the people who made it possible. Your divine guidance and grace sustained me through every step of this journey. As Joshua 1:9 reminds us: "Have I not commanded you? Be strong and courageous. Do not be afraid; do not be discouraged, for the Lord your God will be with you wherever you go."

This book is a testament to the power of family in fostering literacy, and I am profoundly grateful to have such an extraordinary family of my own.

With deepest gratitude,
Lauren

Author's Note

Every journey begins with a single step. My journey to writing *Literacy Roots* began in the most personal of places—my own home. As a parent, I have witnessed firsthand the transformative power of literacy and how early exposure to books, stories, and language will spark a lifelong love of learning. I also observed the struggles children can face when they do not receive strong literacy support from the start.

The contrast is haunting. Some children soared through their reading journey while others stumbled. The achievement gap in literacy was not due to differences in children's natural abilities; instead, it reflected unequal access to literacy resources, learning opportunities, and educational support. This realization became my call to action. Drawing from my experience and research, I set out to create a resource I wish I had as a young parent.

Literacy Roots is more than a book about teaching children to read. It is a guide, a tool kit, and (hopefully) a source of inspiration for families to develop a home where literacy flourishes. This book is designed to grow with your child, beginning with the foundations of early language development and progressing through advanced literacy skills, offering age-appropriate strategies, examples, and practical exercises focusing on how to create a literacy-rich home, navigating digital literacy, and how to support struggling readers and celebrating milestones.

Why is this book needed now more than ever? In our fast-changing world, strong literacy skills are vital. They are not only academic achievements but essential life tools, the keys to opportunity that lay the foundation for critical thinking abilities that build the bridges to understanding our complex world. My goal is to illuminate this process, and with some effort, hopefully, every parent can nurture their children's literacy skills, no matter their own education or reading habits. I believe that literacy is a gift we can give our children that will enrich their lives forever, opening doors to opportunity, understanding, and joy.

This book is my contribution to helping children understand their opportunities in this world and to assisting families in making dreams a reality. Whether you are just beginning your journey with a newborn or want to support an older child's developing skills, I hope you will find in these pages the guidance, encouragement, and practical tools you need to help your child develop strong roots in literacy that will support a lifetime of learning and success.

Together, let us set out on this fundamental journey of nurturing literacy from birth to brilliance!

—Lauren Daugherty (November 2024)

Introduction

Think of your child's first steps into literacy. It does not start with their first word or when they pick up a pencil; it begins much earlier. It happens in those quiet moments when you read them a bedtime story, in their giggles during peek-a-boo games, and in their wide-eyed wonder at picture books. These everyday moments, while seemingly small, are building blocks for their future.

Today's world of literacy is not what it was when we were kids. Sure, reading and writing are still key, but there is more to it now. Our children need to understand websites and figure out what information they can trust, think deeply about what they read, and share their ideas in many different ways. These skills are not just for getting good grades—they are essential for success in life.

I know it can feel overwhelming. As a parent, I have repeatedly heard the same questions: When is the right time to start? What really works? How do we balance books and screens? What if my child struggles with reading? How do we find time for it when life gets busy?

That is why I wrote *Literacy Roots*—to help answer these questions and many more.

This book walks you through your child's literacy journey, from their first baby books to their independent reading adventures. Here are a few key topics we will cover:

- Today's literacy landscape and your crucial role as your child's first teacher
- How to fill your home with literacy opportunities and build essential skills

- Working with schools and helping kids who struggle
- Cultural connections and digital literacy
- Modern skills and community support
- The future of literacy and creating a lasting impact

Each chapter combines research-tested strategies with real stories from families like yours. You will find practical activities to try, solutions to common problems, and ways to celebrate your child's progress. I have also included plenty of resources for when you want to dig deeper.

There is no one-size-fits-all approach to literacy. The strategies in this book are meant to be tailored to fit your family's unique background and needs. Whether you are cuddling with your newborn and a board book or helping your fifth grader with reading challenges, you will find ideas that work for you. We will help you focus on making your home a place where your child's eyes light up at the sight of books, their questions spark exciting discoveries, and learning happens naturally in everyday moments. Those bedtime stories, conversations about new words, and cozy reading sessions on the couch will add up to something remarkable in your child's life.

You know your child best, and you have what it takes to guide their literacy journey. Think of this book as a friendly conversation with someone who has been there, done that, and is doing it all over again. I am here to share what has worked for me and many other parents, offer encouragement when things get tough, and celebrate your successes along the way.

Chapter 1 examines today's literacy challenges and why family involvement matters more than ever. Let us get this adventure started!

Chapter 1: The Literacy Crisis: Understanding the Challenge

Overview
"The man who does not read has no advantage over the man who cannot read." These words, attributed to Mark Twain, echo with newfound urgency in our information age. The literacy crisis—a term that might seem paradoxical in our text-saturated world—quietly shapes destinies, economies, and societies. What exactly constitutes literacy in the 21st century? How has its definition evolved, and why does it matter more than ever?

In this chapter, we will explore the current state of literacy, its wide-ranging impacts, and the various factors contributing to the current literacy challenge. We will also look at parents' important role in addressing this issue while acknowledging that it's just one piece of a much larger puzzle.

Defining literacy in the 21st century
When we talk about literacy today, we're not just referring to the ability to read and write. As technology swiftly advances, literacy has taken on a much broader meaning. Think of it as a Swiss Army knife of skills that allows us to navigate our information-rich world.

So, what does 21st-century literacy look like? It's a combination of several key competencies:
1. Foundational literacy: The basics of reading, writing, and numerical understanding

2. Digital competence: The ability to use and adapt to new technologies and digital tools
3. Information literacy: Knowing how to find, evaluate, and use information analytically
4. Multimodal communication: Interpreting and creating meaning through various forms of media
5. Critical thinking: Analyzing, synthesizing, and problem-solving in digital environments
6. Cultural and ethical awareness: Understanding responsible digital citizenship and cross-cultural communication

This expanded definition reflects the dynamic nature of our digital world. Simply reading words on a page is no longer enough; we need to be able to critically engage with a vast array of information sources and communicate accurately across multiple platforms.

Modern literacy encompasses:
- Basic literacy: Reading and writing
- Digital literacy: Using technology to access, evaluate, and create information
- Media literacy: Analyzing and creating various forms of media
- Information literacy: Locating, evaluating, and effectively using necessary information

Digital literacy is the ability to effectively and judiciously navigate, evaluate, and create information using various digital technologies. It encompasses:
1. Technical skills: Using various digital devices, software, and platforms

2. Information literacy: Knowing how to search for, judge, and use information on computers and the internet
3. Media literacy: Analyzing and creating digital media content.
4. Communication and collaboration: Effectively using digital tools to interact and work with others
5. Digital citizenship: Understanding online safety, ethics, and responsible behavior in digital environments
6. Problem-solving: Using digital tools to address challenges and create innovative solutions

Reflection Question: How many of these literary skills do you use in your daily life?

The Current Literacy Landscape

Despite global progress, the numbers are sobering. A 2019 UNESCO report revealed that 773 million adults and young people worldwide lack basic literacy skills. The economic impact is staggering. A study by the World Literacy Foundation estimated that low literacy costs the U.S. economy a whopping $362 billion annually. That's a billion with a "B," folks. To put it in perspective, that's more than the entire GDP of countries like Denmark and Israel.

Economic Breakdown of Low Literacy Costs

To better understand this $362 billion annual cost, we can break it down into key components:

1. Lost Productivity: Approximately $225 billion, or 62% of the total cost, stems from reduced workplace efficiency. Employees with low literacy skills often struggle to perform tasks effectively, leading to lower output and missed opportunities for innovation.
2. Healthcare Expenses: Around $73 billion, accounting for 20% of the total cost, arises from the correlation between low literacy and poorer health outcomes. Individuals with low literacy skills tend to have higher healthcare use rates, which drives up costs for both individuals and the healthcare system.
3. Unemployment and Welfare Costs: Roughly $47 billion, or 13% of the total cost, relates to increased unemployment and reliance on social services. Those with low literacy skills face more significant challenges in securing stable employment, leading to higher rates of underemployment and dependence on welfare programs.
4. Criminal Justice System Costs: About $17 billion, or 5% of the total cost, is associated with higher incarceration rates among individuals with low literacy. This connection underscores the need for effective literacy programs to help reduce crime and recidivism.

The Power of Literacy: An Investment in Our Future

Imagine a world where everyone has the ability to read, write, and fully participate in society. Literacy is a personal skill and a driving force for national prosperity. Studies show that when nations invest in literacy, the return is extraordinary—both economically and in society's overall well-being.

One of the most compelling pieces of evidence for the value of literacy is its impact on the economy. For every dollar invested in adult literacy programs, the economy sees a return of $7.14. Improved literacy opens doors to better jobs, higher incomes, and increased spending. When individuals have strong reading and writing skills, they contribute more effectively to the workforce, leading to higher productivity and, in turn, economic growth.

Research suggests that even a modest improvement in literacy rates can profoundly affect the economy. If literacy rates were to increase by just 1%, labor productivity could rise by 2.5%, and GDP per capita could grow by 1.5%. These numbers might seem small, but they translate into billions of dollars in a national economy.

However, the case for literacy extends far beyond its economic benefits. Low literacy levels impact a wide range of societal issues. Poor literacy skills are often linked to higher healthcare costs as individuals struggle to understand medical information or instructions. People's inability to navigate job applications or government forms stretches social services thin. The criminal justice system is also affected, with low literacy rates being a predictor of higher crime rates.

These ripple effects show that literacy is more than just an educational issue—it is a foundational social and economic health pillar. By addressing literacy, we invest long-term in a more prosperous, equitable society.

Literacy rates vary significantly across the globe. UNESCO reported in 2023 that the global adult literacy rate was 87.5%, which hides vast differences between regions. While the United States fares better than many countries, it still trails behind other developed nations. This disparity underscores the urgency of tackling the literacy gap at home and abroad.

Literacy is not just a skill; it is an engine for growth, a means of breaking cycles of poverty, and a pathway to stronger communities. The benefits of investing in literacy are clear and extend far beyond the classroom. Investing in literacy must be a top priority if we want a future of shared prosperity.

Let's explore in detail how literacy levels affect health outcomes, economic stability, and social participation.

Health Impacts
Low literacy significantly affects health outcomes. A 2023 meta-analysis published in the *American Journal of Public Health* showed that individuals with low health literacy are 1.8 times more likely to experience poor health outcomes and 2.3 times more likely to misunderstand medical instructions. This leads to higher rates of hospitalization and chronic disease. For example, patients with low literacy might misinterpret medication dosages or not follow preventive health measures, resulting in more frequent and severe health issues.

While literacy levels significantly affect health outcomes, the economic repercussions are equally profound. Low literacy skills can severely limit an individual's financial prospects and contribute to broader economic challenges.

Economic Impacts
Low literacy rates have substantial economic consequences. The World Literacy Foundation (2018) estimated that illiteracy costs the global economy approximately $999.36 billion annually. Low literacy in the United States leads to an estimated $362 billion in annual costs due to lost productivity, increased healthcare expenses, and higher unemployment rates. Low-literacy individuals often face limited job opportunities, lower incomes, and increased dependence on social welfare programs.

Beyond health and economic impacts, low literacy levels can also hinder an individual's ability to engage in society fully. Let's consider how literacy affects civic engagement and social integration.

Crime and Social Issues
Recent research has shed new light on the relationship between literacy and social engagement. A 2022 study published in the *Journal of Education and Human Development* revealed some interesting findings. The study showed that individuals with higher literacy levels are significantly more likely to be active members of their communities.

Specifically, the study found that:
- People with higher literacy levels are 40% more likely to participate in community activities.

- These individuals are also 60% more likely to vote in elections.

These findings suggest that literacy plays a critical role in fostering civic engagement and strengthening democratic processes. Higher literacy levels seem to empower individuals to participate more actively in shaping their communities and participating in the political system.

It's important to note that the relationship between literacy and social engagement is complex. Research from the National Institute of Justice in 2003 showed a strong correlation between low literacy and higher crime rates. However, this connection is influenced by various factors, not just literacy alone. Low literacy can limit economic opportunities, leading some individuals toward criminal activities. However, we must consider this information in the broader context of socioeconomic influences rather than oversimplifying the link between literacy and crime.

Despite these complexities, low literacy continues to contribute to social isolation and difficulties in navigating societal systems. However, the recent findings on increased community participation among those with higher literacy levels indicate that improving literacy could be a powerful way to enhance social cohesion and integration.

To understand the personal toll of these challenges, let's consider a hypothetical case study:

Case Study: John's story
John, now 35, grew up in a low-income neighborhood with scarce educational resources. His parents, working multiple

jobs to make ends meet, had limited time to support his early education. In school, John struggled with reading, but his difficulties went undiagnosed. Feeling ashamed, he began avoiding reading-intensive tasks, further hampering his literacy development.

By high school, John's reading skills were far below grade level. Frustrated and convinced he couldn't succeed academically, he dropped out at 16. The lack of a high school diploma and weak literacy skills limited John's job prospects. He cycled through several low-paying jobs, never earning enough to achieve financial stability.

At 28, John was diagnosed with type 2 diabetes. However, his low literacy made it challenging to understand his condition and follow treatment plans. He often misinterpreted medication instructions and struggled to read nutritional information, leading to poor disease management and frequent hospitalizations.

John's financial instability and health issues strained his personal relationships. Embarrassed about his reading difficulties, he avoided social situations that might expose his challenges. This isolation further limited his opportunities for personal and professional growth.

Now, John is trapped in a cycle of poverty and poor health. His low literacy continues to affect every aspect of his life—from his ability to advance in his career to managing his health and participating fully in his community.

John's story illustrates how low literacy can have cascading effects throughout an individual's life, affecting health, economic opportunities, and social integration. It's a stark reminder of why addressing this issue is so crucial.

The Intergenerational Cycle of Literacy

Picture a world where two-thirds of our children struggle to read at grade level. It sounds like dystopian fiction, doesn't it? Here's the kicker: It's our reality. The 2019 National Assessment of Educational Progress report dropped this bombshell, revealing that only about a third of our fourth and eighth-graders are reading proficiently. It's a wake-up call, folks, and the alarm's been ringing for generations.

We are dealing with what experts call the intergenerational cycle of literacy, a fancy term for a vicious cycle that's as stubborn as it is devastating. Parents who struggle with reading raise kids who struggle with reading, who then grow up to be parents who...well, you get the idea. It's like a literacy version of *Groundhog Day* but far less entertaining. Now, you might be wondering, how does this happen? It's a perfect storm of factors. Parents with limited literacy skills often can't create that cozy, book-filled home environment we all idealize. Bedtime stories? Homework help? It's a challenge when you're grappling with the words yourself. And let's not forget the economic angle; low literacy often walks hand in hand with low income, which means fewer educational resources. A domino effect can topple a family's educational aspirations for generations.

But here's where it gets serious: This isn't just about report cards and reading logs. The ripple effects of low literacy spread far and wide. We're talking about unemployment, poverty, and limited civic engagement—the works. Literacy is the secret ingredient to a functioning society; we're running dangerously low on stock.

What's the solution? Well, if it were simple, we wouldn't be having this conversation. Experts agree it's going to take a village—literally. We need early intervention programs that catch kids before they fall behind. We need family literacy initiatives that boost parents' skills alongside their children. We need communities to step up, with libraries and local organizations creating literacy-rich environments. Let's not forget that our teachers need the training and tools to tackle this head-on.

You may be thinking, why should I care about all this? Because this isn't just someone else's problem. It's a societal issue that affects us all. Whether you're a parent, teacher, policy maker, or concerned citizen, this is your wake-up call. The cycle of low literacy isn't just holding back individuals or families but our entire society. The good news? Knowledge is power. By understanding this cycle, we can start to break it. We can advocate for better education policies, support literacy programs in our communities, and recognize the signs of struggle in our own circles. Because here's the truth: Literacy isn't just about reading words on a page. It's about understanding our world, participating in our democracy, and reaching our full potential as human beings.

Whenever you open a book or help a child figure out a tricky word, you do something significant. You are not just reading; you are helping to address a problem that has persisted for too long. As we spread the love of reading, you're writing a new chapter in our society's story, and that's pretty amazing when you think about it!

Multifaceted Causes of Literacy Issues

While parental involvement plays a crucial role in literacy development, it's essential to recognize that several other vital factors significantly impact literacy outcomes. Let's explore these factors:

1. Socioeconomic Factors: It's no secret that a child's socioeconomic background can profoundly influence their literacy journey. Imagine two children starting school—one from a low-income family and another from an affluent background. The differences in their early literacy experiences can be stark. The child from a low-income family may have had limited access to books, educational toys, or enriching experiences that foster early reading skills.
2. Education System Challenges: Now, consider the schools these children might attend. Schools in low-income communities often grapple with limited resources. Think about the impact of having fewer experienced teachers, outdated textbooks, or understocked libraries. It's like trying to build a house with an incomplete toolbox—possible but much more challenging.
3. Learning Disabilities: Learning disabilities further complicate the path to literacy for some children. Imagine trying to decipher a code where the symbols keep shifting—that's what reading can feel like for a child with dyslexia or other learning challenges. These students may struggle without early identification and targeted support throughout their educational journey.

4. English Language Learners: Consider the complexity of learning to read in a language you're still mastering. This is the reality for many English-language learners. They're not just learning to read; they're learning to read in a new linguistic landscape. It's akin to learning to swim while navigating unfamiliar waters.
5. Systemic Inequalities: How does a school's zip code impact students' literacy outcomes? Schools in wealthier areas often have more resources per student, creating a cycle where affluent communities produce stronger readers, contributing to keeping that affluence.
6. Early Literacy Gaps: Picture two high school freshmen sitting side by side. Would you believe that, on average, a student from a low socioeconomic background might be reading at a level five years behind his or her peer from a high-income family? This stark difference underscores the critical importance of early intervention in literacy development.
7. Digital Divide: In our increasingly digital world, access to technology is becoming as crucial as access to books. Yet, for many low-income students, computers and internet access remain out of reach at home. This digital divide can significantly affect their ability to develop the literacy skills necessary for success in the 21st century.
8. Health and Nutrition: People often say a healthy body supports a healthy mind. This adage holds true for literacy development as well. Poor nutrition and

health issues, more prevalent in low socioeconomic communities, can change cognitive development and, consequently, literacy skills. It's a vicious cycle—lower health literacy often leads to poorer health outcomes, hindering educational achievement.
9. Cultural and Linguistic Diversity: Lastly, let's consider our schools' rich tapestry of cultures and languages. While diversity is a strength, it can also present challenges in literacy development. Students whose home language or cultural literacy practices differ significantly from those emphasized in school may face other hurdles in their literacy journey.

Addressing the literacy crisis requires a nuanced understanding of these intersecting factors. It's not just about teaching children to read; it's about creating an environment where every child, regardless of their background, has the opportunity to become a strong, confident reader. We can create a better future by directly addressing these problems to make reading and writing available to everyone.

The Role of Parents in Addressing the Literacy Crisis

In the face of widespread literacy challenges, parents emerge as pivotal figures in shaping their children's reading abilities and overall educational trajectory. While formal education systems play their part, the home environment is the cornerstone of a child's literacy development. As a child's first and most enduring teacher, parents wield significant influence in nurturing these crucial skills.

Compelling evidence from the National Literacy Trust in 2018 reiterates this point: Children exposed to books and reading from an early age consistently develop more robust language skills and are likelier to become proficient readers. It is worth noting that this early exposure isn't merely about learning to read; it's about cultivating a lifelong passion for reading and learning. The encouraging news? Parents don't need to be literacy experts to make a substantial impact. Small, intentional actions can yield remarkable results.

Let's explore some practical strategies parents can employ to bolster their children's literacy development:

1. Establish a Reading Routine: Perhaps the most straightforward yet powerful tool in a parent's literacy toolkit is reading aloud to their children daily. Even a mere 15 minutes can make a world of difference. This shared reading time exposes children to rich language and strengthens the parent-child bond, creating positive associations with reading.
2. Curate a Home Library: The presence of diverse, age-appropriate books in the home is crucial for encouraging regular reading. Books should be readily accessible and visible, inviting children to explore them independently. Don't let budget constraints deter you—local libraries, book swaps, and secondhand bookstores are excellent resources for building a varied home library.
3. Engage in Interactive Reading: Reading shouldn't be a passive activity. Encourage active engagement

Literacy Roots

by asking questions, discussing illustrations, exploring new vocabulary, and inviting your child to predict plot developments. This interactive approach enhances comprehension skills and maintains children's interest in reading.
4. Model Reading Behavior: Children are natural mimics, often emulating their parents' behavior. When they observe adults regularly engrossed in books, magazines, or newspapers, they're more likely to adopt similar habits. Parents set a powerful example by modeling reading as an enjoyable and valuable activity.
5. Foster Conversation and Play: Language development inextricably links to literacy development. Engaging your child in rich conversations, posing open-ended questions, and encouraging imaginative play contribute to language skills critical for reading proficiency. Incorporate play-based learning, such as telling stories with toys or puppets, to build narrative skills and expand vocabulary.
6. Leverage Technology Judiciously: While balancing screen time is crucial, numerous educational apps and programs can complement literacy learning at home. Interactive e-books and literacy-focused games can be valuable additions to traditional book reading, particularly when used under parental guidance.
7. Participate in Literacy Programs: Parents can take advantage of initiatives like Reach Out and Read, which ingeniously integrate literacy into pediatric

care. This program encourages daily reading and helps bridge the literacy gap early on by providing families with age-appropriate books. Research indicates that children from families participating in this program demonstrate language development three to six months ahead of their peers.
8. Incorporate Writing Activities: Writing is a fundamental component of literacy development. Encourage children to engage in regular writing activities, whether crafting stories, penning letters to family members, or simply captioning their artwork. These exercises help children grasp the connection between spoken and written language.

Support Systems for Parents

It's important to acknowledge that many parents may need support creating a literacy-rich home environment. Schools, community organizations, and healthcare providers can offer invaluable guidance through literacy workshops, parent-teacher collaborations, and accessible resources. Public libraries are precious, often providing story-time sessions, book clubs, and literacy kits to help parents engage their children in reading from an early age.

Programs like Reach Out and Read exemplify how families grappling with time or resource constraints can seamlessly integrate literacy into everyday routines, such as doctor's visits. Moreover, many schools and communities offer free literacy workshops and resources, equipping parents with practical tools and strategies to support their child's learning journey.

The role of parents in children's literacy development is undeniably central. Armed with the right tools and support, parents can play a crucial role in breaking the cycle of low literacy. Simple, everyday actions, such as reading aloud, engaging in meaningful conversations, and providing access to books, can have a profound and lasting impact on a child's future. By fostering a literacy-rich environment at home, parents not only enhance their children's educational prospects but also set them on a path toward lifelong learning and opportunity.

As we continue to address the literacy crisis, let's remember that every bedtime story, shared reading moment, and trip to the library is an investment in our children's future. In the face of this challenge, parents have the power to make a profound difference, one book at a time.

Reflection Question: How did your parents or guardians influence your relationship with reading?

Current Initiatives and Their Effectiveness

Various initiatives aim to address the literacy crisis. For instance:

Reach Out and Read: This program integrates literacy into pediatric care and has shown promising results. A study published in *Pediatrics* in 2014 found that children whose families participated in the program had significantly higher receptive and expressive language scores.

Early Head Start: A 2010 longitudinal study by the U.S. Department of Health and Human Services found that children who participated in Early Head Start had higher vocabulary scores and more positive approaches to learning at age three compared to a control group.

One inspiring success story involves a young girl named Maria, who overcame literacy challenges with the help of the Reach Out and Read program. Maria's family moved to the United States when she was very young and faced numerous challenges, including language barriers. Her pediatrician introduced them to the Reach Out and Read program, which provided them with age-appropriate books and encouraged daily reading.

Through consistent reading sessions with her parents, Maria's literacy skills improved significantly. By the time she started kindergarten, she had developed a strong vocabulary and a love for reading, which set her on a path to academic success. Her parents, initially hesitant due to their limited English ability, found joy in reading together and gradually improved their language skills.

Dr. Joane Cadet, a pediatrician with the Reach Out and Read program, shared her experience: "I incorporate Reach Out and Read when I talk about language development, school readiness, and limiting screen time. Most of the families I meet are surprised to hear that reading a book together is better for language development than an educational television program or video on the phone. The kids always get so excited when I hand them a book, and the parents get to see their child's reaction right away. Almost every child exchanges their tablet for the book" (Cadet, 2024)!

Impact of COVID-19 on Literacy
The COVID-19 pandemic has added another layer of complexity to the literacy crisis. A 2021 McKinsey & Company study estimates that students lost an average of five months of mathematics learning and four months of reading during the 2020-2021 school year due to pandemic-related disruptions.

The National Literacy Trust's key findings include:
- Educational Disruption: Lockdowns and school closures led to significant learning losses, especially for younger and disadvantaged children. Many children missed several months of school, which disrupted their literacy development.
- Inequality in Access: The pandemic highlighted and widened the gap between students from higher and lower-income families. Children from less advantaged backgrounds faced more significant challenges accessing online learning due to lacking resources such as high-quality devices and the internet.
- Reading Attainment Gap: Research showed a learning loss of up to two months in reading for primary and secondary pupils by autumn 2020. Disadvantaged pupils experienced even more significant setbacks, undoing much of the progress in closing the attainment gap over the past decade.
- Parental Support and Home Learning: Many parents struggled to support their children's learning at home, particularly those facing economic hardships and job insecurity. Many families reported

difficulties creating a conducive learning environment despite spending more time at home.

The long-term impacts of these disruptions are yet to be fully understood, but early research suggests they could be significant. It underscores the urgent need for targeted interventions to help children catch up on lost learning and prevent the widening of literacy gaps.

During the COVID-19 pandemic, my family and I lived in Charles County, Southern Maryland. My son, who had recently transferred from an elementary school in Kentucky to a middle school in Maryland, was in 7th grade. In March 2020, the Charles County Public School (CCPS) board announced a two-week shutdown of all schools "to flatten the curve." Little did we know that those two weeks would stretch into nearly two years.

Initially, CCPS lacked the resources for online schooling. They had to distribute laptops and hot spots to students quickly. Due to our home's location, we couldn't get internet access. Fortunately, I had an extensive home library and access to curricula, allowing me to provide my son with more in-depth education than the hastily assembled and often laggy online lessons.

Overall, we were fortunate during the pandemic. However, I'm aware that several of my son's friends and peers experienced significant losses during this challenging time. The pandemic has underscored the urgent need for targeted interventions and support to mitigate these literacy challenges and help children catch up on lost learning.

Reflection Question: How did the pandemic affect your children's learning experiences?

Conclusion

As we have seen, the literacy crisis is a complex, multifaceted issue with significant implications for individuals and society. Low literacy rates contribute to economic instability, poor health outcomes, and social inequality. While parents play a significant role in addressing this crisis, it's essential to recognize and address the broader societal factors contributing to literacy challenges.

Key takeaways to remember:
1. Literacy in the 21st century encompasses a broad range of skills beyond basic reading and writing.
2. Low literacy's economic and social costs are substantial and far-reaching.
3. Families often pass literacy challenges through generations, but proper support and intervention can overcome these challenges.
4. Global perspectives and solutions can inform local efforts to improve literacy rates.
5. The COVID-19 pandemic has highlighted the urgency of addressing literacy gaps.

It's clear that addressing the literacy crisis requires a comprehensive approach. We must consider the evolving nature of literacy in our digital age, address systemic inequalities, provide targeted support for diverse learners, and empower parents to be effective literacy partners. Understanding the complexity of this challenge allows us to work together to create a world where every child can become a robust and confident reader. After all, literacy is not just about reading words on a page; it is about equipping individuals with the skills they need to participate in and contribute to our increasingly complex world fully.

Further Reading

1. *The Reading Mind: A Cognitive Approach to Understanding How the Mind Reads* by Daniel T. Willingham (2017)- This book provides a comprehensive overview of the cognitive processes involved in reading, offering insights into how we can improve literacy instruction.
2. *Proust and the Squid: The Story and Science of the Reading Brain* by Maryanne Wolf (2008)- Wolf explores the history of the reading brain, from the invention of writing to the digital age, providing a fascinating look at how literacy shapes our neural pathways.
3. *The Knowledge Gap: The Hidden Cause of America's Broken Education System—And How to Fix It* by Natalie Wexler (2019)- Wexler examines how the U.S. education system's focus on reading comprehension strategies over content knowledge contributes to persistent achievement gaps.
4. World Literacy Foundation (https://worldliteracyfoundation.org/)- This website offers current research, global literacy statistics, and information on various literacy initiatives worldwide.
5. UNESCO Institute for Statistics - Literacy (http://uis.unesco.org/en/topic/literacy)- A comprehensive global literacy data and analysis resource that provides up-to-date statistics and research on literacy rates worldwide.

Practical Exercises

1. **Literacy Audit**: Conduct a personal or family "literacy audit." For one week, keep a log of all the different types of reading and writing you engage in daily. Include traditional (books, newspapers) and digital (emails, social media) forms. At the end of the week, analyze your log. What types of literacy skills are you using most often? Are there any areas where you feel you could improve?

2. **Digital Literacy Challenge**: Choose a digital tool or platform you're unfamiliar with (e.g., a new social media platform, productivity app, or digital learning resource). Spend 30 minutes exploring it without any guidance. Then, find and watch a tutorial on how to use it effectively. Reflect on the difference between your initial experience and understanding after the tutorial. How does this relate to the concept of digital literacy discussed in this chapter?

3. **Community Literacy Assessment**: Visit your local library or community center and observe the literacy resources available and any programs it offers to support reading and writing skills. If possible, speak with a librarian or community worker about literacy challenges in your area. Write a brief report on your findings and consider how they align with or differ from the global trends discussed in this chapter.

4. **Intergenerational Reading Activity**: If you have children or can borrow a young family member or friend, engage in a shared reading activity. Choose a

book slightly above the child's reading level and take turns reading aloud. Discuss any challenging words or concepts. If you don't have access to a child, consider volunteering for a local reading program. Reflect on how this experience illuminates the role of adult support in literacy development.

5. **Economic Impact Calculation**: Using the figure from the chapter that low literacy costs the U.S. economy $362 billion annually, calculate what this means per capita. Then, consider your local community. Research its population and estimate the potential economic impact of low literacy at the regional level. How might this impact manifest in your community's services, job market, or overall quality of life?

Chapter 2: Parents as First Teachers: The Foundation of Literacy

Overview

"The more that you read, the more things you will know. The more that you learn, the more places you'll go." Dr. Seuss's words ring more accurate than ever as we unlock the secrets of early literacy development. But what if the journey to literacy begins long before a child opens their first book? What if you, as a parent, hold the key to unlocking your child's linguistic potential from the very first lullaby?

This chapter will explore parents' role as their child's first and most influential teachers. We will dig into the science of early brain development, uncover the magic of everyday moments in building literacy skills, and provide practical strategies for nurturing your child's language development. From the power of play to the impact of multilingual environments, I will equip you with the knowledge and tools to set your child on the path to literacy success.

Get ready to discover how your loving interactions today are shaping your child's tomorrow.

The Science of Early Brain Development

Ever wonder what's happening inside your little one's head? It's nothing short of miraculous. Scientists have discovered something truly incredible during our first few years of life. Our brains create more than a million new connections every second, constructing the world's most complex network. The brain grows so rapidly that it reaches 80% of its adult size by age three and expands to nearly 90% by age five. This growth surpasses any other period in human development.

Two key factors actively shape our neural pathways. Our inherited genes provide the basic blueprint, while everyday experiences determine how that blueprint expresses itself. Words we hear and things we touch actively shape how our brain grows. Frequent use strengthens brain connections through repetition and practice, while the brain naturally prunes unused connections. This system actively develops our brains to serve our individual needs and experiences.

The brain follows a specific development order, like how builders construct a complex house. It forms basic foundations first, creating the parts that control seeing, hearing, and moving. The brain then builds more complex sections that control thinking, planning, and problem-solving. Development actively moves from the back of the brain toward the front, with areas maturing at different times. This precise timing helps each new skill build on established abilities.

Scientists at leading research centers actively uncover fascinating insights about this developmental process. Dr. John Hutton at Cincinnati Children's Hospital watches this process unfold in real time using advanced brain scanning technology. Their research shows how children who regularly hear words and stories develop increased activity in areas responsible for language and understanding. Regular book engagement stimulates these areas, revealing more substantial development in crucial learning regions. These findings emphasize how early language and literacy exposure shapes brain development.

Adults actively shape this development process through consistent engagement with children. When adults respond to a baby's babbling, gestures, or emotions, they build important brain connections. These exchanges strengthen neural pathways essential for communication and social understanding. Caring adults provide the stimulus needed for optimal brain development, building strong foundations for future learning and relationships.

Children in language-rich environments develop stronger vocabularies, better reading skills, and enhanced understanding of complex ideas. They excel in school and maintain stronger cognitive abilities throughout their lives. These early advantages lead to better academic performance and stronger social skills throughout their education.

Simple daily activities actively influence brain development when performed consistently and attentively. Reading stories, conversing, exploring new experiences, and responding to curiosity builds stronger brain connections. These everyday moments create a strong foundation that supports lifelong learning. Success depends on regular, quality interactions rather than complex or costly activities.

The Magic of Early Moments

Picture this: a parent gently cradling their newborn, softly singing a lullaby. This tender moment isn't just an expression of love—it's the beginning of a lifelong literacy journey. From day one, every interaction between parent and child, whether it's a lullaby, a whispered word, or a playful exchange of sounds, helps lay the groundwork for the skills that will eventually lead to reading and writing.

Dr. Patricia Kuhl, co-director of the University of Washington's Institute for Learning and Brain Sciences, describes this process as "language nutrition." She explains, "The brain is like a sponge in the first three years of life, absorbing language's sounds, rhythms, and patterns. Parents are serving up this language nutrition with every interaction." These early moments are powerful because they fuel a child's natural ability to learn language, even before they utter their first word. Every coo, babble, and giggle is a building block, contributing to the child's understanding of communication and language.

Everyday Moments as Literacy Building Blocks
The beauty of early language learning is that it doesn't require special tools or resources—just meaningful engagement during everyday moments. A simple walk in the park can be an opportunity to describe the sights and sounds: "Look at the blue sky," or "Can you hear the birds singing?" A trip to the grocery store becomes a chance to name objects: "This is an apple, and this is a banana."

These seemingly small moments are powerful learning experiences. They help babies attach meaning to words and expand their understanding of language. Singing nursery rhymes, reading board books with colorful pictures, and even narrating daily routines ("Now we are washing your hands") all contribute to building vocabulary and comprehension.

Every Interaction Counts

It is essential to understand that literacy development does not start with the ABCs or formal reading instruction. It begins with these early language interactions. Here's how everyday moments contribute to literacy development:

1. **Infant-Directed Speech**: Often called "motherese" or "parentese," this sing-song way of speaking to babies emphasizes important sounds in language, helping infants differentiate between sounds and words.
2. **Responsive Interactions**: Parents engage in conversation when they respond to their baby's coos and babbles. This back-and-forth helps babies understand the turn-taking nature of communication, a fundamental aspect of spoken and written language.
3. **Storytelling and Narration**: Even before babies understand words, hearing stories helps them understand narrative structure and builds vocabulary. Something as simple as narrating your actions as you change a diaper or prepare a meal exposes your baby to a wide variety of words and sentence structures.
4. **Music and Rhymes**: Lullabies, nursery rhymes, and simple songs expose babies to the rhythms and patterns of language. This develops phonological awareness—the ability to recognize and work with sounds in spoken language—which is a crucial precursor to reading.
5. **Book Sharing**: Even with newborns, looking at books together is valuable. It familiarizes babies

with the concept of books and reading and provides an opportunity for close, language-rich interactions.

It's worth noting that the emotional quality of these interactions plays a significant role in language development. Dr. Betty Hart, co-author of the landmark "30 Million Word Gap" study, points out, "It's not just the quantity of words that matters, but also the quality of the interactions. Warm, responsive interactions provide the best context for language learning." This insight comes from her collaborative research with Dr. Todd Risley, published in their 1995 book *Meaningful Differences in the Everyday Experience of Young American Children*. Their study revealed significant disparities in early language exposure across different socioeconomic groups, highlighting the importance of both the number of words children hear and the nature of parent-child interactions in fostering language development.

When parents engage with their babies lovingly and attentively, it creates a positive association with language and communication. This emotional connection can foster a lifelong love of language and learning.

Practical Implications for Parents
Parents who recognize the power of everyday interactions transform simple moments into valuable learning experiences. They discover how each conversation, story, and playful interaction actively builds developing brains. This knowledge transforms routine daily activities into meaningful opportunities for growth and connection.

Here are some practical ways to nurture early language skills:
- Talk to your baby often, describing what you're doing, seeing, and feeling.
- Respond to your baby's coos and babbles as if you're having a conversation.
- Read books together daily, even if it's just for a few minutes.
- Sing songs and recite nursery rhymes.
- Provide a language-rich environment with plenty of opportunities for interaction.

The magic of early moments lies in their cumulative effect. Each interaction, word spoken, and song sung contributes to building a solid foundation for language and literacy. As Dr. Kuhl reminds us, "Parents are serving up this language nutrition with every interaction." So, every coo, babble, and giggle is indeed a step toward literacy—a step toward a future of reading, writing, and lifelong learning.

Key Behaviors That Promote Early Literacy

What can parents do to nurture these vital early literacy skills? Research shows that daily reading, singing songs, and engaging in wordplay create strong neural pathways for language development. Let's break it down:

Reading Aloud
- Start reading to your child from birth
- Make it a daily ritual

- Aim for 10-15 minutes daily; choose age-appropriate books

Singing and Rhyming
- Use songs and nursery rhymes to build phonological awareness

Playing and Exploring
- Engage in hands-on play to build vocabulary
- Describe toys and actions during playtime

Responding to Your Child
- React enthusiastically to babbling and speech
- Expand on what your child says to encourage communication

Consistency is key. Parents who incorporate these activities into everyday routines, from bath time to grocery shopping, transform ordinary moments into powerful learning opportunities.

The Power of Play in Literacy Development

Let's explore the role of play in literacy development more deeply. Play is not just fun and games—it's serious business regarding learning! Through play, children develop crucial skills that form the building blocks of literacy. Dr. Kathy Hirsh-Pasek, co-founder of the Playful Learning Landscapes initiative, emphasizes the importance of play in language development. She says, "Play is the work of childhood. Through play, children learn to take on different roles, use language in various contexts, and understand the power of communication."

Here are some ways play contributes to literacy development:

1. Symbolic play: When a child pretends a block is a phone, he or she is developing symbolic thinking—a crucial skill for understanding that written words represent spoken language.
2. Narrative skills: As children act out stories during pretend play, they learn about story structure, sequencing, and character development.
3. Vocabulary expansion: Play scenarios introduce children to new words in meaningful contexts.
4. Social skills: Through cooperative play, children learn to communicate effectively with others, which is a critical part of literacy.
5. Fine motor skills: Activities like drawing, coloring, and manipulating small objects help develop the fine motor skills needed for writing.

To incorporate literacy-rich play into your child's day:

- Create a dress-up corner with props that encourage storytelling
- Provide materials for drawing and "writing."
- Play word games during daily activities
- Use puppets or stuffed animals to act out stories

The Power of Parent-Child Bonding

It is easy to think of literacy-building activities as purely academic, designed to develop skills that benefit children in school and beyond. However, the true magic of these moments lies in the deep connections they foster between parent and child. As Dr. Mary Ann Abrams, a pediatrician and early literacy advocate, explains: "When parents engage in literacy activities with their children, they are not just teaching skills, they're creating positive associations with reading and learning that can last a lifetime."

Parents who read, sing, or engage in storytelling with their children nurture language skills and strengthen emotional bonds. These interactions create a shared experience that deepens trust, affection, and communication between parent and child. Sitting close, listening to a familiar voice, and discovering stories together give children a sense of security and warmth. This emotional connection is foundational, and it often turns early literacy experiences into lasting memories that influence a child's attitude toward learning for years to come.

The Role of Bonding in Literacy

Alex began reading to his daughter, Sophia, from the day she was born. Reading aloud to a newborn who could not respond initially felt odd, but he persisted. What started as a simple reading activity soon became a cherished ritual, a special time when father and daughter could connect at the end of each day. As Sophia grew, she would climb into Alex's lap, eagerly awaiting their nightly story time.

By age three, Sophia was familiar with the stories they read. She would "read" her favorite books back to her father, using the pictures as cues to retell the story in her own words. This routine nurtured Sophia's early literacy skills. The positive associations she formed with books, stories, and time spent with her dad helped her develop strong reading skills when she started school.

When reading becomes a treasured part of a child's daily routine, it lays the groundwork for a lifelong love of reading. Reading together fosters more than just literacy—it creates an emotional connection between parent and child, influencing how children perceive learning and education.

Emotional Benefits of Shared Literacy Activities
The benefits of shared literacy activities extend far beyond language development. Studies have shown that children who regularly read with their parents experience higher levels of emotional well-being. Reading aloud in a safe and loving environment promotes comfort and happiness, creating positive associations with books and learning. When parents respond to their children's interests during reading, ask questions, and encourage discussion, they validate their children's thoughts and ideas, boosting their self-esteem and confidence.

These bonding moments also allow children to explore emotions and social situations in a safe context. Through stories, children can encounter characters who experience a wide range of feelings—happiness, sadness, anger, fear—and learn how to navigate these emotions. This helps children develop empathy and emotional intelligence, two critical skills that will serve them well in school and life.

Strengthening Parent-Child Relationships Through Routine

Rituals like reading before bed, telling stories after dinner, or singing songs during car rides create predictability and structure in a child's life. These routines comfort children, providing stability in a world that can often feel overwhelming and unpredictable. The consistency of shared literacy activities becomes something a child looks forward to, reinforcing the bond with their parents and creating an anchor in their daily lives.

For parents, these moments of connection are equally valuable. Finding time to connect with their child can be challenging in daily life's hustle and bustle. Literacy activities offer a focused time for parents to slow down, be present, and fully engage with their children. Parents and children share experiences that create moments of mutual joy and discovery, enriching their relationship and forming memories that last long after they put away the storybooks.

When children associate books with feelings of warmth, love, and connection, they are more likely to approach reading as a pleasurable activity rather than a chore. This positive attitude toward reading is crucial as they enter school and begin formal education. Children who enjoy reading are more likely to read for pleasure outside of school, which leads to better academic outcomes and more robust cognitive development. The bond between parent and child, built through early literacy activities, becomes a key driver of academic success.

As Sophia's story shows, these early experiences can translate into solid reading skills later in life. Sophia's love for books, nurtured through her bedtime reading routine with her dad, contributed to her strong literacy skills when she started school. The positive emotions tied to these early moments set her up for success—not just in reading, but in learning.

The Long-Term Impact of Early Parental Involvement

Let's leap into the early literacy story and its incredible ripple effects. Imagine we're sitting down for a chat over coffee, and I'm telling you about this amazing superpower parents possess called "early literacy involvement."

Do you know how superheroes can fly or have X-ray vision? Well, parents who engage their children in early literacy activities are essentially giving them superpowers for life—no cape required! Dr. Hart and Dr. Risley uncovered something mind-blowing: By age three, some children had heard a staggering 30 million more words than others. That's right—30 million! It's as if some kids are getting a head start in a word marathon while others are still trying to find the starting line.

Here's the kicker: It's not just about drowning kids in a sea of words. It's about quality time, engaging conversations, and making learning fun. When parents embark on this literacy adventure with their little ones, magic happens. First off, these kids become academic superstars. They're not just mastering their ABCs; they excel across all subjects. It's like they've been given a secret map to a treasure trove of knowledge. And get this—they're more likely to stay in school and aim for college.

But wait, there's more! (I know, I sound like an infomercial, but I promise this is way better than a set of kitchen knives.) Early literacy doesn't just boost brainpower; it acts like a workout for the entire mind. Kids develop sharper memories, longer attention spans, and problem-solving skills that would make Sherlock Holmes jealous. And let's not forget about creativity—these kids could probably dream up the next Harry Potter series! Now, here's where it gets really interesting. Remember how we said it wasn't just about academics? Well, these literacy-powered kids also become social butterflies. They're better at making friends, staying calm in class, and understanding how others feel. It's as if they've been given a guidebook to the complex world of human interaction. The best part of this is that these benefits don't come with an expiration date. They stick around long after the kids have outgrown their favorite picture books. We're talking better jobs, higher paychecks, and even improved health. It's the gift that keeps on giving!

Here's a plot twist for you—the parents gain superpowers too. They become more confident in their parenting skills, understand their children better, and are often inspired to learn more. It's like a family book club that changes lives. I'm sure you're thinking, this sounds great, but I'm struggling with my reading, or I barely have time to breathe, let alone read stories. As a former single parent, I understand. Don't worry; you're not alone. Schools and communities often offer support through flexible engagement opportunities, resources in multiple languages, adult literacy programs, and the creation of welcoming environments for all families. Programs and resources are available to help every parent become a literacy superhero. Schools, libraries, and community centers act like the S.H.I.E.L.D. of the literacy world, ready to support you on this mission.

So, whether you're reading *Goodnight Moon* for the hundredth time or making up silly rhymes during bath time, know that you're setting your child up for success in school and life.

Adapting Early Literacy Activities for Different Abilities

Every child is unique, and their journey to literacy should be tailored to their individual needs. Early literacy activities can be adapted for children with developmental delays or different abilities to ensure they receive the same benefits as their peers. Dr. Sally Rogers, a developmental psychologist specializing in autism, emphasizes the importance of following the child's lead: "The key is to find what motivates the child and use that as a bridge to literacy activities." Here are some strategies for adapting literacy activities:

1. For children with visual impairments:
   - Use tactile books with different textures
   - Incorporate braille into storytelling
   - Focus on auditory storytelling and word games

2. For children with hearing impairments:
   - Use sign language alongside spoken words

- Emphasize visual storytelling through pictures and gestures
- Utilize technology like closed captioning for video content

3. For children with motor challenges:
   - Use adaptive tools like page-turners or book-holders
   - Explore digital books that can be navigated with minimal motor skills
   - Focus on storytelling and language games that don't require physical manipulation

4. For children with autism spectrum disorders:
   - Use visual schedules to structure reading time
   - Incorporate special interests into literacy activities
   - Use social stories to teach literacy concepts

Making literacy accessible and enjoyable requires understanding that every young learner develops at his or her own unique pace. Parents and educators should focus on creating positive, engaging experiences that celebrate small victories and encourage exploration of language through multiple approaches. Games, songs, movement activities, and interactive storytelling provide diverse paths to learning that accommodate different learning styles and abilities. Meeting learners where they are, rather than pushing toward rigid milestones, builds confidence and maintains enthusiasm for reading and writing.

Disclaimer: While interactive digital media can have some benefits, they cannot replace a parent's interaction and responsiveness. The American Academy of Pediatrics recommends avoiding digital media other than video chatting for children younger than 18 months.

Overcoming Common Misconceptions

Early Literacy: Myths vs. Facts

<u>**Myth**</u>	<u>**Fact**</u>
"My baby is too young to understand."	Even if babies don't understand words, they absorb sounds, rhythms, and language patterns. Early exposure builds a foundation for future language skills.
"I'm not good at reading."	Your enthusiasm and engagement matter more than your reading skills. Your child benefits from your interaction, regardless of your reading ability.
"We don't have time for reading."	Short periods of reading or talking can make a significant difference. For cumulative benefits, incorporate language into everyday activities like mealtimes or bath time.
"Screen time is just as good."	Educational programs can have benefits, they can't replace parental interaction and responsiveness. Personal engagement is crucial for language development.

Literacy Roots

Every time you talk, sing, or play with your child, you create chances for language development. Small actions like singing during car rides, reading labels at the store, or talking about what you see on walks make a big difference in developing reading and writing skills. Parents often don't realize that normal daily activities, from cooking dinner to sorting laundry, offer perfect opportunities to build vocabulary and understanding. These regular interactions wire the brain for learning and create lasting benefits that show up later in reading and writing abilities. The best part? These powerful teaching moments happen naturally during your daily routine.

Supporting Early Literacy with Limited Resources

Do not let limited resources hold you back! You don't need to spend money to help develop strong reading and writing skills. Public libraries offer amazing free resources, including fun story times and tons of books you can check out. Most libraries also have computer access, educational games, and friendly librarians who love helping families find great books and activities.

Sharing stories from your life and culture creates powerful learning moments. Talk about your childhood adventures during dinner, share family history at bedtime, or tell funny stories during car rides. These personal stories mean more than anything you could buy because they connect emotions with learning.

Regular activities become learning opportunities without any extra cost or effort. Try singing while folding laundry, making up rhyming games in the bath, or playing word games on walks. Even grocery shopping turns into a fun learning experience when you read food labels together or make shopping lists.

New words stick better when you learn them in real situations. Talk about what you are doing while cooking dinner, point out interesting things during walks, or explain how things work around the house. These everyday conversations help build a strong vocabulary naturally.

Fathers as Literacy Champions: The Impact of Paternal Involvement

Researchers and educators have often overlooked the critical role of fathers in early literacy development. The research consistently underscores the positive correlation between paternal involvement and children's cognitive and language development (Bus et al., 1995). Fathers contribute uniquely to children's literacy journeys. Unlike maternal engagement, which often centers on nurturing and emotional connection, paternal interactions are more stimulating and challenging (Lamb, 1986). This dynamic fosters critical thinking and problem-solving skills. Additionally, fathers often introduce children to a broader range of vocabulary and complex language structures, enriching their linguistic repertoire (Snow and Ferguson, 1998).

The benefits of father involvement extend beyond early childhood. Children with engaged fathers show higher academic achievement, particularly in literacy, throughout their education (McWayne et al., 2013). Moreover, the shared experience of reading and storytelling strengthens the father-child bond, fostering emotional resilience and social competence (Dadds et al., 1996). Despite these advantages, barriers to paternal involvement persist. Work schedules, lack of confidence in literacy skills, and cultural expectations can hinder fathers' participation (Parrish, 2004). To overcome these challenges, tailored programs, flexible engagement opportunities, and the strategic use of technology can be effective (Dadds et al., 1996).

Early childhood educators play a crucial role in promoting father involvement. By creating inclusive environments, organizing father-focused events, and acknowledging diverse family structures, educators can empower fathers to become active participants in their children's literacy development (Epstein, 1995).

In conclusion, recognizing and supporting fathers' unique contributions to early literacy is essential for fostering optimal child development. Creating a culture that values paternal involvement can strengthen families, enhance children's educational outcomes, and build a foundation for lifelong learning.

Looking Ahead: Building on the Foundation

As we move forward in this book, we will explore how to create a literacy-rich home environment (Chapter 3) and develop comprehensive literacy skills (Chapter 4). The foundation you lay in these early years will support all future efforts. Your love, attention, and everyday interactions are the most powerful tools for building early literacy skills.

Conclusion

Parents truly are the first and most influential teachers in a child's literacy journey. By understanding the science of early brain development and embracing their role as literacy nurturers, parents can give their children an invaluable gift—a strong foundation for lifelong learning and literacy.

As we wrap up this chapter, let's recap the essential points:

1. Early brain development: Your child's brain forms millions of neural connections daily. Every interaction matters.
2. Language nutrition: All verbal exchanges provide crucial "language nutrition" for development.
3. Key behaviors: Talking, reading, singing, playing, and responding all promote early literacy.
4. Play's importance: Play is vital for literacy development, fostering various skills.
5. Long-term impact: Early involvement affects academic, cognitive, and social-emotional development.
6. Adaptability: Parents and educators can tailor literacy activities for children with different abilities.
7. Overcoming barriers: Limited resources aren't obstacles; there are many ways to support literacy.
8. Multilingual advantage: Using heritage languages at home strengthens language development.

Keep in mind that every interaction, shared story, and loving conversation is a building block in your child's literacy development. You have the power to shape your child's future, one word, story, and interaction at a time.

Whether reading a bedtime story, singing a silly song during bath time, or simply chatting about your day, you're laying the foundation for your child's literacy skills. It's not about being perfect—it's about being present, engaged, and consistent in your efforts. Let us embark on this exciting literacy journey together! Embrace your role as your child's first teacher, and enjoy the wonderful world of words, stories, and learning that you will explore together.

Further Reading

1. *Thirty Million Words: Building a Child's Brain* by Dana Suskind (2015)- This book explores the critical role of early language exposure in brain development and provides practical strategies for parents to enhance their child's language environment.
2. *How Babies Talk: The Magic and Mystery of Language in the First Three Years of Life* by Roberta Michnick Golinkoff and Kathy Hirsh-Pasek (2000)- A comprehensive look at language development in the crucial first three years, offering insights into how babies learn to talk and how parents can support this process.
3. *Growing a Reader from Birth: Your Child's Path from Language to Literacy* by Diane McGuinness (2004)- This book provides a research-based approach to fostering literacy from birth and offers practical advice for parents on supporting their child's language and reading development.
4. Zero to Three (https://www.zerotothree.org/)- An organization that ensures all babies and toddlers have a strong start in life. Its website offers a wealth of resources on early childhood development, including language and literacy.
5. Reading Rockets (https://www.readingrockets.org/)- A national multimedia project offering information and resources on how young kids learn to read, why there are so many struggles, and how caring adults can help. It includes a section specifically for parents.

Literacy Roots

Practical Exercises

1. **Language Nutrition Log**: For one week, keep a daily log of your verbal interactions with your child. Note the types of interactions (e.g., reading, singing, conversation) and their duration. At the end of the week, reflect on your patterns. Are there times of day when you could incorporate more language-rich activities? Set a goal to increase your "language nutrition" in the coming week.
2. **Everyday Object Storytelling**: Choose five everyday objects from around your home. Create a simple story incorporating all these objects—practice telling this story to your child using animated voices and gestures. Encourage your child to participate by making sounds or movements related to the objects. This exercise helps develop narrative skills and vocabulary while making storytelling a part of daily life.
3. **Literacy-Rich Play Scene**: Create a play area that encourages literacy. This could be a pretend restaurant with menus and order pads, a post office with envelopes and stamps, or a library with books and cards. Spend time playing in this area with your child, emphasizing literacy-related activities. Observe how your child engages with the literacy elements and how you can naturally incorporate language and pre-reading skills into play.
4. **Multilingual Family Tree**: If you speak multiple languages or have a multicultural background, create a family tree highlighting the languages spoken by different family members. Use this to

discuss your family's linguistic heritage with your child. For monolingual families, create a "language wish list" tree featuring languages you and your child might like to learn. This activity promotes language awareness and celebrates linguistic diversity.

5. **Sensory Alphabet Exploration**: Create sensory experiences for learning letters. This could involve tracing letters in sand or shaving cream, forming letters with Play-Doh, or going on a letter hunt around your home or neighborhood. As you explore each letter, discuss its sound and the words that start with it. This multi-sensory approach helps make abstract letter concepts more concrete for young children.

Chapter 3: The Home Literacy Environment: Setting the Stage for Success

Overview

"The most important work you will ever do will be within the walls of your own home." This quote, frequently attributed to Harold B. Lee, underscores the profound impact of the home environment on a child's development. As we've established, parents are their children's primary and most influential educators. But how can this understanding be translated into practical, everyday actions? How can we transform our homes into nurturing environments for cultivating lifelong readers and learners?

In the following sections, we will embark on a comprehensive exploration of the home literacy environment. This concept encompasses all literacy-related experiences, interactions, and resources available to a child within their home. We will explore practical strategies for enhancing this environment, from utilizing "environmental print" to creating literacy-rich play spaces. Prepare to gain new insights into how your living space and your role within it can become dynamic catalysts for your child's literacy development. Through this journey, everyday moments will reveal their potential as powerful tools in fostering a love for reading and learning.

The Power of the Home Literacy Environment

Imagine walking into two different homes. In the first, you see bare walls, a television blaring in the background, and not a book in sight. In the second, colorful alphabet posters adorn the walls, a cozy reading nook invites you to curl up with a good book, and a child-sized writing desk stands ready for creative expression. Which environment is more likely to foster a love of reading and writing?

The home literacy environment encompasses all literacy-related experiences, interactions, and resources available to a child within their home. Research consistently shows that children raised in literacy-rich homes have significant advantages in language development, reading readiness, and overall academic success (Niklas and Schneider, 2017).

The good news? Creating such an environment doesn't require extensive resources or a degree in education. Every family can set the stage for literacy success with some creativity and commitment.

Reflection question: Think about your own home. What elements of a literacy-rich environment do you already have in place?

Components of a Literacy-Rich Home Environment

Imagine walking into a home where every corner whispers stories, creativity flows as freely as conversation, and the love of language is as palpable as the aroma of freshly baked cookies. This is the essence of a literacy-rich home environment, a place where reading and writing are not just activities but a way of life.

Access to Reading Materials
At the heart of this literary haven lies an abundance of reading materials. Picture shelves lined with books of various shapes, sizes, and subjects; magazines fanned out on coffee tables; and cozy reading nooks inviting exploration. As Jim Trelease, author of *The Read-Aloud Handbook*, eloquently puts it, "For the impoverished child lacking the travel portfolio of affluence, the best way to accumulate background knowledge is by either reading or being read to." These words remind us that books are not just paper and ink but portals to worlds beyond our immediate reach.

To cultivate this literary landscape in your own home, consider these strategies:
1. Carve out a dedicated reading corner, complete with a comfortable chair and good lighting
2. Keep your book collection fresh by rotating titles regularly, much like a museum curator changes exhibits
3. Make library visits a cherished family ritual, allowing each member to select books that pique his or her interest
4. Introduce variety through magazine subscriptions tailored to different age groups and interests
5. Embrace the digital age by incorporating e-books and educational apps into your reading repertoire

Writing Materials and Spaces

While reading often takes center stage in literacy discussions, writing deserves equal billing. Imagine your home not just as a library but as a vibrant writing workshop where words come to life. Like any skilled craftspeople, budding writers require their own tools and dedicated areas to hone their craft and express their ideas.

Picture a child-sized desk adorned with an array of writing implements—crayons, markers, pencils, and pens—each offering a unique way to capture thoughts on paper. This writing station becomes a launching pad for creativity, a place where ideas take flight and imagination knows no bounds.

To nurture the writer within, consider these approaches:
1. Set up a writing station with paper, pencils, colored pens, etc.
2. Create a gallery wall to showcase your child's written works, celebrating their progress and creativity.
3. Weave writing into the fabric of daily life, from composing grocery lists to penning thank-you notes.
4. Provide a chalkboard or whiteboard for spontaneous scribbling.

Having a dedicated writing area in your home invites regular practice and makes writing feel like a normal part of daily life. This simple setup encourages natural self-expression and helps develop strong, lasting writing habits.

Environmental Print

Step outside your front door, and you will immerse yourself in a sea of text. From street signs to billboards, our world is awash in what educators call "environmental print." This everyday text serves as a powerful tool for connecting the abstract concept of reading to real-world applications.

Harness the power of environmental print with these strategies:
1. Turn your daily commute into a reading adventure by pointing out and discussing signs and billboards.
2. Create a word wall at home featuring familiar logos and labels, bridging the gap between known brands and written language.
3. Engage in playful "I Spy" games focused on letters and words in your surroundings, making literacy a fun, everyday activity.

Reflection Question: How might your perspective on everyday literacy learning change if you viewed each trip outside your home as an opportunity to "read the world" rather than just navigate it?

Play: Where Literacy Comes to Life
In the world of children, play is a serious business. It is their primary mode of learning, exploring, and making sense of the world around them. Reading together should feel like a special treat, not a daily chore. Make story time fun and exciting by using different voices, asking questions, and snuggling close together. These enjoyable moments create positive connections with reading that spark a natural love for books and stories. When reading becomes a treasured part of your daily routine, learning happens naturally through the joy of sharing stories. Bring literacy to life through play with these ideas:

1. Transform a corner of your home into a bustling restaurant with menus to read and order pads for writing.
2. Set up a mock post office where writing letters becomes an exciting game of pretend.
3. Incorporate alphabet blocks, magnetic letters, or letter-themed toys into playtime, making letter recognition a natural part of fun.

Creating a Culture of Reading

While a well-stocked bookshelf is a great start, the true magic happens when reading becomes woven into the very fabric of family life. It's about creating an atmosphere where books are present, celebrated, discussed, and treasured. Trelease emphasizes the power of this approach, stating, "Reading aloud is the single best investment of parental time and energy" (Trelease 2019, 4). This simple act of sharing stories aloud creates bonds, sparks discussions, and lays the foundation for a lifelong love of reading.

To cultivate this reading culture, consider:
1. Establishing a daily family reading time, where everyone gathers to read together or independently
2. Sharing your own reading experiences, letting your enthusiasm for books become contagious
3. Making book discussions a regular part of family conversations, perhaps over dinner or during car rides
4. Drawing connections between books and real-life experiences, helping children see the relevance of what they read

Technology and Digital Literacy

In this digital world, technology offers opportunities and challenges for literacy development. While debates continue about the role of screens in early literacy, a balanced approach can harness the benefits of technology while maintaining the irreplaceable value of traditional reading practices. As S.B. Neuman (2012) suggests, judicious use of technology can enhance the home literacy environment. The key lies in thoughtful selection and interactive engagement with digital content.

Consider these guidelines for incorporating technology into your literacy-rich home:
1. Curate a collection of high-quality educational apps and e-books, treating them with the same discernment you'd use for physical books.
2. Make screen time an interactive experience by discussing digital content, just as you would with a physical book.
3. Maintain a balance between digital and traditional literacy activities, recognizing the unique benefits of each.
4. Establish clear boundaries for technology use, ensuring it enhances rather than replaces other literacy experiences.

Creating a literacy-rich home environment is about more than just filling shelves with books. It's about crafting a space where words come alive, stories spark imagination, and the joy of reading and writing is as natural as breathing. Create a nurturing ecosystem where literacy thrives and flourishes by weaving literacy into the everyday fabric of family life through books, writing spaces, environmental print, play, shared reading experiences, and thoughtful use of technology. In this environment, children don't just learn to read and write; they discover the power and beauty of language, setting the stage for a lifetime of learning, creativity, and self-expression.

Making Time for Literacy: Strategies for Busy Families
Finding time for literacy activities can feel like trying to squeeze water from a stone. As a busy parent, you're likely juggling work, school schedules, and many extracurricular activities. Adding "literacy time" to your already packed day might seem overwhelming. However, here is the good news: Fostering your child's literacy does not require huge chunks of time. It's about making the most of the moments you already have.

The Time Crunch Challenge
Let's face it: Time is often in short supply for many families. According to a 2018 Pew Research Center study, 56% of parents say they don't have enough time with their children (Livingston, 2018). This time crunch can make dedicated literacy activities feel like an impossible luxury. However, research suggests that small, consistent efforts can be highly effective. A study published in the *Journal of Educational Psychology* found that just 15 minutes of daily shared reading significantly improved children's literacy skills over six weeks (Mol and Bus, 2011).

Dr. Rebecca Daniels, a literacy specialist at the University of Michigan, emphasizes this point: "The key to fostering literacy isn't time in large quantities but consistency. Short, regular reading sessions can have a profound impact on a child's literacy development" (personal communication, May 15, 2023). By shifting our mindset from finding large blocks of time to seizing small, regular moments, we can make literacy a natural part of daily life without significant stress.

Let's explore some evidence-based strategies for incorporating reading and literacy into the busyness of life, ensuring that even the most time-strapped families can still nurture their children's love for reading.

Integrating Literacy into Daily Routines
One of the easiest ways to build literacy into family life is by incorporating it into existing routines. These practices do not require extra time, just a little creativity.

- **Breakfast Book Club**

    Mornings may be hectic, but using breakfast time to read together can be both nourishing and educational. A study in the *Early Childhood Education Journal* found that families who engaged in shared reading during meals reported stronger family bonds and increased interest in reading among children (Aram and Levin, 2012).

    The Johnson family, participants in a 2022 literacy intervention study at Boston University, succeeded with this strategy. "We started with just two minutes of reading at breakfast," shares Sarah Johnson. "After three months, our kids' vocabulary scores improved by 22%, and now they wake up early, excited to find out what happens next in our current book!" (Boston et al. Lab, 2022).

- **Commute Storytelling**
    Whether in the car or on the subway, commutes provide perfect moments for literacy. A 2020 study in the Journal of Research in Reading found that children who listened to audiobooks during commutes significantly improved their vocabulary and comprehension compared to a control group (Smith et al., 2020).

- **Bedtime Wind-Down**
    Despite the busyness of the day, bedtime remains a sacred time for reading in many families. Research published in *Pediatrics* found that incorporating reading into bedtime routines improved children's literacy skills and improved sleep quality (Garrison and Christakis, 2012).

    Simple daily activities create powerful learning opportunities that strengthen reading and writing skills. From sharing stories over breakfast to playing word games during car rides, incorporating literacy into regular routines takes little extra time but makes a big difference. Studies show that families who make reading and language activities part of their daily schedule see impressive vocabulary, reading skills, and overall learning improvements.

Maximizing "Hidden" Moments
Simple moments in your day can become great chances to learn about reading and writing. Reading street signs on walks, playing rhyming games during chores, or making grocery lists together turns regular activities into fun learning time. These everyday moments of talking, reading, and playing with words help develop strong reading and

writing skills, showing how learning happens naturally throughout the day. Here are a few examples:

- **Waiting Time Activities**

    A study in the *Journal of Applied Developmental Psychology* found that parents who engaged their children in word games or storytelling during waiting periods (e.g., at a doctor's office) reported less stress and more positive interactions (Brown et al., 2019).

- **Chore-Time Rhymes**

    Incorporating language play into chores can make them more enjoyable while supporting literacy. Research in *Applied Psycholinguistics* shows that exposure to rhymes and wordplay significantly enhances phonological awareness, a crucial precursor to reading (Melby-Lervåg et al., 2012).

- **Bath Time Literacy**

    A 2021 study in *Early Childhood Research Quarterly* found that families who incorporated literacy activities into bath time reported increased engagement with books and improved letter recognition in their children (Taylor and Francis, 2021).

    Dr. Susan Neuman, professor of childhood and literacy education at New York University, notes, "These small moments of engagement add up. They not only build skills but also reinforce the idea that literacy is a natural, enjoyable part of everyday life" (Neuman, 2021).

Addressing Potential Challenges

While these strategies can be effective, it's important to acknowledge that families may face significant challenges in implementing them. Recent studies have highlighted several common obstacles:

1. Children's Reluctance: A study in the *Journal of Literacy Research* found that 42% of parents reported their children being reluctant to engage in reading activities (Johnson et al., 2022). Solution: The same study found that allowing children to choose their reading material increased engagement by 57%. Dr. Katie Davis adds, "Make it fun and low-pressure. Let children choose books they're interested in, and don't force reading if they're not in the mood. Consider alternative formats like graphic novels or interactive e-books."
2. Consistency: Research published in *Applied Cognitive Psychology* showed that families who set specific literacy goals were three times more likely to maintain consistent reading habits than those who didn't (Lee and Thompson, 2022). Solution: Setting reminders or creating a visual schedule can help families stay on track. The study found that families using digital reminder apps maintained consistent reading habits 28% longer than those who didn't.
3. Digital Distractions: A 2023 report from Common Sense Media found that children ages 8-12 spend an average of 5 hours and 33 minutes per day on entertainment screen media, up from 4 hours and 44 minutes in 2019 (Rideout and Robb, 2023). Solution: Establishing tech-free times or zones in the home can help create space for literacy activities. The report also found that families

implementing "device-free dinner" rules reported 40% more time spent on shared reading activities.
4. Multilingual Families: Supporting English literacy can be challenging for families where English is not the primary language at home. However, a 2022 study in *Bilingualism: Language and Cognition* found that reading in any language supports overall literacy development (Garcia and Wei, 2022). Solution: Encourage reading in the home language as well as English. The study found that children who were read to in multiple languages showed stronger overall literacy skills than monolingual peers.

Technology as a Time-Saver
While it's important to balance screen time, technology can be a valuable ally in time-crunched literacy efforts when used thoughtfully:

- **Quick Literacy Apps**

    A meta-analysis published in *Reading Research Quarterly* found that high-quality literacy apps can significantly improve early reading skills, primarily when used in short, focused sessions (Furenes et al., 2021).

- **Audiobooks for Passive Learning**

    Research in the *Journal of Educational Psychology* suggests that audiobooks can be as effective as print books for language comprehension and vocabulary development, making them an excellent option for busy families (Moore and Cahill, 2016).

- **Strategic Use of Educational Shows**

A 2022 study in *Child Development* found that educational shows designed to teach literacy skills can have positive effects, particularly when parents co-view and discuss the content with their children (Anderson et al., 2022).

Dr. Lisa Guernsey, director of the New America Teaching, Learning, and Tech program, advises, "The key is to use technology as a tool to enhance, not replace, human interaction around literacy" (Guernsey and Levine, 2020).

Modern technology offers exciting new ways to help develop reading and writing skills. Research shows that digital tools can save time and create fun, interactive learning methods. Apps, e-books, and learning games make reading more engaging while adapting to individual learning styles and needs. These digital resources work alongside traditional methods like books and writing activities to create more learning opportunities. Using simple technology can help make reading and writing practice more interesting and effective for everyone.

Integrating artificial intelligence into literacy tools has marked a significant leap forward. A groundbreaking 2023 study published in *NPJ Science of Learning* has shed light on the effectiveness of AI-powered reading apps. Zhang et al. (2023) found that these apps, which adapt to a child's reading level and interests, can increase reading engagement by an impressive 45% compared to traditional methods. This personalized approach saves time in identifying appropriate reading materials and significantly boosts motivation and sustained interest in reading.

Virtual reality (VR) has transcended its gaming roots to become a powerful educational tool. Research from Stanford's prestigious Virtual Human Interaction Lab has revealed VR's potential in literacy education. Bailenson and Chen's 2023 pilot study demonstrated that children engaging with VR storytelling experiences showed a remarkable 32% improvement in story recall compared to traditional reading methods. This immersive approach saves time in capturing and maintaining attention and creates lasting impressions that enhance vocabulary retention and reading comprehension.

The rise of educational podcasts has introduced a new dimension to literacy development, particularly beneficial for auditory learners. Mahmoud Patel's 2022 study, published in the Journal of Research on Technology in Education, highlighted the significant improvements in listening comprehension and vocabulary acquisition through podcast use. This trend underscores the time-saving aspect of integrating literacy practice into various daily activities, allowing for learning on the go.

The social aspect of reading has been digitally transformed through platforms that enable children to share and discuss books with peers. The Joan Ganz Cooney Center's 2023 report by Levine et al. revealed a striking statistic: children using social reading apps read 27% more books per month than non-users. This trend saves time in encouraging reading habits and creates a self-sustaining ecosystem of literary engagement among young readers.

Integrating smart speakers in literacy development has opened new avenues for interactive storytelling. A 2023 study published in *Computers & Education* by Brown and Patel demonstrated the effectiveness of this approach. Their research found a 38% increase in story comprehension when children interacted with AI-driven narratives compared to passive listening. This technology saves time in story delivery and significantly enhances engagement and comprehension, particularly for younger children.

Carving out time for literacy in a busy family schedule may seem challenging, but with creativity and intention, it can become an organic part of daily life. Families can foster their child's literacy development without feeling overwhelmed by integrating reading into routines, seizing hidden moments, and utilizing technology and community resources. It's the accumulation of small, consistent efforts that will make the most significant impact on your child's literacy development. Your commitment to finding time for literacy is one of the greatest gifts you can give your child, no matter how hectic life becomes.

Moving forward, keep in mind that these time-management strategies will be crucial in implementing developmental support for your child's literacy journey. Prioritize literacy and find creative ways to incorporate it into your daily life.

Understanding and Supporting Literacy Milestones

As we cultivate a literacy-rich home environment, it's essential to understand the developmental stages of literacy and how to recognize your child's progress. This knowledge will help you tailor your efforts and celebrate your child's growth along his or her unique literacy journey.

Recognizing Developmental Stages
Every child's path to literacy is unique, but there are common milestones that can guide our expectations and support:
- Infants (0-12 months): Babies are developing listening skills and language awareness at this stage. They respond to sounds, recognize voices, and enjoy listening to stories, even if they don't understand the words.
- Toddlers (1-3 years): This is when children start recognizing familiar words and "reading" pictures in books. Their vocabulary expands rapidly, and they may begin repeating words from stories.
- Preschoolers (3-5 years): Children typically start recognizing letters and understanding that words are made of sounds. They may identify words in familiar books and enjoy rhymes and repetition.
- Early Elementary (5-7 years): This is when most children begin reading independently, sounding out words, and recognizing sight words. Their comprehension deepens as they start grasping the meanings behind the stories.
- Mid to Late Elementary (7-10 years): Reading becomes more fluent, vocabulary expands, and children develop more complex comprehension skills. They start understanding different genres and analyzing texts more deeply.

Celebrating Progress

As parents and caregivers, it's crucial to celebrate each milestone along your child's literacy journey. These celebrations boost your child's confidence and reinforce the joy of reading and learning. Celebrate when infants start babbling or responding to your voice during story time. Toddlers rejoice when they point to familiar objects in picture books or attempt to "read" to their stuffed animals. Preschoolers might delight you by recognizing their names in print or identifying rhyming words. These are moments worthy of praise.

Make it a special occasion when your early elementary child reads his or her first book independently. Consider creating a reading nook or presenting him or her with a special bookmark to commemorate the achievement. For older elementary students, celebrate their ability to discuss books in depth or their growing interest in specific genres.

Signs of Literacy Progress

As you engage in literacy activities with your child, look for these indicators of progress:
- Use of new vocabulary: Do they use new words from books in everyday conversations?
- Letter and word recognition: Can they recognize letters and familiar words in their environment?
- Comprehension and discussion: How well do they understand, retell, and discuss stories?
- Reading interest: Are they becoming more interested in reading and eager to do it independently or be read to?

- Narrative understanding: Do they try to predict what will happen next in a story, showing their understanding of narrative structure?
- Print awareness: Have they learned that text is read from left to right and top to bottom? Do they point to words as you read them aloud?
- Phonological awareness: Can they identify individual sounds in words and play with them (e.g., rhyming)?
- Early writing attempts: Are they attempting to write, even if it's just scribbles or random letters at first?
- Book handling skills: Do they hold books correctly and turn pages properly, showing an understanding of how books work?
- Connecting stories to life: Can they relate events or characters from stories to their own life experiences?

These signs of progress align with the earlier developmental stages and provide concrete examples of what to look for as your child's literacy skills develop. Remember, every child progresses at his or her own pace, and it's important to celebrate each milestone along the way.

Simple Ways to Track Reading and Writing Progress
Parents can easily monitor reading and writing development through everyday activities and natural observations. Watch for excitement about books, the ability to follow stories, and growing interest in asking questions about what was read. Keeping simple reading logs with

drawings or brief thoughts about stories provides a fun way to track progress over time while writing journals offer space for creative expression and skill development.

Regular conversations during daily activities reveal naturally growing vocabulary and understanding. Ask questions about favorite stories, discuss interesting topics, and encourage sharing thoughts and ideas. Make assessment fun by turning it into games like word puzzles, letter scavenger hunts, or storytelling activities. These playful approaches help track progress without feeling like tests or formal evaluations.

Remember that progress happens at different rates, so focus on celebrating small victories and maintaining enthusiasm for learning. Watch for growing confidence in reading independently, increased interest in writing stories or notes, and expanding vocabulary during regular conversations. These natural observations provide valuable insights into developing literacy skills while keeping learning enjoyable and stress-free.

Supportive Strategies for Literacy Growth

Create a nurturing learning environment with these approaches:
- Positive Reinforcement: Celebrate every step of progress, no matter how small.
- Goal Setting: Work with your child to set achievable literacy goals, like reading several books per week, month, or year, depending on their age.
- Feedback and Encouragement: Focus on effort and growth rather than mistakes.

Collaborating with Educators
You're not alone in supporting literacy development. Regular communication with teachers helps align goals and share observations. Take advantage of school resources like literacy workshops and parent-teacher meetings. By understanding these milestones and using these strategies, you can better support reading and writing skills at home. The goal is to teach these essential skills while fostering a lifelong love of learning and literacy.

Overcoming Challenges

Creating a literacy-rich home environment isn't without its challenges. Limited space, tight budgets, or competing priorities can all pose obstacles. However, with creativity and resourcefulness, these challenges can be overcome. Here are a few examples of literacy-rich environments in small spaces:

- Use Wall Space: Hang alphabet charts, word walls, or inspirational quotes to utilize vertical space effectively.
- Cozy Reading Nook: Create a small area with floor cushions and a compact bookshelf to encourage reading.
- Hanging Organizers: Employ hanging organizers for books and writing materials to save floor space.
- Rotate Materials: Regularly rotating books and literacy materials keeps the space engaging.
- Magnetic Letters: Use magnetic letters on a refrigerator or magnetic board for interactive learning.

- Portable Writing Station: Develop a portable writing station using a small box or basket that can be moved around the home.

Tight budget
For families on a budget, purchasing new books, games, or technology may seem out of reach. However, several low-cost or free alternatives can help create a literacy-rich environment:
- Local Libraries: Libraries are treasure troves of resources. Most offer books and free access to audiobooks, e-books, and literacy programs. Regular library visits can expose children to a wide variety of reading materials without the cost of purchasing new books.
- Book Swaps: Organizing book swaps with neighbors, family members, or school groups is a great way to refresh your home library without spending money. Swaps allow families to exchange gently used books, introducing children to new stories and topics.
- DIY Literacy Tools: Simple, everyday materials can be turned into literacy tools with a bit of ingenuity. For instance, homemade flashcards made from index cards or re-purposing cereal boxes and magazine clippings for word games can be as effective as store-bought materials. You can also create a word wall in your home by using sticky notes to label household objects, helping children connect words with everyday items.

- Digital Resources: Many websites and apps offer free books and literacy games. Apps like Libby allow families to check out e-books from local libraries, and websites like Project Gutenberg provide free access to thousands of classic works. These digital tools provide various reading materials without a financial investment.

Time Constraints
With some resourcefulness, a rich literacy environment is attainable for all families, regardless of their circumstances. Parents can overcome the obstacles posed by tight budgets and busy schedules by seeking free or low-cost resources, being creative with everyday materials, and finding ways to weave literacy into daily life. Ultimately, consistent exposure to words, stories, and the joy of reading makes the most significant difference in a child's literacy journey—not the cost or complexity of the materials.

Case Study: The Thompson Family's Literacy Haven
Sarah and Mike Thompson lived with their two children, 4-year-old Emily and 6-year-old Jack, in a small one-bedroom apartment in the heart of the city. Despite their limited space and tight budget, the Thompsons were determined to create a rich literacy environment for their kids. "At first, I felt overwhelmed," Sarah admitted. "How could we compete with families who had entire playrooms dedicated to learning? However, then I realized it's not about the space you have; it's about how you use it."

The Thompsons got creative. They sectioned off a corner of their living room using a colorful curtain from a secondhand store. This became their "book nook"—a cozy retreat filled with soft cushions and a small bookshelf they found at a yard sale. Mike explained, "We wanted the kids to have a special place associated with reading. Even though it's just a corner, to them, it's like a magical portal to other worlds."

The family ruled that the book nook was a screen-free zone, encouraging the children to focus on books and storytelling. They rotated the books regularly, mixing favorites with new finds from the library to keep things fresh. Their efforts didn't stop at the book nook. Sarah and Mike turned their entire neighborhood into a literacy playground. During their walks, they made a game of spotting and discussing street signs, store logos, and advertisements.

"It's amazing how much environmental print is out there once you start looking," Mike said. "We play 'I Spy' with letters and words; the kids love it. They're learning without even realizing it."

The Thompsons also got creative with writing opportunities. They hung a large piece of butcher paper on one wall, creating a family message board. Everyone was encouraged to write notes, draw pictures, or practice letters. "Jack was reluctant to write at first," Sarah shared. "But seeing his little scribbles beside our notes made him feel so proud. Now he's always asking how to spell things so he can add to the board."

The impact of these efforts became clear when Emily started preschool. Her teacher was impressed by her letter recognition and early reading skills. "The teacher asked what program we were using at home," Sarah laughed. "I told her it was just us, making the most of what we have." In first grade, Jack developed a deep love for reading. "He used to complain about bedtime, but now he begs for 'just one more story,'" Mike said proudly.

The Thompsons' experience shows that creating a literacy-rich environment doesn't require a lot of space or money, just creativity and commitment. "Our apartment might be small," Sarah reflected, "but it's big enough to foster a love of learning. That's what matters most."

It is not about perfection or comparison. Every small step toward a more literacy-rich environment can significantly impact your child's development. The goal is to make literacy flow as smooth as chocolate, not medicine.

Conclusion: Your Home, Your Child's Literacy Launchpad

As we have explored in this chapter, the home literacy environment plays a pivotal role in setting the stage for a child's literacy success. When you thoughtfully curate space and incorporate literacy into daily life, you foster a culture of reading and provide your child with a solid foundation for lifelong learning. Research consistently shows the impact of these efforts. A more recent study by Niklas Schneider and Hans-Jürgen Schneider (2017) found that the home literacy environment significantly predicted children's linguistic competencies and letter knowledge. This shows the long-term impact of early literacy experiences in the home.

By creating a literacy-rich home environment, you're not just teaching your child to read and write; you're opening doors to worlds of imagination, knowledge, and possibility. You're equipping them with the tools to become lifelong learners, critical thinkers, and confident communicators.

Key takeaways:
- Provide abundant access to diverse reading materials
- Create spaces and opportunities for writing
- Engage with environmental print
- Incorporate literacy into play and daily activities
- Foster a culture of reading within the family
- Use technology thoughtfully to support literacy
- Celebrate linguistic diversity in multilingual homes
- Recognize developmental stages and signs of literacy progress
- Use practical, nonintrusive methods to assess and support your child's growth
- Collaborate with educators to align home and school literacy efforts

These simple strategies create powerful foundations for lifelong reading and writing success. Parents who provide consistent support and encouragement help develop strong literacy skills that last through school and beyond. Each person learns to read and write at his or her own pace, so focus on creating positive experiences, celebrating progress, and offering plenty of opportunities to explore language through daily activities. Every book shared, word discussed, writing attempt celebrated, and milestone recognized is a step toward raising a confident, capable reader and learner. Jim Trelease reminds us that it's the "single best investment" you can make in your child's future.

Further Reading

1. *Reading Magic: Why Reading Aloud to Our Children Will Change Their Lives Forever* by Mem Fox (2008)- This book provides insights into the importance of reading aloud and offers practical tips for making it a meaningful experience. Fox's engaging style makes complex concepts accessible to all parents.
2. *Literacy Beginnings: A Prekindergarten Handbook* by Gay Su Pinnell and Irene C. Fountas (2011)- While aimed at educators, this comprehensive guide offers valuable insights for parents on creating literacy-rich environments and supporting early literacy development.
3. *The Read-Aloud Family: Making Meaningful and Lasting Connections with Your Kids* by Sarah Mackenzie (2018)- Mackenzie provides practical strategies for building a culture of reading in your home, including book lists and conversation starters for different age groups.
4. Reading Rockets (https://www.readingrockets.org/)- This website offers a wealth of research-based information on reading and strategies to help kids become strong, confident readers. It includes sections specifically for parents.
5. National Association for the Education of Young Children (NAEYC) (https://www.naeyc.org/resources/topics/literacy)- NAEYC provides evidence-based resources on early literacy development, including articles and practical tips for parents and educators.

Practical Exercises

1. **Home Literacy Audit**: Conduct a "literacy audit" of your home. Walk through each room with a notepad, jotting down existing literacy-rich elements and potential opportunities for improvement. Consider available reading materials, writing spaces, environmental print, and literacy-related play areas. After your audit, create an action plan to enhance your home's literacy environment based on your findings.
2. **Environmental Print Scavenger Hunt**: Create a family scavenger hunt focused on environmental print. Make a list of common words or logos found on household items (e.g., "STOP" on a stop sign, brand names on food packaging). Have family members photograph or write down each item they find. Discuss the words and their meanings together. For younger children, focus on letter recognition; for older ones, discuss the purpose and design of the text.
3. **DIY Reading Nook Challenge**: Challenge yourself to create a cozy reading nook in an underutilized space in your home. This could be a corner of a room, under a staircase, or even in a large closet. Use items you already have, like pillows, blankets, and a small bookshelf. Involve your children in the process, letting them help decorate and choose books to feature. Document the before and after and reflect on how this new space might encourage more reading time.

4. **Family Literacy Time Capsule**: Create a "literacy time capsule" as a family. Each family member contributes something literacy-related: a favorite book, a piece of writing, a list of current favorite words, or a recording of a story or poem. Include a letter to your future selves about your current literacy goals and experiences. Seal the time capsule and set a date (perhaps a year from now) to open it. This activity encourages reflection on literacy growth over time.
5. **Weekly Literacy Theme Nights**: Implement a weekly "Literacy Theme Night" in your family routine. Each week, choose a different theme (e.g., Rhyme Time, Letter of the Week, Storytelling Night). Plan activities, snacks, and decorations around the theme. For example, on Rhyme Time night, read rhyming books, play rhyming games, and even try writing simple rhymes together. This exercise helps integrate literacy into family fun time in creative ways.

Chapter 4: Beyond Reading: Comprehensive Literacy Skills

Overview

"The limits of my language mean the limits of my world," said philosopher Ludwig Wittgenstein. But what if we could expand those limits, pushing the boundaries of our children's worlds through the power of comprehensive literacy? As we have seen, creating a literacy-rich environment at home lays an essential foundation. Now, it is time to build on that foundation, constructing a solid framework of skills that extends far beyond the printed page.

This chapter will broaden our understanding of literacy to encompass more than just reading. We will examine the interconnected web of skills that define true literacy, highlighting how reading, writing, speaking, and listening are codependent. Our exploration will reveal how progress in one domain can stimulate growth in others. Through creative exercises that integrate multiple skills and strategies for embedding literacy across various learning contexts, we'll equip you with practical tools to foster comprehensive literacy at home. Get ready to reframe your perspective on literacy and discover how nurturing these interrelated skills can help your child become a proficient reader and a confident, articulate, and empathetic communicator.

The Literacy Mosaic

Imagine literacy as a beautiful mosaic. Each tile represents a different skill: the blue tiles for reading, green for writing, red for speaking, and yellow for listening. While the blue reading tiles might catch your eye first, it's the combination of all colors that creates the whole picture. Just as a mosaic is incomplete without all its pieces, true literacy requires ability in all these interconnected skills. Dr. Catherine Snow, a literacy researcher at Harvard University, emphasizes this point: "Literacy is not just about decoding words on a page. It's about understanding, creating, and communicating meaning across multiple contexts and mediums" (Snow, 2017).

Reflection question: Think about your literacy skills. Which piece of your mosaic feels strongest? Which might need more attention?

Components of Comprehensive Literacy

Comprehensive literacy is a multifaceted skill set that forms the foundation of effective communication and learning. This section explores the four key components of comprehensive literacy: reading, writing, speaking, and listening. Each component plays a primary role in developing the ability to understand, express, and engage with the world. When we nurture these interconnected skills, parents and educators can help children build a strong foundation for lifelong learning and success.

1. Reading: The Gateway Skill

Reading is often regarded as the gateway skill that unlocks access to information and learning across all domains. It's like the foundation of our mosaic, supporting all other pieces. To develop reading skills, it is essential to read aloud daily, even with older children, as this fosters engagement with books together. Providing a variety of reading materials caters to different interests and reading levels, ensuring that children have access to diverse texts. Additionally, modeling reading for pleasure demonstrates that reading is a lifelong activity, encouraging children to make time for it themselves.

2. Writing: From Scribbles to Stories

Writing is the expressive counterpart to reading. It begins with early scribbles and evolves into complex composition. Dr. Steve Graham, author of *Writing Next*, emphasizes: "Writing is thinking made visible. When we encourage children to write, we are helping them clarify their thoughts and ideas" (Graham, 2020).

To encourage writing, keep crayons, pencils, and paper easily accessible. Celebrate all forms of writing, from scribbles to invented spelling, as all attempts at writing are valuable. Writing together, such as composing shopping lists, thank-you notes, or stories, can also be an effective strategy to develop this skill.

3. Speaking: Finding Their Voice

Oral language skills form the foundation for all other literacy components. Speaking involves vocabulary, pronunciation, and the ability to express ideas clearly and engage in meaningful dialogue. To nurture oral language skills, engage in conversations about a variety of topics to expand vocabulary. Play word games to make learning fun. Encourage storytelling to foster imagination through both real and fictional stories and ask questions that require more than a one-word response.

Reflection Question: What's your child's favorite topic to talk about? How could you use this interest to expand his or her vocabulary?

4. Listening: The Often-Overlooked Skill

Active listening is crucial for comprehension and critical thinking. It involves not just hearing words but understanding, analyzing, and responding to them. To develop listening skills, practice whole-body listening by encouraging attentive listening through eye contact and proper body language. Play listening games like Simon Says to make listening fun and engaging. Encourage reflection by discussing what was heard and understood after stories or conversations.

Dr. Donna Ogle, an expert in literacy education, notes: "Listening is not a passive activity. It requires focus, interpretation, and response. By teaching children to listen actively, we're preparing them for success in all areas of literacy and learning" (Ogle, 2019).

Reflection question: When did you last practice whole-body listening with your child? How did it affect your interaction?

Integrating Multiple Literacy Skills

Developing a robust set of literacy skills involves more than just honing each skill in isolation. Engaging in activities that blend reading, writing, speaking, and listening can create a richer, more integrated literacy experience. Here are a few practical ideas to help weave these skills together:

1. Create a Family Newsletter

Think of a family newsletter as a mini-journalistic endeavor where everyone contributes to the narrative of your household. This activity is a dynamic way to merge multiple literacy skills. Members can write articles, share personal stories, or interview each other about recent events or interesting topics. This process incorporates writing and reading, while interviews and discussions enhance speaking and listening skills. It's akin to running your small newspaper, where each family member plays the reporter, editor, and reader role. Imagine the fun and learning that comes from creating and sharing a newsletter filled with family updates, accomplishments, and creative contributions!

2. Host a Family Book Club

A family book club transforms reading into a shared experience, much like a mini-literary salon within your home. Choose a book to read together and then engage in discussions about its themes, characters, and plot. This activity fosters reading and writing (creating reviews or summaries) and speaking and listening during discussions. Think of it as a way to blend the warmth of family bonding with the intellectual stimulation of literary analysis.

Imagine the joy of discussing your latest read over dinner or the lively debates about characters' decisions and plot twists that bring everyone closer together.

3. Perform Plays or Puppet Shows

Performing plays or puppet shows offers a creative avenue to integrate literacy skills in a fun and engaging way. This activity involves reading scripts, writing dialogue, performing roles, and listening to cues. It's like stepping into the world of theater, where each participant contributes to the production. Children and adults alike can enjoy the process of scripting and acting out stories, whether it's a classic fairy tale or an original creation. Picture a family gathering where everyone gets into character with homemade puppets or costumes, and the living room transforms into a stage. The laughter, creativity, and collaboration can turn a simple play into a memorable literacy experience.

Simple activities folded into your daily routine nurture both literacy skills and cherished memories, igniting a lifelong passion for learning. Each interaction opens the door to deeper connection, richer communication, and shared growth, transforming ordinary moments into extraordinary learning experiences.

The Role of Metacognition in Literacy

As children cultivate their literacy skills, it is essential to help them develop an awareness of their thinking processes. This concept, known as metacognition, involves learning and reflecting on how one learns. Dr. John Flavell, who introduced the term in the 1970s, aptly describes it as "thinking about thinking." Metacognition enables children to recognize when they don't understand something and to choose appropriate strategies to improve their comprehension (Flavell, 1979).

Imagine metacognition as a personal coach for the mind, guiding learners to navigate their cognitive landscape. Here are some practical steps to nurture this vital skill:

- Model Your Thinking

Think of modeling your thinking as offering a behind-the-scenes tour of your cognitive processes. When you read a book or solve a problem, verbalize your thought process out loud. For example, if you're reading a challenging passage, you might say, "I didn't quite get that part, so I'll reread it and break it down into smaller sections." This approach demonstrates to children how to approach problems and understand text critically. It's like showing them the blueprint for building their mental toolkit.

- Ask Reflective Questions

Engage children with questions that prompt them to reflect on their thinking, much like guiding them to see the map of their cognitive journey. Questions like "How did you figure that out?" or "What made you think of that?" encourage them to articulate their thought processes and reasoning. This reflective practice helps them gain insight into their strategies and recognize their problem-solving methods. It is just like discussing a shared experience with a friend, helping them analyze and learn from it.

- Encourage Self-Assessment

Empower children to evaluate their work and set goals for improvement, like teaching them to be their own critics and coaches. When they review their writing or problem-solving attempts, guide them in identifying strengths and areas for growth. For example, after completing a writing assignment, you might ask, "What parts of your essay do you think are strong? What could be improved?" This process fosters a habit of self-reflection and goal-setting, helping them become more autonomous learners.

- Teach Problem-Solving Strategies

Equip children with various problem-solving strategies, much like providing them with a toolkit of techniques for tackling challenges. Show them different approaches to overcoming obstacles, such as breaking tasks into smaller steps or using graphic organizers for complex information. For instance, if they are struggling with a math problem, you might demonstrate how to draw a diagram or use a step-by-step approach to solve it. This guidance helps them develop a repertoire of strategies they can apply independently in future situations.

These practices help students become better learners while building their reading and writing skills. Like a trusted guide, you support them in discovering how they learn best and what strategies work for them. Over time, students grow more confident and independent, able to tackle new challenges because they understand their own learning styles and strengths.

Literacy Across the Curriculum

Literacy is often associated primarily with language arts, but its significance extends far beyond the boundaries of reading and writing classes. Integrating literacy into subjects like math, science, and social studies allows students to apply their skills in various contexts, enriching their overall learning experience. Think of literacy as the thread that weaves through the fabric of all academic disciplines, connecting and enhancing each one.

Here is how literacy can be effectively integrated into different subject areas:

Math

Imagine math as a language with its own set of symbols and rules. Just as we read and write in everyday life, we can apply these skills to math. Encourage students to read and write math problems, which helps them understand and articulate the steps involved. For instance, have them write out the problem-solving process in detail when tackling a complex equation. They can also explain their solutions verbally, like narrating a story, reinforcing their understanding and communication skills. Participating in discussions about mathematical concepts and listening to others' explanations further deepen their comprehension. This transforms math from abstract symbols into a dynamic and communicative activity.

Science

Science is a world of exploration and discovery, and literacy plays a crucial role in navigating it. When students read science texts, they are not just absorbing information;

they are learning to decode the language of scientific inquiry. Writing lab reports helps them organize their observations and conclusions, like crafting a narrative others can follow. Discussing hypotheses and listening to scientific explanations are like collaborative brainstorming sessions, where ideas are exchanged and refined. Picture a classroom where students conduct experiments and engage in lively discussions and detailed write-ups, making the scientific process both a practical and communicative experience.

Social Studies
Social studies focus on history, culture, and society, and literacy is essential for exploring these dimensions. Reading historical texts allows students to step into different eras and perspectives, much like opening a time capsule. Writing reports on historical events helps them combine the past into coherent narratives. Discussing cultural differences and listening to diverse perspectives enriches their understanding of the world, akin to having a global conversation where every voice contributes to the collective story. Envision a classroom where students analyze historical documents, engage in debates about cultural practices, and reflect on their findings, creating a vibrant tapestry of historical and cultural awareness.

Strong reading and writing skills grow stronger when students use them in all their classes. When students read about science experiments, write out math solutions, or discuss history topics, they build these important skills without even thinking about them. Using reading and writing across different subjects helps students see how these skills matter in the real world. The more they practice, the better they get at understanding tough topics and explaining their ideas clearly—skills they will need for any subject or future career.

Influence of Culture and Background on Literacy Development

Cultural and familial backgrounds deeply influence children's literacy development. Diverse cultural experiences can enrich literacy by introducing different storytelling traditions, languages, and communication styles.

Examples of Cultural Influences:
- **Storytelling Traditions:** Different cultures have unique storytelling practices that can enhance narrative skills.
- **Bilingualism:** Exposure to multiple languages can support literacy development and cognitive flexibility.
- **Family Practices:** Cultural practices around reading and writing can shape a child's approach to literacy.

Resources for Parents
Here are some additional resources to support comprehensive literacy development:
- **Books:**
  - *The Read-Aloud Handbook* by Jim Trelease
  - *Writing Magic: Creating Stories that Fly* by Gail Carson Levine

- **Websites:**
  - Reading Rockets: Offers resources and strategies for developing reading skills
    https://www.readingrockets.org/
  - National Writing Project: Provides resources for improving writing instruction
    https://www.nwp.org/
- **Organizations:**
  - International Literacy Association: Focuses on literacy research and advocacy
    https://www.literacyworldwide.org/
  - Zero to Three: Supports early literacy and developmental milestones
    https://www.zerotothree.org/

The Connection Between Literacy and Social-Emotional Development

Literacy and social-emotional development are like two sides of the same coin. They are not separate aspects of a child's growth but instead profoundly connected and reinforce one another in profound ways. For parents and educators, recognizing this relationship can help us support our children's overall well-being more effectively, fostering academic success, emotional intelligence, and social resilience.

Take, for example, the relationship between emotional expression and vocabulary. A child with a rich vocabulary can articulate his or her feelings with much more precision. Rather than simply saying they feel bad, they might recognize they are feeling frustrated, disappointed, or anxious. This ability to label emotions is essential for developing emotional intelligence, allowing them to understand and manage their feelings more effectively.

Another powerful connection is the link between reading and empathy. When children engage with stories, they are exposed to diverse characters and situations, which helps them see the world from different perspectives. This exposure to various viewpoints fosters empathy, a key skill in navigating social interactions. A child who understands the feelings of others is better equipped to manage relationships, whether with peers or adults.

Self-regulation is another skill that literacy can enhance. The simple act of sitting still and focusing on a book helps a child develop concentration and impulse control. These same skills are crucial for managing emotions and behavior in social situations. Similarly, as children read stories presenting conflicts and resolutions, they gain valuable problem-solving models they can apply to their lives.

Literacy also plays a role in building self-confidence. As children master reading and writing, they develop a sense of competence, and this newfound confidence spills over into other areas of their lives, including social interactions. They begin to believe in their abilities, whether it's speaking up in class or joining a group activity. Active listening, another skill honed by storytelling, becomes second nature, enhancing their ability to communicate effectively and build stronger relationships.

Practical Strategies for Fostering Literacy and Social-Emotional Growth

With an understanding of how literacy and social-emotional development intersect, there are several strategies parents can implement to nurture both areas simultaneously. One effective method is emotion-focused reading. When reading with your child, take the time to discuss the characters' emotions. Ask questions like, "How do you think the character feels right now?" or "Have you ever felt like that?" This helps your child think about feelings in more detailed ways. It builds their emotional vocabulary—the words they use to describe feelings. It also helps them understand the emotions of others better, which is called empathy.

Journaling is another fantastic tool. Encouraging your child to keep a journal enhances writing skills and gives them a private space to express their emotions. This practice can be incredibly cathartic and helps children make sense of their feelings in a structured way. Role-playing is a fun and engaging way for younger children to explore different perspectives. Acting out scenes from books allows them to embody different characters, helping them to understand and empathize with different points of view. Storytelling, whether reading aloud or inventing new stories, is also a powerful method for encouraging emotional expression and creativity. For older children, starting a family book club can create opportunities for deeper discussions around both literary elements and emotional themes.

Lastly, something as simple as letter-writing can blend literacy with relationship-building. Encouraging your child to write letters or emails to friends and family improves their writing and nurtures their social connections.

Case Study: The Coley Family's Literacy Journey
The Coley family embraced this holistic approach to literacy. They decided to prioritize reading and communication at home by establishing a daily "story time" ritual, during which each family member would take turns reading aloud, telling a story, or sharing something about their day. As Mrs. Coley shares, "We're not just raising readers; we're raising confident communicators and compassionate listeners."

Indeed, the family saw tremendous benefits from this practice. Their children became more articulate in school and expressed their emotions and thoughts at home. Storytime gave them the tools to understand their feelings better, and reading diverse stories enhanced their empathy toward others. They also became more adept at resolving conflicts, often referencing characters or situations from books when facing challenges.

Beyond academics, the ritual strengthened the Coley family's bond. It created a space for open communication and shared experiences, something Mr. Coley noted had a noticeable effect on their family dynamic. He reflected, "We've noticed that our kids are not only doing better in school but are also more attuned to each other's feelings. It's amazing how our focus on literacy has positively impacted many areas of their lives."

Understanding the connection between literacy and social-emotional development opens the door to more effective, holistic strategies for supporting children's growth. Every story you read, discussion you have, and emotion you explore with your child contributes to their development as both skilled communicators and socially and emotionally intelligent individuals. As you continue on your literacy journey with your family, remember that you're doing more than teaching your children how to read and write. You are equipping them with the tools to understand themselves, relate to others, and navigate the complex world around them.

Looking Ahead: Literacy in the Digital Age

As we stand on the threshold of an increasingly digital world, the literacy landscape is evolving at a breathtaking pace. It's as if we have been teaching our children to navigate familiar city streets, and suddenly, we find ourselves in a sprawling metropolis with gleaming skyscrapers, intricate subway systems, and virtual highways stretching as far as the eye can see. The foundational skills we've explored throughout this book are still crucial, but they now serve as the bedrock on which a new, multifaceted literacy must be built.

Imagine literacy as a tree. The roots and trunk represent our traditional reading and writing skills, firmly grounded in the soil of language and comprehension. However, this tree has sprouted new branches in the digital age, each representing a different aspect of digital literacy, from navigating online information to creating digital content, from understanding cybersecurity to engaging in virtual collaboration. Dr. Kristen Hawley Turner, a leading researcher in digital literacy, puts it succinctly: "Digital literacy isn't about replacing traditional literacy; it's about expanding it. We're not abandoning the book; we're giving it a whole new set of companions" (Turner, 2020).

The Chen family's experience beautifully illustrates this evolving landscape. When 10-year-old Mei was assigned a project on local ecosystems, her parents expected her to check out books from the library and perhaps visit a nearby park. Instead, Mei proposed a multifaceted approach that left them astounded. "Mei suggested we use a nature identification app during our park visit," Mrs. Chen recounts. "She wanted to create a digital ecosystem map, complete with embedded videos of wildlife we observed. She even proposed creating a blog to share her findings with her classmates and engage with local environmental groups."

It's not just about consuming content but about creating, collaborating, and connecting in a global digital community. However, this new frontier comes with its own set of challenges. Just as we teach children to navigate physical spaces safely, we must now guide them through the virtual world, which has its own set of opportunities and pitfalls.

The Thompson family learned this lesson the hard way when their teenage son, Jake, fell for an online scam. "We had taught Jake about stranger danger in the real world, but we hadn't addressed online safety," Mr. Thompson admits. "It was a wake-up call for us. We realized that digital literacy isn't just about using technology; it's about using it wisely and safely."

This incident led the Thompsons to implement "Digital Literacy Dinners," weekly family discussions about online experiences, digital citizenship, and critical evaluation of online content. "It's opened up amazing conversations," Mrs. Thompson shares. "We're learning as much from Jake as he is from us!"

Dr. Sonia Livingstone, a professor of social psychology, emphasizes the importance of this collaborative approach: "Digital literacy isn't something parents can simply 'teach' to their children. It's a journey of co-learning, where parents and children navigate this new terrain together, each bringing their strengths to the table" (Livingstone, 2021).

It's clear that digital literacy will be an integral part of our children's future. But it's important to remember that it builds on, rather than replaces, the foundational skills we've discussed throughout this book. Critical thinking, comprehension, creativity—these skills are more important than ever in the digital age. Consider digital literacy, a new language that our children need to be fluent in to thrive in the 21st century. Just as bilingualism enhances cognitive flexibility, mastering both traditional and digital literacy can provide our children with a more comprehensive, adaptable skillset.

The Garcia family embraced this bilingual approach to literacy with enthusiasm. They established a "Tech and Tale Time," a daily family ritual where they would read a traditional story and then explore a related digital resource. "One day, we're reading The Very Hungry Caterpillar and the next, we're using an augmented reality app to watch a virtual caterpillar transform into a butterfly in our living room," Mr. Garcia explains. "It's bringing stories to life in ways we never imagined possible."

As we venture into this new literacy chapter, remember that your role as a parent remains crucial. You are the guide, the co-explorer, and sometimes the student in this digital journey. Your curiosity, willingness to learn, and critical thinking will model the approach your children need in this new literacy landscape.

Reflection Questions: Think about your family's current approach to digital technology. How do you balance traditional literacy activities with digital experiences? How might you incorporate this into your family's literacy practices to enhance, rather than replace, traditional literacy skills?

Conclusion: The Literacy Mosaic

As we have explored throughout this chapter, comprehensive literacy is like an intricate mosaic, with each skill representing a vital piece of the overall picture. The blue tiles for reading, the green for writing, the red for speaking, and the yellow for listening combine to create a beautiful, complete image of literacy. By nurturing all these skills, parents can help their children become proficient readers and masterful creators of their literacy mosaics.

Educator and philosopher Paulo Freire once said, "Reading the world always precedes reading the word, and reading the word implies continually reading the world." This powerful quote reminds us that our literacy mosaic extends beyond the pages of a book or the strokes of a pen. It extends to how we interpret and engage with the world around us. As a mosaic artist carefully selects and places each tile, parents play a crucial role in helping their children develop and integrate each literacy skill. The result is a robust, multifaceted literacy that enables children to become effective communicators, critical thinkers, and lifelong learners.

Key Takeaways:

- Literacy is a comprehensive skill set that includes reading, writing, speaking, and listening.
- Each literacy skill reinforces and enhances the others.
- Parents play a crucial role in developing their child's literacy mosaic.
- Everyday interactions provide opportunities to strengthen literacy skills.
- A well-rounded literacy foundation prepares children for lifelong learning and effective communication.

Consider how you can continue to add diverse and colorful tiles to your child's literacy mosaic, creating a masterpiece that will serve them well throughout their lives. In the next chapter, we'll explore how to extend this mosaic beyond the home, collaborating with educators to ensure that all aspects of your child's literacy development flourish.

Self-Assessment: Supporting Comprehensive Literacy Skills

Take a moment to reflect on how you're currently supporting each literacy skill in your home:

1. Reading: Do you have a daily reading routine? Is there a variety of reading materials available?
2. Writing: Are writing materials easily accessible? Do you encourage different forms of writing?
3. Speaking: How often do you engage in meaningful conversations? Do you provide opportunities for storytelling?
4. Listening: Do you model and encourage active listening? Do you reflect on stories or conversations together?

Rate your support for each skill on a scale of one to five, with five being the strongest. Which areas might you focus on improving?

_____
_____
_____
_____
_____
_____
_____
_____
_____
_____
_____
_____

Further Reading

1. *Proust and the Squid: The Story and Science of the Reading Brain* by Maryanne Wolf (2008)- This book is a fascinating exploration of the history and science of reading, offering insights into how literacy shapes our brains and our civilization.
2. *The Reading Strategies Book: Your Everything Guide to Developing Skilled Readers* by Jennifer Serravallo (2015)- This book is aimed primarily at educators. A practical guide, it offers 300 strategies for comprehension, fluency, word work, and more, many of which can be adapted for home use.
3. *Bringing Words to Life: Robust Vocabulary Instruction* by Isabel L. Beck, Margaret G. McKeown, and Linda Kucan (2013)- This book provides research-based strategies for vocabulary development, a crucial component of comprehensive literacy.
4. International Literacy Association (ILA) (https://www.literacyworldwide.org/)- The ILA website offers a wealth of resources, research, and advocacy information related to literacy education.
5. Reading Rockets (https://www.readingrockets.org/)- A comprehensive website that provides research-based strategies, articles, and resources for parents and educators to help children become strong, confident readers.

Practical Exercises

1. **Family Literacy Mosaic Project**: Create a visual representation of your family's literacy skills. Use colored paper or digital tools to create "tiles" representing different literacy activities (e.g., blue for reading, green for writing, red for speaking, yellow for listening). Over a week, add a tile each time a family member engages in a literacy activity. At the end of the week, arrange these tiles into a mosaic. Discuss the balance of colors and identify areas for growth.

2. **Story Round Robin**: Engage in a family storytelling activity incorporating all four literacy skills. Start by having one family member read the beginning of a story aloud. The following person then writes a continuation, read aloud by the next person, who then adds to the story verbally. Continue this pattern, switching between reading, writing, speaking, and listening. This exercise demonstrates how these skills interconnect in creating and understanding narratives.

3. **"Four Corners" Literacy Game**: Designate four corners of a room for reading, writing, speaking, and listening. Call out various activities (e.g., "writing a grocery list," "listening to a podcast," "reading a menu," "giving directions"). Family members move to the corner that best represents the primary literacy skill used in that activity. Discuss why they chose that corner and how other skills might also be involved, highlighting the interconnected nature of literacy skills.

4. **Literacy Skills Scavenger Hunt**: Create a scavenger hunt that requires using all four literacy skills. Include tasks like "Read a product label and write down its main ingredients," "Listen to a short audio clip and verbally summarize it," or "Speak to a family member about your day and write down their response." This activity shows how we use multiple literacy skills in everyday situations.
5. **Metacognition Journal**: Encourage family members to keep a "thinking about thinking" journal for a week. After engaging in any literacy activity, they should write a short reflection answering questions like "What strategy did I use?" "What was challenging?" and "What did I learn?" At the end of the week, share insights as a family, discussing how awareness of our thinking processes can enhance literacy skills.

Chapter 5: School/Home Connections: Building Strong Partnerships

Overview
"It takes a village to raise a child," goes the age-old proverb. Regarding literacy development, that village is centered around two crucial pillars: home and school. But how do we ensure these pillars work in harmony rather than in isolation? This chapter unlocks the secrets of forging powerful partnerships between parents and educators, transforming your child's literacy journey from a solo trek to a well-supported expedition.

We will explore practical strategies for understanding your child's school curriculum, communicating effectively with teachers, and aligning home practices with classroom instruction. You will discover how to turn everyday moments into rich literacy experiences that complement school learning. Whether you're navigating the challenges of remote education or seeking to enhance traditional schooling, this chapter will equip you with the tools to build a robust bridge between home and school, ensuring your child's literacy journey is supported by a united front of caring adults.

The Power of Partnership
Imagine two boats rowing across a shimmering lake. In one boat, the rowers' strain against their oars, their movements disjointed and chaotic. They expend enormous energy, yet the ship zigzags erratically, making little progress. In the other boat, the rowers move as one, their oars dipping and

rising in perfect synchronization. This boat glides smoothly across the water, covering distance gracefully and efficiently.

This vivid image encapsulates the stark difference between disjointed and aligned efforts in supporting a child's literacy development. When parents and educators row in different directions, the child's journey becomes arduous and confusing. But when home and school synchronize their strokes, the literacy voyage transforms into an exhilarating adventure of discovery and growth.

Dr. Joyce L. Epstein, a leading figure in school, family, and community partnerships, effectively expresses this collaboration: "When parents, teachers, students, and others view one another as partners in education, a caring community forms around students and begins its work" (Epstein 2018, 12). This community becomes the wind in the sails of our literacy boat, propelling it forward with collective wisdom and shared purpose.

Just as a championship rowing team must practice together, fine-tuning their movements until they achieve perfect synchronization, building a solid school/home partnership requires dedication, communication, and consistent effort. It's about creating a shared language around literacy, aligning goals, and working together to support the child's unique learning journey. This partnership can take many forms. It might look like a weekly email exchange between parent and teacher, sharing observations and strategies. It could be a family literacy night at school, where parents learn alongside their children. It might also involve a shared online platform where teachers post daily literacy activities that parents can reinforce at home.

This partnership isn't about perfection—it's about progression. Even small steps toward alignment can yield significant results. You could start by asking your child's teacher about the current focus in reading instruction and inviting the teacher to share one strategy you can practice at home. These actions are like a slight adjustment to your oar, bringing you more in sync with your child's educational journey.

Reflection Question: How would you describe your current partnership with your child's school? What areas could be strengthened?

Take a moment to visualize your literacy partnership boat. Are you and the teacher rowing harmoniously, or do you feel out of sync? You may be somewhere in between, occasionally finding your rhythm but still working toward consistency.
Consider specific areas of your partnership:
1. Communication: How often and in what ways do you interact with the teacher about literacy development?
2. Shared strategies: Are you aware of the reading and writing strategies being taught in class? Do you reinforce these at home?
3. Goal alignment: Have you and the teacher discussed shared goals for your child's literacy growth?

4. Home/school connection: Do you engage in literacy activities at home that complement classroom learning?

Identifying areas for improvement is the first stroke toward a more harmonious partnership. Remember, every excellent rowing team started with practice and patience. Your journey to a solid school/home literacy partnership is no different. With each synchronized stroke, you're propelling your child toward literacy success, creating ripples extending far beyond the shores of their educational journey.

Understanding the School's Literacy Curriculum

The first step in building a strong partnership is understanding what's happening in the classroom. Today's literacy instruction often looks quite different from what many parents experienced in their school days.

Key aspects to understand:
1. Balanced Literacy Approach: Many schools use a balanced literacy approach, which combines phonics instruction with whole language experiences. Think of it like a balanced diet for reading and writing:
    - Phonics instruction is like protein, building strong foundational skills.
    - Whole language experiences are like fruits and vegetables, providing rich, varied exposure to language.

- Comprehension strategies are complex carbohydrates, fueling deeper understanding.
- Writing activities are like healthy fats, essential for well-rounded literacy development.

Just as a balanced diet nourishes different aspects of physical health, a balanced literacy approach nurtures various components of literacy skills. According to a 2020 survey by the International Literacy Association, 68% of U.S. schools reported using this balanced approach. Schools often use a leveled reading system to match students with appropriate texts. The Fountas and Pinnell system is used in approximately 50% of U.S. elementary schools. Writing instruction typically involves brainstorming, drafting, revising, editing, and publishing. In terms of digital literacy, many schools integrate technology into literacy instruction. A recent study found that 85% of K-12 teachers use digital learning tools in their literacy instruction at least weekly.

To stay involved, attend curriculum nights or parent workshops offered by the school. Request a copy of the literacy curriculum or standards for your child's grade level. Additionally, ask the teacher to explain their approach to literacy instruction.

Effective Communication with Teachers

Clear, open communication is the foundation of any strong partnership. Let's examine strategies for fostering effective dialogue with your child's teacher. Karen Mapp, author of *Beyond the Bake Sale: The Essential Guide to Family-*

School Partnerships, notes, "Effective family engagement is not a one-time event. It's an ongoing process that requires mutual trust, respect, and shared responsibility" (Mapp 2017, 45). This perspective underscores the importance of consistent, meaningful communication. Key strategies include:

1. Establish Early Contact: Don't wait for problems to arise. Reach out early in the school year to introduce yourself and express your interest in supporting your child's literacy development.
2. Use Multiple Channels: Take advantage of various communication methods—email, phone calls, in-person meetings, or digital platforms used by the school. A study by Thompson et al. (2020) found that parents who used multiple communication channels reported higher satisfaction with school/home partnerships.
3. Be Proactive: Share insights about your child's reading habits, interests, and challenges at home.
4. Ask Specific Questions: Instead of general inquiries like "How is my child doing in reading?" ask targeted questions such as "What specific reading strategies is my child working on right now?"
5. Listen Actively: Remember that communication is a two-way street. Listen carefully to the teacher's insights and recommendations.

Reflection Question: Which of these communication strategies do you currently use? What could you implement to enhance your partnership with your child's teacher?

Aligning Home and School Literacy Practices

Imagine your child's literacy journey as a grand expedition, with home and school serving as two vital base camps. When these camps are in sync, sharing supplies, strategies, and goals, the journey becomes smoother and more rewarding. This alignment is not just helpful; it's transformative. Sonnenschein and Schmidt's research (2000) illuminates that when home literacy practices harmonize with school instruction, children's reading achievement soars.

Let's explore how we can create this powerful synergy, turning your home into an extension of the classroom and vice versa.

1. Speaking the Same Language: The Power of Shared Terminology

Imagine trying to navigate a foreign city where you don't speak the language. That's how children can feel when literacy terms used at school differ from those at home. By learning and using classroom terminology, you're essentially providing your child with a reliable map for their literacy journey.

The Johnson family discovered this firsthand. "When Ethan kept talking about chunking words, I was lost," chuckles Mr. Johnson. "It turned out it was a decoding strategy he learned at school. Once we understood and started using the term at home, Ethan's confidence in tackling new words skyrocketed. It was like we'd cracked a secret code together!"

Try this: Create a Literacy Lingo chart with your child featuring key terms from their classroom. Make using these terms during your home reading time a fun family challenge.

2. Practicing Current Skills: Reinforcing the Learning Rhythm

Think of literacy skills as dance steps. Your child learns new moves at school, but practicing at home helps them master the dance. You're providing the perfect practice space by aligning home activities with current classroom focus areas.

Ms. Rodriguez, a second-grade teacher, shares an inspiring anecdote: "I was teaching my class about descriptive writing. Little did I know Sophia's parents had turned it into a dinnertime game. They'd take turns describing their food using vivid adjectives. Sophia's writing blossomed, and soon, the whole class was playing Dinner Descriptions!"

Try this: Set up a quick weekly check-in with your child's teacher (email works great) to learn about current focus areas. Then, weave these skills into daily life—grocery lists become exercises in phonics, car rides turn into storytelling sessions, and bedtime stories become opportunities for predicting and inferencing.

3. Extending School Projects: From Seedling to Mighty Oak

School projects are like seedlings of knowledge. With a little nurturing at home, they can grow into mighty oaks of understanding. Expanding on school projects reinforces learning—you're showing your child how classroom knowledge connects to the wider world.

The Li family turned this idea into a delightful family tradition. When 9-year-old Mei studied poetry at school, they instituted Poetry Picnics every Sunday. "We'd pack a lunch, head to the park, and take turns reading poems and even trying to write our own," Mrs. Li recalls. "It became less about homework and more about enjoying language together. Mei's teacher was amazed at her appreciation for poetry."

Try this: Create a Project Extension Corner in your home. When your child brings home a new school project, brainstorm together how you might explore the topic further through books, outings, experiments, or creative activities.

4. Sharing Home Literacy Activities: Closing the Loop

Communication between home and school shouldn't be a one-way street. By sharing your home literacy activities with teachers, you're helping them build bridges between home and classroom learning. Mr. Patel, the father of twin first-graders, found an innovative way to do this. "We started a family blog about our reading adventures," he explains. "The kids would post about books we read, literacy games we played, and even funny wordplay we encountered. Their teacher subscribed to and often used our posts as conversation starters in class. It made the kids feel like their home reading mattered."

Try this: Create a simple Literacy Log where you and your child can jot down home literacy activities. Encourage your child to share this with his or her teacher regularly. It could be as simple as a notebook or as high-tech as a shared online document.

Sara's, another parent acquaintance, experience with "making connections" during bedtime stories beautifully illustrates the power of this alignment. She and her daughter's teacher were rowing in perfect sync, propelling her daughter's literacy boat forward with powerful, coordinated strokes.

Dr. Patricia Edwards sums it up perfectly: "When home and school literacy practices align, we're not just teaching children to read and write. We're showing them that literacy is a valued, integral part of life in and out of the classroom. We're cultivating skills and a lifelong love of learning" (Edwards, 2016). Aligning home and school practices doesn't mean turning your living room into a classroom. It's about creating a seamless, supportive literacy environment that bridges the two worlds your child inhabits. It's about showing them that reading and writing are not just school subjects but keys that unlock doors to imagination, knowledge, and success in all areas of life.

Reflection Question: What literacy activities do you currently do at home? How might these align with your child's school curriculum?

Supporting School Literacy Initiatives at Home

Your involvement at home greatly enhances the literacy skills your child develops at school. A meta-analysis by Senechal and Young (2008) confirms this, showing that parent involvement in literacy activities at home significantly boosts reading acquisition. Working together, at home and in school, creates the perfect environment for your child's literacy skills to flourish.

Here are some common initiatives and ways to support them:
1. Reading Logs: If your child's school uses reading logs, make them a positive part of your routine rather than a chore.
2. Sight Word Practice: Early elementary classrooms focus on sight word recognition. Create fun games at home to practice these words.
3. Summer Reading Programs: Summer reading isn't about preventing a "slide"; it's about taking an exciting literacy leap! Embrace your local library's summer reading program as a family adventure.
4. Author Studies: If your child's class is studying a particular author, seek out more books by that author for home reading.

Dr. Richard Allington, a literacy researcher, emphasizes the importance of volume in reading development: "Kids not only need to read a lot, but they also need lots of books they can read accurately, fluently, and with comprehension right at their fingertips" (Allington 2012, 7). Think of this as creating a literary feast for your child—the more varied and abundant the "menu" of books, the richer their reading diet becomes.

Supporting school initiatives at home isn't about replicating the classroom experience. It's about extending and enriching it in ways that fit your family's lifestyle and your child's interests. You're supporting literacy and weaving it into the fabric of your family life.

Here are a few more ideas to spark your creativity:

- Create a "Word of the Day" ritual at dinner, incorporating vocabulary from your child's current school reading.
- Start a family book club, reading and discussing books related to your child's author studies.
- Use car rides as opportunities for storytelling games that reinforce narrative skills.
- Incorporate sight words or vocabulary into daily chores or routines.

You're creating a powerful echo chamber of literacy by aligning your home activities with school initiatives. Each word read, story shared, and game played reverberates between home and school, amplifying your child's learning. You're supporting school literacy initiatives by co-creating a rich, immersive literacy environment that extends far beyond the classroom walls.

So roll up your sleeves and dive into these literacy adventures with your child. You're not just helping with homework; you're cultivating a lifelong love of reading and writing. And that, dear parents, is a gift that will continue to be given long after the school bells fall silent.

Addressing Challenges in School/Home Partnerships

School/home partnerships face real challenges in supporting student literacy. Hornby and Lafaele (2011) observed that time constraints, language barriers, and differing expectations can create significant obstacles. However, with the right tools and strategies, we can overcome these challenges and build more productive relationships to support student learning.

Let's dive deeper into these challenges and explore some innovative solutions:

1. Time Constraints: The Whirlpool of Busy Schedules

In our fast-paced world, time is often the scarcest resource. Many parents juggle multiple jobs, care for extended family, or face long commutes. Schools, too, grapple with packed curricula and administrative demands.

Solution: Flexible Communication Options

Think of communication as a bridge that can be built with various materials. Some families might prefer the sturdy wood of in-person meetings, while others need the flexibility of a rope bridge they can access anytime.

Johnson Elementary School in Springfield, Illinois, embraced this approach with remarkable results. At the beginning of the year, they introduced "Communication Choice Forms," where parents could select their preferred methods and times for teacher interactions. Options included traditional parent-teacher conferences, video calls, messaging apps, or even weekend email updates.

2. Cultural Competence: Navigating Diverse Waters

Our educational landscape is beautifully diverse, but this diversity can sometimes lead to misunderstandings or unintentional exclusion.

Solution: Cultural Competency Training

Cultural competency is like a sophisticated GPS for educators, helping them navigate the rich, varied terrain of their school community. Maple Grove Middle School in Maple Grove, Minnesota, implemented a year-long cultural competency program for its staff. It wasn't just about one-off workshops; the school created ongoing learning circles where teachers could discuss real-life scenarios and learn from each other's experiences.

3. Differing Expectations: When Maps Don't Align
Sometimes, schools and families have different ideas about parent involvement, leading to frustration on both sides.

Solution: Clear, Mutually Agreed Upon Expectations
Think of this as co-creating a detailed travel itinerary for your educational journey together. Sunnyvale High in Sunnyvale, Texas, took an innovative approach. At the start of the school year, it hosted a "Partnership Planning Night." Families and educators worked together to draft a "Family-School Compact," outlining shared responsibilities and goals.

4. Language Barriers: When Words Create Walls
Language differences in our linguistically diverse communities can create significant obstacles to effective communication.

Solution: Comprehensive Language Support
Think of language support as building a universal translator for your school community. Riverdale Elementary in Germantown, Tennessee, went beyond just offering translators for major events. It created a "Language Buddy" system, pairing bilingual parents with those less confident in English. It also invested in a multi-language communication app that could translate real-time messages.

Action Step: Identify the primary challenge in your school-home partnership and brainstorm three potential solutions.

Take a moment to reflect on your school/home partnership journey. What's the biggest rapid you're currently facing? Is it the whirlpool of time constraints? The diverse waters of cultural differences? The misaligned maps of differing expectations? Or perhaps the wall of language barriers?

Once you have identified your primary challenge, let your creativity flow. Brainstorm three potential solutions, no matter how out-of-the-box they might seem. Remember, sometimes, the most innovative solutions come from thinking beyond traditional boundaries.

For instance, if time is your biggest constraint, you might consider:

1. Proposing a rotating evening or weekend "office hours" schedule for teacher-parent check-ins.
2. Suggest a voice message system where parents and teachers can leave updates for each other to be listened to at convenient times.
3. Create a private social media group for your child's class, where updates, questions, and discussions can happen asynchronously.

Addressing these challenges is not about finding perfect solutions but about making continuous progress. Each small step you take helps build a stronger bridge between home and school, creating a more supportive environment for your child's literacy journey.

As you navigate these waters, keep in mind the words of Margaret Mead: "Never doubt that a small group of thoughtful, committed citizens can change the world; indeed, it's the only thing that ever has." Your efforts to strengthen your school/home partnership, no matter how small they might seem, are creating ripples that can transform your child's educational experience and future.

So, what challenge will you tackle first? And what creative solutions will you find? Let's start working together to build strong school/home partnerships!

Partnerships Across Socioeconomic Backgrounds

It's important to recognize that the nature and challenges of school/home partnerships can vary across socioeconomic backgrounds. Research by Lareau (2011) found that middle-class families often have more resources and are familiar with the educational system to engage with schools effectively. This includes things like:

- Understanding how schools operate
- Knowing how to communicate with teachers and administrators
- Being comfortable advocating for their children
- Having social networks that include education professionals

Working-class and poor families, on the other hand, may face more barriers. These could include:

- Less familiarity with the education system
- Time constraints due to work schedules
- Language barriers
- Less confidence in interacting with school staff

Schools can address this imbalance by:

- Providing resources (e.g., books, educational materials) for families to use at home

- Offering workshops on how to support literacy in homes with limited resources
- Ensuring that communication and engagement opportunities are accessible to all families

Reflection Question: How can you support more equitable school/home partnerships in your community?

Supporting Diverse Learners

Diverse learners, such as those with learning disabilities or English Language Learners (ELLs), often need tailored approaches to reach their full potential in literacy. The bridge between school and home becomes even more crucial for these students, providing an environment where specialized strategies can be effectively implemented and developed.

For Students with Learning Disabilities: Cultivating Strength Through Collaboration

Supporting a child with a learning disability requires specialized attention and care. With the right approach, these children can achieve remarkable growth and success. Regular communication about Individualized Education Program (IEP) goals provides a detailed framework for supporting the child's unique needs. When parents and teachers agree on these goals, the child receives consistent, targeted support that helps him or her thrive. The Thompson family's experience illustrates this beautifully. Their daughter, Emma, has dyslexia, and initially, they felt overwhelmed. "It was like we were given a map in a language we couldn't read," Mrs. Thompson recalls.

However, regular meetings with Emma's special education teacher transformed their approach.

"We learned about the multisensory reading techniques they were using at school," Mr. Thompson shares. "Suddenly, our home reading time became a fun exploration of touch, sight, and sound. We'd trace letters in shaving cream, build words with Lego, and sing phonics songs. Emma's progress was remarkable, and more importantly, she started enjoying reading."

Sharing specific strategies used in school that can be reinforced at home ensures that the child receives consistent, effective support across all environments. This approach provides tailored assistance that enhances the child's learning and development in both educational and home settings. Dr. Sally Shaywitz, a leading expert in dyslexia, emphasizes this point: "Consistency and repetition are key for students with learning disabilities. When school and home reinforce the same strategies, we're essentially creating a 'surround sound' of support for the child" (Shaywitz, 2020).

Try this: Create a "Strategy of the Week" board at home. Each week, feature a new learning strategy from school and find creative ways to incorporate it into daily life.

For English Language Learners (ELLs): Supporting English Language Learners (ELLs) involves nurturing two languages simultaneously, with each language enhancing and complementing the other. The key is to develop both languages, allowing them to intertwine and strengthen each other. Encouraging home language use alongside English language development is crucial. This approach ensures that both languages receive equal care and attention, promoting balanced bilingual growth and cognitive development. The Nguyen family's story is a powerful testament to this approach. When 8-year-old Minh started struggling with reading in English, his parents were advised to speak only English at home.

"It felt wrong," Mrs. Nguyen admits. "Like we were uprooting half of our family's identity."

Thankfully, Minh's ESL teacher intervened. She encouraged the family to maintain rich conversations in Vietnamese while supporting English learning. "We started a beautiful routine," Mr. Nguyen shares. "We'd read a book in English, then discuss it in Vietnamese. Minh's comprehension improved in both languages, and he became proud of his bilingual abilities."

This approach aligns with what Dr. Jim Cummins calls the "interdependence hypothesis." He explains, "Skills developed in the home language transfer to the new language, serving as a foundation for literacy in both languages" (Cummins, 2000).

Providing bilingual resources empowers families to actively participate in their child's literacy development, regardless of their English proficiency. These materials enable parents and caregivers to support learning in both languages, fostering a rich, bilingual educational environment at home.

The Garcia family found an innovative way to leverage bilingual resources. "We started a Language Swap club with other ELL families," explains Mr. Garcia. "We'd meet monthly, share bilingual books, and exchange ideas for language learning. It became a supportive community where our children saw the value of their home languages while improving their English."

Try this: Create a "Language of the Day" calendar. Alternate between English and the home language, featuring a new daily word or phrase. Make it a family game to use the word as often as possible.

Dr. Guadalupe Valdés, a leading researcher in bilingualism, beautifully summarizes the importance of this inclusive approach: "When we support both the home language and English, we're not just teaching language; we're nurturing the child's entire identity and cognitive potential" (Valdés, 2018).

Supporting diverse learners is not about fixing deficits; it's about recognizing and nurturing unique strengths. By aligning school and home approaches, we create a robust support system that celebrates diversity and fosters success.

Reflection Question: Consider your child's unique learning needs or language background. How might you collaborate with your child's teacher to ensure consistency between home and school approaches?

Case Study: Enhancing ELL Student Literacy Through School/Home Partnership

Eight-year-old Maria stared at her desk, surrounded by unfamiliar English words that filled her with uncertainty. Since moving from Mexico, reading has transformed from a joy into a daily challenge in her new American classroom. Her classmates' voices swirled around her in an overwhelming stream of strange sounds, making each lesson feel like navigating through the fog.

Ms. Johnson, Maria's third-grade teacher, noticed Maria's struggle and crafted a plan for success. During one gentle afternoon conversation, she proposed a special reading adventure involving Maria's parents. The Garcias enthusiastically embraced this partnership to support their daughter's literacy journey, though they wondered how to turn their excitement into effective action.

Weekly video calls in both English and Spanish built the foundation of their shared mission. Ms. Johnson introduced bilingual books that claimed a cherished place in the Garcia home, sparking nightly family reading sessions. These stories created bridges between cultures. Ms. Johnson's reminder that "Spanish is a superpower for learning English" inspired the family to weave both languages into their daily lives through dinner conversations and bedtime stories.

The Garcia household created a daily 20-minute reading routine that turned their home into a learning sanctuary. They brought story characters to life with different voices, created word games, and connected vocabulary between languages. Ms. Johnson supplied interactive worksheets, online games, and writing prompts. Maria completed these activities at her kitchen table as her parents guided her progress, transforming every task into a family adventure.

Maria's transformation unfolded like a beautiful story over the following months. Her quiet classroom whisper grew into a confident voice. Her vocabulary flourished in both languages as naturally as flowers in spring. Reading comprehension became clear and natural. The once-shy newcomer evolved into an engaged, bilingual storyteller who shared tales with her classmates.

Mrs. Garcia reflected through tears on their remarkable journey during the final parent-teacher conference. "Our whole family has learned to read anew," she shared, describing how the experience enriched their household. Ms. Johnson smiled, explaining how the partnership between school and home created the perfect environment for Maria's growth. Together, they celebrated Maria's achievement in becoming a bridge between two cultures, her literacy flourishing through the powerful collaboration between school and home.

Digital Communication Tools and School/Home Partnerships

Recent research has highlighted the growing role of digital tools in facilitating school/home communication. A 2015 study by Kraft and Rogers found that weekly text message updates to parents about their child's academic progress significantly increased student achievement.

Popular digital communication tools used by schools include:
- Class Dojo
- Remind
- Google Classroom
- School-specific apps

Here is a real-world example using Class Dojo:

Sarah, the parent of a second grader named Alex, uses Class Dojo to stay connected with her child's literacy progress. Here's how it works:

1. Daily updates: Alex's teacher posts a quick summary of the day's reading lesson. For instance, "Today we practiced making predictions while reading *Charlotte's Web*."
2. Individual progress: Sarah receives a private message that Alex struggled with some vocabulary words in today's reading. The teacher suggests a fun word game they can play at home to reinforce these words.
3. Homework reminders: The app notifies Sarah that Alex needs to read for 20 minutes tonight and complete a short book response.
4. Sharing successes: The teacher uploads a photo of Alex's latest writing piece, allowing Sarah to see her child's progress in sentence structure and creativity.
5. Quick questions: Sarah uses the messaging feature to ask the teacher about Alex's reading level progress, getting a prompt response that helps her choose appropriate books for home reading.
6. Resource sharing: The teacher posts links to online reading games that reinforce skills taught in class, which Sarah and Alex can explore together at home.

While these tools can enhance communication, it's important to ensure they don't replace face-to-face interactions entirely.

Adapting Partnerships in the Wake of COVID-19

The COVID-19 pandemic has significantly transformed the dynamic between schools and homes, creating challenges and collaboration opportunities. As education shifted to remote and hybrid learning models, the roles of parents and teachers became more intertwined than ever before. The lines between home and school have blurred, leading to an urgent need for closer, more effective partnerships to support children's learning.

Key Adaptations in School/Home Collaboration

Several key adaptations have emerged in response to the demands of pandemic-era education. These adjustments helped bridge the gap during a time of crisis but also revealed strategies that may continue to strengthen school/home partnerships moving forward.

- **Increased Use of Video Conferencing for Parent-Teacher Meetings**: With schools unable to host in-person meetings, video conferencing became a critical tool for maintaining communication between parents and teachers. Platforms like Zoom and Google Meet allowed for more frequent and flexible check-ins, making it easier for working parents to attend meetings without needing to take time off or arrange childcare. Virtual meetings provided a more accessible option for parents to engage with their child's education, especially for those who might have previously faced barriers to in-person attendance.

- **More Frequent, Often Daily, Communication About Learning Activities**: Communication between schools and homes became more consistent and detailed during remote learning. Teachers would send daily or weekly updates about lessons, assignments, and expectations, allowing parents to stay informed and better equipped to assist their children. This regular flow of information helped parents feel more connected to their child's learning process and created opportunities for immediate feedback or support if difficulties arose.

- **Greater Emphasis on Supporting Parents as Co-Educators**: As classrooms moved into the home, parents were thrust into the role of co-educators, often taking on tasks like guiding lessons, helping with technology, and managing schedules. Recognizing this shift, many schools began providing resources and training to help parents navigate their new responsibilities. Educators offered practical guidance on everything from setting up a productive learning environment to troubleshooting technical issues, helping parents feel more confident and capable of supporting education at home.

The Impact of Strong School/Home Communication
Research highlights the importance of effective communication between schools and families during remote learning. "COVID-19 and Remote Learning: Experiences of Parents with Children during the Pandemic" by Garbe, Ogurlu, Logan, and Cook, published in 2020 in

the *American Journal of Qualitative Research*, found that successful remote learning during the pandemic was characterized by strong school/home communication and clear guidance for parents on how to support their child's learning at home. When teachers provided explicit instructions and maintained regular contact, parents felt more empowered to assist with learning activities, leading to better student outcomes. The study also highlighted that frequent communication helped identify and address challenges early on, preventing students from falling behind.

In addition to logistical support, strong communication fostered a partnership between parents and educators. Both groups had to rely on one another in unprecedented ways, with parents acting as the eyes and ears on the ground while teachers adapted lesson plans for at-home instruction. This partnership was often key to student success, especially in households where technology issues or learning disabilities created additional hurdles.

Get Parents Engaged in Literacy Activities
Studies show that when parents get involved, kids do better with reading and writing. As educators, we need to find ways to connect what happens in class with what happens at home. So how can we do this?

One idea is to have Family Literacy Nights. These are fun events where families come to school to do reading and writing activities together. Imagine families working on stories or puzzles. It's a great way for everyone to learn and bond. We can also send home literacy kits. These are like take-home packages with books and activities. They help turn regular home time into learning time.

Keeping in touch with parents is super important. A class newsletter can share tips and updates about reading and writing, helping parents know how to help their kids at home. These days, we can use technology to stay connected. Apps and social media make it easy to share updates and resources with parents quickly.

Another good idea is to have parents volunteer in class. It gives them a chance to see how we teach reading and helps in the classroom, too. Parent-child book clubs are neat because they get families to read together. This can help kids enjoy reading more, even when it's not for school.

Lastly, it's important to have resources in different languages for families who speak languages other than English at home. This shows we respect all cultures and want everyone to be included. By doing all these things, we're helping kids read better while creating a community where everyone values reading and writing, both in school and at home.

Reflection Question: What do you think works best to get families involved in literacy?

Building a Framework for Future Partnerships
The adaptations made during the pandemic will likely leave a lasting impact on school/home partnerships. As we move forward, several lessons can be carried into future practices to strengthen collaboration between schools and families:

- **Maintaining Flexibility with Communication**: The success of video conferencing and more frequent communication suggests that schools should continue offering flexible options for parent engagement. Virtual meetings can supplement traditional in-person conferences, making it easier for all parents to participate regardless of their schedules or personal circumstances. Continuing to offer regular updates about student progress can also help keep parents informed and engaged.

- **Empowering Parents as Partners in Education**: The pandemic emphasized the role of parents as critical partners in their child's education. Schools can build on this momentum by providing resources and support for parents, helping them remain active participants in their child's learning even when students return to in-person classes. Offering workshops, guides, and online resources can ensure that parents feel equipped to contribute meaningfully to their child's educational journey.

- **Personalized Support and Communication**: The pandemic highlighted families' varying needs, from access to technology to differing levels of time and expertise available for home instruction. Going forward, schools may benefit from adopting more personalized approaches to communication and support. Understanding the unique challenges that each family faces allows educators to tailor their interactions and provide the necessary tools to help each student succeed, whether through differentiated communication methods or specialized resources.

Redefining School/Home Collaboration Post-COVID
The pandemic highlighted the importance of strong, ongoing communication and parents' critical role in supporting their children's education. The adaptations made during remote and hybrid learning have revealed new pathways for effective collaboration that can continue to benefit students in the post-pandemic era. By building on these practices through flexible communication options, empowering parents, and offering personalized support, schools and families can create stronger, more resilient partnerships that enhance student learning and well-being for the long term.

Conclusion: The Bridge to Literacy Success

Building strong connections between home and school is like constructing a sturdy bridge. It requires effort, communication, and ongoing maintenance, but the results are transformative. When parents and educators work harmoniously, children receive consistent support, encouragement, and instruction, leading to more robust literacy development.

Key takeaways from this chapter include:
1. Understanding your child's school literacy curriculum is crucial for effective support at home.
2. Effective communication with teachers involves using multiple channels, being proactive, and asking specific questions.

3. Aligning home literacy practices with school instruction significantly boosts reading achievement.
4. Supporting school literacy initiatives at home, such as reading logs and sight word practice, enhances their effectiveness.
5. Addressing challenges in school/home partnerships, including time constraints and language barriers, is essential for inclusive collaboration.
6. Digital communication tools can enhance school/home connections but should not replace face-to-face interactions entirely.
7. Adapting partnerships to changing circumstances, as seen during the COVID-19 pandemic, is crucial for continuing to support children's literacy development.

As we move forward in our exploration, remember that you are not alone on this journey. Your child's teachers are valuable allies, bringing expertise and daily classroom experience to complement your deep knowledge of your child and your home literacy efforts.

Further Reading:

1. *Beyond the Bake Sale: The Essential Guide to Family-School Partnerships* by Anne T. Henderson, Karen L. Mapp, Vivian R. Johnson, and Don Davies- This comprehensive guide offers practical strategies for building strong school-family partnerships.
2. *Home, School, and Community Collaboration: Culturally Responsive Family Engagement* by Kathy B. Grant and Julie A. Ray- This book provides insights into creating culturally responsive partnerships with diverse families.
3. *The Reading Strategies Book: Your Everything Guide to Developing Skilled Readers* by Jennifer Serravallo- While primarily for teachers, this resource can help parents understand and support various reading strategies used in schools.
4. National Association for Family, School, and Community Engagement (NAFSCE) website: https://nafsce.org/- This organization offers resources, research, and best practices for effective family engagement in education.
5. Reading Rockets website: https://www.readingrockets.org/- A comprehensive site offering a wealth of research-based information on reading and strategies for parents and educators.

Practical Exercises

1. **Communication Audit**: Review your current communication methods with your child's teacher. List them out and evaluate their effectiveness and identify any gaps or areas for improvement. Set a goal to implement one new communication strategy (e.g., weekly email check-ins) for the next month.
2. **Curriculum Scavenger Hunt**: Obtain a copy of your child's literacy curriculum or standards for their grade level. Create a simple checklist of key skills or topics and, over a week, try to identify how these skills are being practiced at home in everyday activities. This will help you align home activities with school learning.
3. **Literacy Environment Assessment**: Take a "tour" of your home, looking at it through the lens of literacy support. Identify areas where you could enhance literacy engagement (e.g., creating a cozy reading nook, setting up a writing station, displaying alphabet charts in frequently used spaces). Make a plan to implement at least two improvements.
4. **Teacher Interview**: Prepare a list of 5-10 questions about your child's literacy instruction and progress and schedule a brief meeting (in-person or virtual) with your child's teacher to discuss these questions. Focus on understanding current strategies used in class and how you can support them at home.
5. **Family Literacy Night**: Plan and host a "Family Literacy Night" at home. Include activities that mirror school literacy practices (e.g., read-aloud,

writing prompts, word games) and invite your child to be the teacher for part of the evening, explaining a concept or leading an activity he or she has learned at school.

Chapter 6: Overcoming Challenges: Addressing Literacy Difficulties

Overview
"The human brain is resilient, but there is no question that early intervention is more effective than later intervention," asserts Dr. Sally Shaywitz, co-director of the Yale Center for Dyslexia & Creativity. These words underscore the critical importance of addressing literacy difficulties promptly and effectively. In this chapter, we embark on a journey to understand, confront, and overcome some children's challenges in developing reading and writing skills.

From recognizing early warning signs to understanding common learning disabilities, we'll begin by exploring the early signs of reading and writing difficulties, equipping you with the knowledge to spot potential issues before they become entrenched. You'll discover practical strategies to support struggling readers at home, learn how to effectively collaborate with schools, and explore the role of professional assessments and interventions. Along the way, we'll address the crucial emotional aspects of literacy challenges and share inspiring success stories. By the end of this chapter, you'll be armed with the insights and approaches needed to empower every child to become a confident, capable reader and writer.

Early Signs of Reading and Writing Difficulties
Parents can learn to recognize early indicators of literacy struggles, much like they notice other developmental

milestones in their children. By being attentive to their child's reading and writing behaviors, parents can identify potential challenges early on and seek appropriate support when needed.

Some early signs of literacy struggle to watch for include:
- Difficulty recognizing and producing rhymes
- Struggles with letter recognition and sound-letter correspondence
- Persistent reversal of letters or numbers beyond age 7
- Difficulty remembering sight words
- Slow, laborious reading
- Avoidance of reading activities

Remember, occasional struggles are normal. It's persistent difficulties that warrant attention.

Reflection Questions: Have you noticed any of the early signs of reading difficulties in a child you know? How might you approach addressing these signs?

Common Learning Disabilities Affecting Literacy

While every child's journey to literacy is unique, certain learning disabilities frequently stand in the way of progress. These conditions don't define a child's potential but can influence the way they experience learning. By understanding these challenges, parents, teachers, and caregivers can offer better support, helping students build confidence and find ways to thrive academically.

One of the most common learning disabilities affecting literacy is dyslexia, a neurological condition that impairs word recognition, spelling, and decoding abilities. Contrary to misconceptions, dyslexia has nothing to do with intelligence. Imagine a bright, imaginative child who struggles to read, perhaps feeling frustrated or embarrassed as his or her classmates breeze through books. Yet, with the right support—like structured literacy instruction—this child can unlock the joy of reading, overcoming the difficulties that once seemed insurmountable.

Another common learning disability is attention deficit hyperactivity disorder (ADHD). While ADHD is most often associated with attention and behavior regulation, it can have a profound impact on literacy. Students with ADHD might struggle to focus during reading assignments or find it difficult to organize their thoughts in writing. Think of a student who reads a paragraph multiple times but finds their mind wandering before fully understanding the content. For these students, strategies like breaking tasks into smaller, manageable parts and using graphic organizers can be game changers.

Another lesser known but equally important condition is Auditory Processing Disorder (APD). This affects how the brain processes spoken language, which can impact a child's ability to hear sounds correctly and link them to corresponding letters. A child with APD might be able to hear perfectly well but may have trouble understanding a fast-paced classroom discussion or remembering multi-step instructions. In literacy, APD can impede phonological awareness—the critical ability to hear and manipulate sounds, which is key to learning to read. Providing these children with clear, concise instructions and using multisensory learning methods can help bridge the gap.

Visual Processing Disorder (VPD) presents another set of challenges. This condition affects how the brain interprets visual information, which can interfere with reading fluency and comprehension. A child with VPD might see words clearly but have trouble making sense of them, skipping lines, or confusing similar-looking letters like "b" and "d." They might struggle with reading maps, charts, or even the words on a page. For these students, using color-coded text, reading guides, or highlighting key sections can help them navigate the text more effectively.

Having a learning disability doesn't mean a child is destined for academic struggles forever. Dr. Louisa Moats, a leading expert in literacy education, reminds us: "Learning disabilities are not a prescription for failure. With the right kinds of instruction, guidance, and support, there are no limits to what individuals with LD can achieve" (Moats 2017, 132). Dr. Moats' insight is both a call to action and a message of hope. Consider the story of a student with dyslexia who, after years of battling low self-esteem due to reading difficulties, finally receives the right intervention. With the help of a dedicated teacher and tailored instruction, they begin to read fluently and gain confidence in the classroom and every aspect of their life.

For parents, it's important to remember that early identification and intervention are key. By working with educators and specialists, you can help your child develop the strategies and resilience they need to navigate their learning disability and experience academic success. These disabilities do not define a child's future. With the right tools, guidance, and persistence, every child can discover their strengths and reach their full potential.

Creating a Supportive Home Environment for Children with Literacy Challenges

The home environment plays a pivotal role in a child's literacy development, especially for those facing challenges. As parents and caregivers, we have the power to transform our homes into nurturing spaces that foster a love for reading and writing. Let's explore some strategies to create this supportive environment, bringing them to life with real-world examples and expert insights.

1. Make Reading a Positive Experience

The key to nurturing a love for reading lies in making it an enjoyable, stress-free activity. This involves a well-thought-out selection of reading materials and creating a cozy, inviting reading atmosphere. Dr. Maria Montessori once said, "The greatest sign of success for a teacher...is to be able to say, 'The children are now working as if I did not exist.'" This principle applies beautifully to parents supporting their children's reading journey.

Consider the story of Jake, a 9-year-old struggling reader. His mother, Sarah, shares: "We used to battle over reading time. Then, we discovered Jake's passion for dinosaurs. We filled his bookshelf with dinosaur books at various reading levels and paired them with dinosaur audiobooks. Now, I often find Jake curled up in his 'reading nest'—a cozy corner we created together—lost in a world of prehistoric creatures."

Strategies to try:
- Create a dedicated, comfortable reading space
- Allow children to choose their reading material
- Pair audiobooks with print books for a multisensory experience
- Read aloud to your child, regardless of his or her age

2. Break Tasks into Smaller Steps

Large tasks can overwhelm children with literacy challenges. Breaking these tasks into smaller, manageable steps can make learning less daunting and more achievable. Dr. Carol Dweck, known for her work on growth mindset, emphasizes the importance of praising effort and progress: "The way we explain success and failure critically impacts a child's motivation."

Emily, a reading specialist, shares a success story: "I worked with a 10-year-old, Mia, who panicked at the sight of a full page of text. We started using a window tool, a piece of card with a small rectangle cut out. Mia would slide this over the text, revealing just one sentence at a time. Gradually, we increased the window size. Mia's confidence soared within months, and she could tackle whole paragraphs without anxiety."

Try these steps:
- Use a window tool for reading
- Break writing tasks into brainstorming, drafting, and editing stages
- Set small, achievable daily goals

3. Embrace Multisensory Approaches

Incorporating multiple senses into literacy activities can enhance learning and make it more engaging. This approach is rooted in the Orton-Gillingham method, which was developed in the 1930s and is still widely used today. Dr. Samuel Orton and Anna Gillingham believed that children with dyslexia learn best when lessons engage multiple senses simultaneously. Modern neuroscience research has since supported this theory.

Lisa, a mother of twins with dyslexia, shares her experience: "We turned our kitchen into a literacy lab. The boys trace letters in shaving cream on the counter, mold sight words with Play-Doh, and jump on letter mats while spelling words. Their progress has been remarkable, and more importantly, they're having fun while learning." Some multisensory activities to try:
- Create letter shapes with pipe cleaners or Play-Doh
- Play hopscotch with sight words
- Use body movements to represent different sounds in words

4. Focus on Phonological Awareness

Phonological awareness is a critical foundation for reading success. It involves recognizing and manipulating the sounds in spoken language. Dr. Linnea Ehri, a professor of educational psychology, emphasizes: "Phoneme awareness is essential for learning an alphabetic writing system. It's like a glue that helps children secure the connections between letters in spellings and sounds in pronunciations of words in memory."

John, the father of a 6-year-old with a language processing disorder, shares: "We play sound games every day. Our favorite is the odd-one-out game. I say four words, and Emma has to identify the one that doesn't share a sound with the others. It's amazing to see her ears perk up as she listens intently to the sounds."

Try these phonological awareness activities:
- Play rhyming games
- Clap out syllables in words
- Practice blending and segmenting sounds in words
- Play I Spy with beginning sounds

5. Leverage Assistive Technology

Various technological tools can support children with literacy challenges in our digital age. These tools can help level the playing field, allowing children to access content and express their ideas more easily. Dr. Todd Rose, a developmental neuropsychologist, advocates for using assistive technology: "These tools don't just compensate for weaknesses; they allow students to capitalize on their strengths."

Michael, a high school student with dyslexia, shares his experience: "Text-to-speech software changed my life. I went from dreading reading assignments to actually enjoying literature. Now, I listen to the text while following along in the book. It's improved my comprehension and my spelling."

Some helpful assistive technologies:
- Text-to-speech software
- Speech-to-text tools
- Digital graphic organizers
- Spell-checkers and word-prediction software

6. Celebrate Progress

Acknowledging and celebrating progress, no matter how small, can significantly boost a child's confidence and motivation. This aligns with the principles of positive reinforcement in psychology. Dr. Robert Brooks, a psychologist specializing in motivation, advises: "We must create islands of competence for children with learning challenges. These are areas where they feel capable and confident, which then generalize to other areas of their lives."

Sarah, a reading tutor, shares a heartwarming story: "I work with a 7-year-old, Zoe, who struggled with sight words. We created a word wall in her room. Every time she mastered a new word, she'd write it on a colorful star and add it to her wall. Seeing that wall grow has been incredibly motivating for Zoe. Now, she eagerly asks to learn new words!"

Ways to celebrate progress:
- Create a visual representation of achievements (like Zoe's word wall)
- Keep a journal of reading victories
- Share successes with family members or friends
- Plan small rewards for reaching goals

As we implement these strategies, it's important to remember consistency. Dr. Reid Lyon, a neuroscientist specializing in learning disabilities, reminds us: "It's not that some students can't learn; it's that sometimes we don't use methods that teach them in the ways they learn best" (Lyon 2018, 45). Consistency doesn't mean rigidity. It means creating a reliable, supportive environment where learning is a natural, ongoing process. It's about weaving these strategies into your daily life in a way that feels organic and sustainable for your family.

Remember, every child's journey is unique. What works for one might not work for another. The key is to remain patient, observant, and flexible, always ready to adjust your approach based on your child's needs and responses.

Reflection Questions: Take a moment to reflect on your experiences and comfort level in supporting a child with literacy challenges. How comfortable do you feel collaborating with schools on these issues? What steps could you take to improve this collaboration?
Perhaps you could:
- Schedule regular meetings with your child's teachers
- Join a parent support group for children with learning differences
- Attend workshops or webinars on literacy support strategies
- Share successful home strategies with your child's educational team

You are your child's most important advocate. By creating a supportive home environment and fostering strong school/home connections, you're laying the foundation for your child's success in literacy and lifelong learning.

As you embark on this journey, keep in mind Dr. Seuss's words: "You're off to Great Places! Today is your day! Your mountain is waiting, So...get on your way!" With patience, persistence, and the right strategies, every child can climb their mountain of literacy challenges and discover the joy of reading and writing.

Working with Schools to Address Literacy Challenges

When difficulties arise in your child's literacy development, it can be confusing and frustrating. However, you create a clear path forward by forging a strong partnership with the school. This collaboration provides guidance and support, turning potential obstacles into opportunities for growth. Let's explore how to build this crucial partnership, which can transform challenges into stepping stones for success.

1. Requesting a Comprehensive Evaluation

A comprehensive evaluation helps identify specific areas where your child might be struggling, providing a clear understanding of their literacy challenges. The Thompsons' experience illustrates the power of this step. When 9-year-old Jake struggled to keep up with his peers in reading, his parents felt helpless. "We knew he was having trouble, but we couldn't pinpoint exactly where," Mrs. Thompson recalls. After requesting a comprehensive evaluation, the family finally got clarity. "The evaluation gave us the answers we needed," Mr. Thompson shares. "We discovered Jake had dyslexia. We had a name for what he was experiencing and a plan for how to help him."

2. Understanding Your Rights

Familiarizing yourself with special education laws helps you understand the often-complicated world of educational support. These laws explain what your child is entitled to and what schools must provide. When you know these rules, you can better speak up for your child and make sure they get the right help and adjustments at school. This knowledge is like a tool kit that helps you work with the school to get your child the support they need to succeed.

3. Participating in IEP or 504 Plan Development

If your child qualifies for an Individualized Education Program (IEP) or a 504 plan, think of this process as co-creating a detailed roadmap through the literacy labyrinth. Your input is crucial in ensuring this map accurately reflects your child's needs and strengths.

The Garcia family's story beautifully illustrates the importance of this collaboration. When their daughter Sophia was diagnosed with a language processing disorder, they felt overwhelmed by the IEP process. "At first, it felt like we were trying to read a map in a foreign language," Mr. Garcia admits. But something remarkable happened as they actively participated in the meetings, asking questions and sharing insights about Sophia's home behaviors. "We realized we weren't just passive recipients of a plan," Mrs. Garcia explains. "We were essential contributors. Our understanding of Sophia complemented the teacher's expertise. Together, we created a plan that really worked for her."

4. Maintaining Open Communication

Open communication with teachers and specialists is crucial for helping your child with literacy challenges. It creates a strong connection between school and home, allowing information, strategies, and support to flow smoothly. You might want to use a communication notebook that goes back and forth between home and school or set up regular email or phone check-ins. The most important thing is to keep communication consistent and clear. This way, everyone stays on the same page about the child's progress and needs, making it easier to provide the right support at school and home.

5. Requesting Progress Updates and Advocating

Regular progress updates are important for tracking your child's literacy development. They help you see if your child is improving and allow you to adjust their support if needed. These updates show you if the current strategies are working or if something different should be tried. Don't be afraid to speak up for your child if you think they're not getting the help they need. You know your child best, so if you feel the school's approach isn't working, it's okay to talk to teachers or administrators about your concerns.

Dr. Maryanne Wolf, co-founder of Curious Learning: A Global Literacy Initiative, points out, "The most successful interventions occur when there is a seamless connection between what happens in school and at home" (Wolf 2019, 201). This means that working closely with your child's school and staying informed about their progress can really help improve their reading and writing skills.

The Patel family learned the power of advocacy when their son Arjun's progress seemed to stall. "We noticed Arjun wasn't making the gains we'd hoped for," Mrs. Patel shares. "At first, we were hesitant to speak up, but we realized that our observations at home were valuable insights." They requested a meeting with Arjun's teaching team and shared their concerns and observations. This led to a reevaluation of Arjun's intervention strategies and, ultimately, a breakthrough in his reading progress. "It was like we'd been trying to solve a puzzle with some pieces missing," Mr. Patel reflects. "We provided those missing pieces by advocating for Arjun and sharing our perspective. Suddenly, the whole picture became clearer."

Addressing literacy difficulties is not a solo journey. It's a collaborative expedition involving you, your child, teachers, and specialists. By working together, sharing insights, and maintaining open communication, you create a powerful support network to guide your child through the literacy labyrinth. Keep in mind the words of Dr. Shaywitz: "Difficulties in reading are not a reflection of intelligence or effort. With the right support and interventions, every child can find their path to literacy success" (Shaywitz, 2020).

Reflection Question: Consider your current relationship with your child's school regarding literacy support. What's one step you could take this week to strengthen this partnership? How might you leverage your unique knowledge of your child to contribute to their literacy support plan?

The Role of Professional Assessments and Interventions

While parents play an imperative role in supporting their child's literacy development, professional support is often necessary when addressing significant literacy challenges. This may include various specialists and interventions:

1. Educational Psychologists:
   - Conduct comprehensive cognitive and academic assessments
   - What to expect:
     - In-depth evaluation of cognitive abilities, including memory, processing speed, and reasoning
     - Academic achievement testing in reading, writing, and math
     - Attention and executive functioning assessments
     - Detailed report with findings and recommendations
   - Typically involves multiple sessions, including interviews, testing, and feedback meetings

2. Speech-Language Pathologists (SLPs):
   - Perform language and phonological processing evaluations
   - What to expect:
     - Assessment of receptive and expressive language skills
     - Evaluation of phonological awareness and processing
     - Screening for articulation and fluency issues
     - Recommendations for therapy or classroom accommodations
   - May involve both standardized tests and informal observations

3. Occupational Therapists (OTs):
   - Assess fine motor and visual processing skills

- What to expect:
  - Evaluation of handwriting and fine motor coordination
  - Assessment of visual perception and visual-motor integration
  - Screening for sensory processing issues that may impact learning
  - Practical strategies to improve classroom performance
- Often includes both clinical assessment and functional observations

4. Specialized Reading Tutors or Interventionists:
   - Provide targeted skill development
   - What to expect:
     - Initial assessment to identify specific areas of difficulty
     - Customized intervention plan based on the child's needs
     - Regular one-on-one or small group sessions
     - Progress monitoring and adjustment of strategies as needed
   - May use various research-based programs and approaches

5. Multidisciplinary Team Approach:
    - In many cases, a combination of these professionals may work together to provide a comprehensive evaluation and intervention plan
    - What to expect:
        - Coordinated assessments to avoid duplication
        - Team meetings to discuss findings and recommendations
        - Collaborative development of an Individualized Education Program (IEP) or 504 plan if appropriate

6. Early Intervention Programs:
    - As emphasized by Dr. Nadine Gaab, early identification and intervention are crucial
    - What to expect:
        - Screening programs in schools or pediatric settings
        - Rapid response with targeted interventions for at-risk children
        - Focus on foundational skills like phonological awareness and phonics
        - Regular progress monitoring and communication with parents

7. Ongoing Support and Reevaluation:
    - Professional involvement often extends beyond the initial assessment
    - What to expect:
        - Regular check-ins and progress updates

- Adjustment of interventions based on response
- Periodic reevaluations to track progress and identify any new concerns

Gaab, an associate professor of pediatrics at Boston Children's Hospital, stresses the importance of early, targeted intervention: "The key is to catch struggling readers early and provide them with systematic, explicit, and intensive instruction in phonological awareness and phonics" (Gaab 2021, 78).

Assistive Technologies for Literacy Support

Technology has emerged as a powerful ally for struggling readers and writers in our increasingly digital world. These innovative tools don't just offer convenience; they provide essential support that can transform a child's educational experience. Imagine a student who once shied away from complex texts is now eagerly engaging with new ideas, all thanks to a device that reads aloud to them. For children grappling with traditional reading and writing methods, these technologies serve as bridges, connecting them to academic success and boosting their confidence as learners.

A Tool Kit for Success

Assistive technologies have emerged as powerful allies in supporting students with diverse learning needs. These innovative tools are essential components in creating an inclusive and effective learning environment. For students grappling with literacy challenges, these technologies can be the bridge that connects their capabilities with their potential, transforming obstacles into opportunities. Let's explore some of the most impactful assistive technologies:

1. **Text-to-Speech (TTS) Software**: These tools breathe life into written words, converting them into spoken language. For a child struggling with decoding, this can be the key to unlocking a world of knowledge previously shrouded in frustration.
2. **Speech Recognition Programs**: These programs that transcribe spoken words into text offer a lifeline to students who struggle with fine motor skills or traditional spelling. Suddenly, the barrier between thought and written expression dissolves, allowing ideas to flow freely.
3. **Digital Graphic Organizers**: These visual aids provide a structure for planning essays or stories, breaking down the writing process into manageable steps. For students who feel overwhelmed by a blank page, these tools can be the scaffolding they need to build confidence and competence.
4. **Reading Pens**: These portable devices scan and read text aloud, empowering students to work independently. Imagine a child who once needed constant support navigating through books independently, with a sense of autonomy growing with each page.
5. **Specialized Fonts**: Fonts like Dyslexie or OpenDyslexic are designed with the needs of dyslexic readers in mind. By altering the visual appearance of letters to reduce misreading, these

fonts can clear the path to comprehension for many students.

Each of these tools meets students where they are, providing tailored support that can unlock their potential and transform their relationship with learning.

The Human Touch: Balancing Technology and Instruction

While these technological aids offer tremendous support, it's crucial to remember that they complement, rather than replace, expert instruction and human connection. Dr. Linda Siegel, a renowned expert in learning disabilities, wisely notes, "Technology should supplement, not replace, systematic instruction in reading and writing skills" (Siegel 2016, 156). Dr. Siegel's words serve as an essential reminder. While a speech recognition program might help children transcribe their ideas, it can't teach them the phonemic awareness fundamental to becoming an independent reader. The most effective approach combines technological support with skilled, personalized instruction.

The impact of assistive technologies extends beyond academic performance; it can profoundly affect a child's self-perception as a learner. Consider a student with dysgraphia who once dreaded writing assignments but now eagerly participates in using a speech-to-text program. Or imagine a child with dyslexia who, after years of struggling to read fluently, discovers a new world of literature through a reading pen. These technologies don't just make education accessible; they transform how children see themselves as learners, showing them that success is within reach.

Given the rapid pace of technological advancement, parents and educators must stay informed about emerging tools. Following educational technology blogs, attending workshops, and regularly consulting with your child's educational team are excellent ways to stay up-to-date. By being proactive, we can ensure that students can access the most effective tools to support their literacy journeys.

Assistive technologies offer a new chapter in the story of literacy support. They provide powerful tools that can level the playing field for struggling readers and writers, opening doors to learning that may have once seemed firmly shut. However, it's important to remember that these technologies are most effective when used as part of a comprehensive approach to literacy instruction, guided by skilled educators and supported by engaged parents. Let's embrace these innovations while remembering the irreplaceable value of human connection and expert instruction in every child's learning journey. With this balanced approach, we can empower every child to write their success story.

The Emotional Impact of Literacy Difficulties

We should recognize that literacy challenges can significantly affect the emotional well-being of a child. Struggling readers may experience frustration, anxiety, low self-esteem, and even depression. These emotional impacts can make learning even more difficult for students who are already facing reading challenges. Dr. Ryan Spencer, a literacy expert from the University of Canberra, puts it eloquently: "Learning to read is not just about decoding words; it is about decoding one's self-worth. When children struggle with reading, they are not just grappling with text; they are wrestling with their identity" (Spencer, 2018). Let's address these emotional challenges:

1. Validate their feelings

Think of validation as creating a safe harbor in the turbulent sea of literacy struggles. It's about letting your child know their feelings are valid and understood.

Nine-year-old Zoe's story beautifully illustrates the power of validation. Zoe, a bright girl with dyslexia, would often dissolve into tears during reading time. Her mother, Sarah, shares a turning point in their journey: "One day, instead of trying to cajole Zoe into reading, I sat with her and said, 'Reading can be tough, can't it? It's okay to feel frustrated.' The relief on Zoe's face was immediate. It was like she could finally let out a breath she'd been holding. From that day on, Zoe became more open about her struggles, which allowed us to address them together."

2. Focus on strengths

While addressing literacy difficulties, it's essential to help your child explore and develop their talents in other areas. Think of it as helping them discover new, exciting islands in their ocean of abilities.

The story of Alex, a 12-year-old struggling reader, exemplifies this approach. Alex's parents noticed his knack for solving puzzles and enrolled him in a robotics club. "Seeing Alex light up as he programmed his first robot was incredible," his father recounts. "It reminded us—and more importantly, reminded Alex—that reading challenges don't define his intelligence or potential."

3. Provide a supportive environment

Ensuring your child feels safe to make mistakes and ask for help is like creating a protected cove where they can practice navigating the waters of literacy without fear of judgment.

The Chen family transformed their living room into a "Mistake Celebration Zone" for their daughter, Mei. "We hung a sign that said," 'Mistakes are proof you're trying,'" Mrs. Chen explains. "Whenever Mei stumbled over a word or misunderstood a passage, we'd ring a little bell and cheer. It sounds silly, but it completely changed her attitude towards reading challenges."

4. Teach positive self-talk

Helping your child develop by encouraging internal dialogue is like equipping them with an inner compass that always points toward self-compassion and perseverance.

Eleven-year-old Jamal's journey with positive self-talk is particularly inspiring. His teacher taught the class to be their own "reading coaches." Jamal's mother shares, "Now, when Jamal encounters a difficult word, I hear him whisper to himself, 'You've got this, Coach Jamal. Take it step by step.' It's beautiful to witness him encouraging himself."

5. Consider counseling

If emotional struggles persist, professional support can act as a lighthouse, helping your child navigate the complex emotions associated with literacy difficulties. The Rodriguez family's experience highlights the value of professional support. When their son Carlos' reading struggles led to anxiety and not wanting to go to school, they sought help from a child psychologist. "It was like

Carlos had been lost in a fog of negative emotions," Mr. Rodriguez reflects. "The counselor helped him find his way back to clearer skies. She gave him tools to manage his anxiety and rebuild his confidence. Now, Carlos approaches reading challenges with resilience instead of fear."

Dr. Moats emphasizes the importance of addressing the emotional aspect of literacy difficulties: "We must remember that behind every struggling reader is a child with hopes, fears, and infinite potential. By nurturing their emotional well-being and literacy skills, we give them the best chance to thrive" (Moats, 2020).

We must guide our children through these emotional challenges while teaching them to read and explore their world with confidence. When we focus on learning and emotional support, we help create strong readers who are ready to tackle any challenge that comes their way.

Reflection Question: Considering the emotional impact of literacy difficulties, how might you better support a struggling reader's emotional well-being?

Building Confidence and Motivation in Struggling Readers

When a child struggles with reading, it's not just their literacy skills that are affected. Their self-esteem, motivation, and overall attitude toward learning can take a significant hit. As parents, our role extends beyond teaching reading strategies—we must also nurture these children's confidence and kindle their motivation to learn. Let's dig deeper into Dr. Robert Brooks' suggestions and explore how we can implement them effectively.

Focus on Strengths
Recognizing and developing a child's talents across various areas can significantly boost his or her confidence. When children are aware of their strengths, they are more likely to approach reading with a positive attitude. Educators and parents can celebrate these strengths by providing opportunities for students to shine, even in small ways, which helps build a sense of achievement and self-worth.

Provide Choices
Allowing children to have some control over their learning can significantly enhance their motivation. Providing choices in reading materials or activities can make learning more engaging and personalized. This autonomy helps students feel more invested in their learning journey.

Set Realistic Goals
Setting attainable goals is crucial for building competence and confidence. By breaking tasks into smaller, manageable steps, educators can create opportunities for immediate success. These goals might include:
- Reading for 15 minutes without interruption
- Learning five new sight words a week
- Successfully sounding out all the words on a page of a leveled reader

The key is to make these goals challenging enough to require effort but achievable enough to ensure success.

Celebrate each time a child reaches a goal! These celebrations reinforce a sense of progress and competence.

Model a Growth Mindset
Demonstrating a growth mindset by viewing challenges as opportunities for learning can inspire students to adopt the same perspective. Encouraging students to embrace mistakes as part of learning can reduce anxiety and build resilience. This approach helps students understand that their abilities can improve with effort and practice.

Encourage and Reward Risk-Taking
Creating a safe and supportive learning environment where mistakes are seen as learning opportunities can encourage students to take risks without fear of failure. This approach helps develop resilience and perseverance, which are essential for overcoming reading challenges.

Build Positive Relationships
Establishing strong, supportive relationships with students can significantly impact their motivation and confidence. When students feel valued and understood, they are more likely to engage in reading activities. Frequent conversations about books and personalized feedback can foster a sense of connection and encouragement.

Engage the Reader
Activating a student's interest in reading by making stories come alive can be the first step in building confidence. Engaging materials and interactive reading experiences can make reading more enjoyable and less daunting for struggling readers. While these strategies are powerful, the real magic happens when we integrate them into a holistic approach to supporting struggling readers. By consistently focusing on strengths, providing choices, setting achievable goals, and modeling a growth mindset, we create an environment where children feel empowered to tackle their reading challenges.

Remember Dr. Brooks' wise words: "All children want to succeed. It's our job to help them discover how they can" (Brooks 2018, 89). As parents and educators, we have the privilege and responsibility of guiding children on this journey of discovery. Through nurturing their confidence and motivation, we're not just helping them become better readers; we're empowering them to become lifelong learners who approach challenges with resilience and enthusiasm. Fairness is not giving every child the same thing; it's giving each child what they need. When we tailor our approach to each child's unique needs and strengths, we can help every struggling reader find their path to success.

Success Stories: Overcoming Literacy Challenges

Let's conclude with an inspiring story of triumph over literacy difficulties. Meet Jamie, a bright 10-year-old who struggled with reading early in school. Despite her best efforts, Jamie found herself falling behind her peers,

leading to frustration and a growing dislike of reading. Jamie's parents noticed her struggles and worked closely with her teachers to have her evaluated. The assessment revealed that Jamie had dyslexia. Armed with this knowledge, her parents and teachers developed a plan that included:
- Specialized reading instruction using a structured literacy approach
- Regular practice with phonological awareness activities at home
- Use of audiobooks paired with print books to build comprehension and vocabulary
- Text-to-speech software for homework assignments

Most importantly, Jamie's parents and teachers consistently encouraged her efforts and celebrated her progress. Within a year, her reading skills improved dramatically, and she regained her confidence and developed a love for stories. Jamie's mother shares: "The journey wasn't easy, but seeing Jamie curl up with a book she chose herself, reading for pleasure...that makes it all worthwhile. We learned that every child can become a reader with the right support."

Conclusion: Empowering Every Child to Read

As we have explored in this chapter, literacy difficulties can present significant challenges but are not insurmountable barriers.

The key takeaways:
1. Early identification is crucial: Recognize the signs of literacy difficulties and seek help promptly.

2. Understanding is power: Knowing about different learning disabilities can help you better support your child.
3. Home strategies matter: Consistent, positive support at home can make a significant difference.
4. Professional help is valuable: Don't hesitate to seek expert assessments and interventions.
5. Technology can be a powerful ally: Explore and utilize appropriate assistive technologies.
6. Emotional well-being is paramount: Address the emotional impact of literacy challenges.
7. Confidence and motivation are key: Foster a positive attitude toward reading and learning.

Everyone's journey is unique. What works for one may not work for another. The key is to remain patient, persistent, and positive. Celebrate every step of progress, no matter how small it may seem.

In the face of literacy challenges, always remember that every child has the potential to succeed. With your support, understanding, and advocacy, you can help your child unlock the transformative power of literacy, opening doors to a world of knowledge, imagination, and opportunity.

Reflection Question: After reading this chapter, what is the most essential action you plan to take to support a child with literacy challenges?

Further Reading

1. *Overcoming Dyslexia (2nd Edition).* Shaywitz, S. E., and Shaywitz, J. (2020). Knopf. A comprehensive guide to understanding and addressing dyslexia, written by leading experts in the field.
2. *Reader, Come Home: The Reading Brain in a Digital World.* Wolf, M. (2018). Harper. An exploration of how digital technology is changing the way we read and process information.
3. *Basic Facts About Dyslexia and Other Reading Problems.* Moats, L. C., and Dakin, K. E. (2017). International Dyslexia Association. A concise overview of reading difficulties and evidence-based interventions.
4. National Center on Improving Literacy (https://improvingliteracy.org/): A website offering a wealth of research-based information and resources for supporting children with literacy difficulties.
5. Understood.org (https://www.understood.org/) is a comprehensive resource for parents and educators that provides information on various learning and attention issues, including reading difficulties.

Practical Exercises

1. **Early Signs Checklist:** Create a checklist of early signs of reading difficulties based on the information provided in this chapter. Use the checklist to observe a child you know (your own child, a student, or a family friend) over a week. Note any signs you observe and reflect on what they might mean.
2. **Home Reading Environment Audit:** Evaluate your home reading environment. Make a list of ways to improve it to support a struggling reader. Consider factors like:
    - Availability of age-appropriate books
    - Comfortable reading spaces
    - Reduction of distractions
    - Presence of literacy-rich materials (labels, posters, etc.) Implement at least three improvements over the next month.
3. **Multisensory Phonics Activity:** Design a multisensory activity to teach specific phonics skill. For example:
    - Use Play-Doh to form letters while saying their sounds
    - Create a hopscotch game where each square represents a different letter or sound
    - Use sandpaper letters for tactile letter recognition

    Try out your activity with a child and reflect on its effectiveness.
4. **Emotional Support Role-Play:** With a partner, role-play scenarios where a child expresses

frustration or anxiety about reading. Practice validating his or her feelings and offering encouragement. Switch roles and discuss your experiences and insights.

5. **Technology Exploration:** Research and test out one assistive technology tool mentioned in this chapter (e.g., text-to-speech software, digital graphic organizers). Write a brief review of its features, ease of use, and potential benefits for struggling readers.

Chapter 7: Cultural Literacy: Honoring Diverse Practices

Overview

"Literacy is not just about reading words on a page. It's about reading the world, and every child brings their own world to the literacy experience," asserts Dr. Gloria Ladson-Billings, a pioneering researcher in culturally relevant pedagogy. This powerful insight opens the door to a dimension of literacy that goes beyond phonics and grammar: cultural literacy.

Imagine literacy as a vibrant tapestry woven from threads of diverse colors and textures. Each thread represents a different cultural practice, language, or tradition. Together, they create a rich, complex picture that reflects the beautiful diversity of our world. This is the essence of cultural literacy. In our diverse, globalized society, navigating and appreciating different cultural contexts is not just enriching; it's essential.

This chapter will guide you through the landscape of cultural literacy, showing how it intertwines with and enhances traditional literacy skills. We'll explore the benefits of multilingualism, strategies for maintaining home languages while acquiring new ones, and ways to bridge cultural gaps between home and school. Through inspiring family stories and practical advice from experts, you'll discover how to weave cultural literacy into your child's learning journey. Our goal is to prepare children not just to read books but to read and thrive in our multicultural world.

The Value of Cultural and Linguistic Diversity in Literacy

Cultural diversity isn't just a buzzword; it's a powerful asset in literacy development. Research consistently shows that children exposed to multiple languages and cultural practices often develop stronger metalinguistic awareness—the ability to think about language as an object of thought. This skill is fundamental for reading comprehension and overall academic success.

Dr. Jim Cummins, a professor at the University of Toronto, notes: "Bilingualism is not a zero-sum game. When we support a child's home language, we are also supporting their development in the school language" (Cummins, 2000).

Key benefits of cultural and linguistic diversity in literacy include:

- Enhanced cognitive flexibility
- Improved problem-solving skills
- Greater empathy and cultural understanding
- Expanded vocabulary across languages
- Stronger family bonds through shared cultural practices

Honoring Home Languages and Cultural Practices in Literacy Development

Picture a child's literacy journey as a vibrant garden, where each language and cultural practice is a unique flower, contributing to a diverse and beautiful landscape. As parents and educators, our role is to nurture this garden, ensuring each flower thrives. But how do we balance honoring home languages and cultural practices while supporting literacy development? Let's explore some strategies that can help us cultivate this rich linguistic and cultural garden.

- Treating All Languages as Treasures

First and foremost, we need to value all languages equally. It's like treating each language as a precious gem in a treasure chest. Showing the same respect for the home language as we do for the community's dominant language sends a powerful message. We need to tell our children, "Your linguistic heritage is valuable." This recognition can spark pride and confidence, motivating children to dive deeper into both languages.

- Creating a Multilingual Print Paradise

Imagine transforming your home into a print-rich wonderland, where every corner tells a story in multiple languages. Books, labels, signs—all in the languages your family speaks. It's like creating a linguistic scavenger hunt that children engage in daily. This inclusive space supports language development and reinforces the idea that all languages are equally important. It's a constant reminder of the family's linguistic diversity, making language learning a natural, everyday occurrence.

- Weaving Cultural Stories into Daily Life

Think of cultural stories and traditions as the threads that weave together the fabric of a child's identity. Regular family storytelling creates strong bonds and teaches life lessons that stick. These shared moments help everyone understand their family values and feel like they truly belong. It's like giving children a cultural compass to navigate their world.

A parent once told me, "When we started telling our family stories at dinner time, in both English and Mandarin, our children became more curious about their heritage. They started asking questions about their grandparents and life in China. It opened up a whole new world of conversation."

- Embracing the Many Faces of Literacy

Let's broaden our view of literacy. It's not just about reading words on a page or writing essays. It's a multifaceted gem that includes cultural knowledge, oral traditions, and even digital literacies. Recognizing and celebrating diverse forms of communication helps children understand the power of expression. Each new method they discover adds to their growing set of tools, building confidence and skill in sharing their ideas with the world.

- The Bilingual Reading Adventure

Encouraging children to read in both their home language and the dominant language is like sending them on a bilingual adventure. It's not just about understanding two sets of words; it's about navigating between two worlds, enhancing cognitive flexibility, and building a bridge between cultures. Bilingual books or translations of favorite stories can be excellent vehicles for this journey.

- Tapping into Community Resources

Remember, it takes a village to raise a child, especially for multilingual and multicultural children. Engaging with community resources—cultural centers, language classes, and heritage festivals—can provide additional support and enrichment. It's like expanding the child's cultural garden beyond the home, allowing them to interact with others who share their linguistic and cultural backgrounds. This fosters a sense of belonging and community that's crucial for a child's development.

- Cultivating a Growth Mindset

Finally, let's encourage children to see language learning as an exciting journey rather than a daunting challenge. Children learn to see mistakes as opportunities for growth when we encourage resilience and persistence. Each error becomes a natural part of learning, helping students build confidence and problem-solving skills. It's about helping them see that their ability to learn and use languages can grow with effort and practice.

As Dr. Sonia Nieto, author of *Affirming Diversity: The Sociopolitical Context of Multicultural Education*, reminds us, "When children's language, culture, and experience are valued, their learning flourishes" (Nieto, 2010). Honoring home languages and cultural practices supports literacy development and nurtures a child's sense of self.

In essence, we are creating an environment where children feel valued and empowered to succeed, not just in reading and writing but in understanding and navigating our diverse world. This holistic approach recognizes each child as a unique individual with a rich linguistic and cultural heritage to share with the world.

Reflection Question: How do you currently incorporate your cultural heritage into your child's literacy journey?

Bridging Home and School Literacy Practices

Open communication with teachers about your family's cultural practices and languages creates a strong foundation for learning. You can help your child succeed by finding connections between home and school literacy practices while encouraging them to use all their language skills to understand and express ideas. Share with teachers how your family approaches reading and writing and support your child in bringing their cultural knowledge into the classroom. Remember that using multiple languages to communicate is a valuable skill that enhances learning. This approach, known as translanguaging, helps children develop strong literacy skills across languages. Here are some practical examples:

1. **Code-switching in storytelling:** A child might begin a story in English but switch to Arabic for culturally specific terms or expressions that don't have direct English equivalents

2. **Multilingual word walls:** Teachers can create word walls in classrooms that include vocabulary in multiple languages, helping students make connections between concepts across languages

3. **Bilingual journaling:** Encourage students to write journal entries using whichever language feels most natural for expressing different thoughts or emotions

4. **Comparative language analysis:** Guide students in comparing idioms or proverbs across languages, fostering metalinguistic awareness.

Dr. Ofelia García, author of *Translanguaging: Language, Bilingualism, and Education*, explains: "Translanguaging is not just about moving between languages, but about constructing and using complex, interrelated discursive practices to make meaning" (García & Wei, 2014).

Strategies for Educators to Support Cultural Literacy

Educators play an important role in fostering cultural literacy, which helps students appreciate and engage with diverse perspectives. Teachers create welcoming classrooms when they include everyone's background in their lessons. Students learn better when they see connections between schoolwork and their own lives, and everyone benefits when the classroom respects all students' voices and ideas. Here are some comprehensive strategies to support cultural literacy:

1. Conduct a Cultural Audit of Your Curriculum: Start by evaluating your teaching materials for diversity and inclusion. A cultural audit involves assessing whether your resources reflect a range of perspectives, particularly those from underrepresented groups. Ensure that textbooks, media, and lesson plans showcase different cultures, identities, and viewpoints, moving beyond a single-story narrative.

2. Integrate Global Literature: Incorporating books from diverse cultures into your reading lists and classroom library is a powerful way to expose students to global perspectives. Include literature that reflects different traditions, histories, and experiences, offering students a broader understanding of the world. Pairing this with reflective discussions allows students to explore the themes and lessons embedded in these stories, deepening their cultural literacy.

3. Celebrate Cultural Holidays and Traditions: Recognizing cultural holidays and traditions in the classroom fosters respect and understanding. Use literature and activities to highlight celebrations from various cultures, allowing students to learn about and honor the practices of their peers. For instance, reading stories about the Lunar New Year or Diwali and incorporating art or music from these cultures brings these celebrations to life and makes them relatable.

4. Use Music, Art, and Food: Cultural elements like music, art, and food can make learning more engaging and relatable. Incorporating these elements into literacy activities brings a sensory and emotional dimension to the learning experience. For example, reading about a particular culture could be accompanied by listening to its traditional music or trying a simple recipe from that region. These experiences help deepen students' understanding and appreciation of different cultures.

5. Encourage Sharing of Cultural Stories: Allowing students to share their cultural stories, traditions, and experiences fosters an inclusive classroom environment. Create opportunities for students to tell stories from their own cultural backgrounds through written narratives, oral storytelling, or presentations. This practice promotes pride in their heritage and encourages classmates to listen, ask questions, and learn from one another.

6. Organize Cultural Literacy Projects: Consider organizing larger-scale cultural literacy projects, such as fairs or festivals celebrating diversity within the school community. These events could involve students researching different cultures, creating displays, preparing traditional foods, or performing cultural dances and songs. These projects help raise awareness of global cultures while celebrating the rich diversity in the classroom.

Teachers create rich learning environments when they fill classrooms with diverse books, encourage cultural sharing, and welcome multiple languages. These practices not only support student learning but prepare children to thrive in our interconnected world. When students see their cultures and languages valued in the classroom, they develop stronger literacy skills and a deeper appreciation for learning.

Cultural Literacy in Action: A Family's Journey
From Vietnam to the USA

The Nguyen family's journey from Vietnam to the USA exemplifies the delicate balance of preserving cultural heritage while embracing a new environment. When five-year-old Mai Nguyen began her education in the United States, her parents implemented a thoughtful strategy to ensure her success while maintaining their Vietnamese roots.

They fostered a bilingual home environment, speaking Vietnamese while supporting Mai's English acquisition. To encourage literacy in both cultures, a dedicated reading corner with books in both languages was established. The parents shared Vietnamese folktales as a springboard for discussions about cultural values and differences. Collaborating with Mai's teacher, they integrated Vietnamese culture into classroom activities, such as Mai's mother demonstrating the traditional *áo dài* during a unit on cultural clothing. The family also actively participated in community events celebrating diversity.

By the time Mai reached middle school, she had achieved fluency in Vietnamese and English, developing a profound appreciation for her cultural heritage and an openness to other cultures. Mai's mother reflects: "At first, we worried that focusing on our home culture might hold Mai back. However, we discovered that embracing our heritage while engaging with our new community gave Mai a unique strength. She doesn't just read words; she reads cultures."

Literacy Roots

From Nigeria to Canada

The Okafor family's approach to cultural literacy offers an inspiring example of how immigrant families can maintain their heritage while embracing their new home's culture. Originally from Nigeria, the Okafors settled in Toronto with their son, Chidi, and implemented a multifaceted strategy to nurture his cultural identity and literacy skills. At home, they consistently spoke their native Igbo language, creating an immersive environment for Chidi to retain his linguistic roots. Simultaneously, they actively supported his acquisition of English and French, recognizing the importance of multilingualism in Canada's diverse society. The family's commitment extended beyond their household, as they organized a monthly "Culture Day" in collaboration with other Nigerian families. This event became a vibrant celebration of their heritage, where children like Chidi had the opportunity to learn traditional Nigerian dances, music, and cooking, fostering a strong sense of community and cultural pride.

The Okafors took an active role in Chidi's school, working with educators to introduce a "Global Reading Challenge." This innovative program encouraged students to explore literature from various cultures, broadening their worldviews and promoting cross-cultural understanding. Through these concerted efforts, the Okafors not only preserved their Nigerian heritage but contributed to the multicultural fabric of their new community, exemplifying how cultural literacy can be a bridge between diverse worlds.

Digital Literacy and Cultural Diversity

- Digital literacy opens exciting opportunities for cultural exchange and learning that extend from classrooms into our daily lives. Technology helps families explore and understand different cultures, enriching their knowledge and connections to the world. Let me share some effective ways you can use technology to support cultural literacy:
- Use language learning apps to explore new languages as a family. Language is a gateway to culture, and language learning apps provide a fun and interactive way for families to explore new languages together. These apps offer more than just vocabulary lessons—they often include cultural notes, pronunciation guides, and even stories from different regions, helping users better understand the language's context. Learning a new language as a family strengthens your bond and opens up a world of cultural insights and global perspectives.
- Connect with relatives or cultural communities. Video calls have revolutionized how we maintain relationships, making it easier than ever to stay connected with relatives or cultural communities, no matter the distance. These digital interactions provide a rich opportunity for children to practice language skills in real time and learn about traditions, customs, and histories directly from family members or community elders. This form of communication can also help bridge generational gaps, as younger family members learn about their

heritage and cultural identity from those who have lived it.
- Explore virtual museums and cultural sites. The digital age has made it possible to visit museums and cultural landmarks from around the globe without leaving your home. Virtual tours and interactive exhibits allow families to explore art, history, and cultural artifacts in an immersive way. Whether you're walking through the halls of the Louvre, exploring ancient ruins, or viewing Indigenous art from remote regions, these experiences make cultural learning accessible and engaging for all ages. These virtual explorations can spark conversations about history, art, and the interconnectedness of different cultures.
- Create digital stories that incorporate your family's cultural traditions. Digital storytelling is a powerful tool for preserving and sharing cultural traditions. Families can work together to create digital stories that reflect their cultural heritage, whether it's through writing, photography, video, or a combination of media. This process allows children to actively document and curate their cultural narratives, fostering a deeper connection to their roots. As Dr. Lalitha Vasudevan, an expert in adolescent literacies, notes: "Digital tools allow young people to be not just consumers of culture, but creators and curators of their own cultural narratives" (Vasudevan, 2015). By crafting and sharing these stories, families can contribute to the ongoing dialogue about culture in the digital age,

ensuring their unique traditions and experiences are preserved and celebrated.
- Engage with cultural content on social media. Social media platforms are brimming with content that showcases diverse cultural expressions, from traditional dances and music to contemporary art and fashion. Families can follow cultural influencers, participate in cultural challenges, and engage in discussions that broaden their understanding of global cultures. This enhances cultural literacy and helps children develop a critical eye for how culture is represented and consumed in the digital space.
- Participate in online cultural events. Many cultural festivals and events have transitioned to virtual formats, offering live streams, workshops, and interactive sessions. Families can participate in these online events to experience cultural practices firsthand, such as cooking classes, dance workshops, or storytelling sessions. These events provide an interactive way to learn about and appreciate different cultures, fostering a sense of global citizenship and empathy.

Families can weave digital tools and resources into daily activities, creating engaging and educational cultural experiences. Technology connects us to diverse communities, helping us understand and celebrate the richness of our global society. When we use these tools thoughtfully, we build bridges between cultures and deepen our appreciation for different perspectives.

Reflection Question: What digital tools have you found helpful in exploring your cultural heritage?

Challenges and Considerations

Cultural literacy encompasses many aspects of identity: language, traditions, values, and experiences. While building cultural understanding creates rich learning opportunities, it also presents unique challenges. Let's explore how families navigate these complexities.

1. Societal Pressures to Assimilate

Picture society as a giant melting pot where various cultures are expected to blend into a uniform mixture. For many families, this creates a tension between maintaining their cultural heritage and fitting into the dominant culture. The Nguyen family's experience poignantly illustrates this challenge. When 10-year-old Mai started refusing to speak Vietnamese at home, her parents were heartbroken. "It felt like she was trying to erase a part of herself," Mrs. Nguyen recalls. "She told us that speaking Vietnamese made her feel different at school."

Dr. James Banks, a pioneer in multicultural education, explains this phenomenon: "Children often feel pressure to conform to the dominant culture, especially in educational settings. This can lead to a sense of cultural shame or denial" (Banks, 2019). The Nguyens tackled this challenge creatively. They organized a multicultural fair at Mai's school, where students could showcase their heritage. "Seeing her classmates excited about her Vietnamese culture was a turning point for Mai," Mr. Nguyen shares. "She realized her difference was something special."

2. Limited Resources in Minority Languages

For many families, finding resources in their heritage language can feel like an endless scavenger hunt. It's as if they're searching for rare gems in a vast desert of English-language materials. The Ahmadi family, originally from Iran, faced this challenge when trying to maintain their children's Farsi literacy. "Finding age-appropriate books in Farsi was like looking for a needle in a haystack," Mr. Ahmadi sighs. Their solution? They started a community lending library of Farsi books, with families pooling their resources and even translating English books into Farsi.

3. Balancing Multiple Cultural Identities

For children growing up in multicultural families, balancing different cultural identities can feel like walking a tightrope between worlds. It's a delicate act of embracing multiple heritages without feeling torn between them. Sophia, a 14-year-old with a Greek father and Brazilian mother, describes her experience as follows: "Sometimes I feel like I'm switching channels between different versions of myself—Greek Sophia, Brazilian Sophia, American Sophia—it can be exhausting."

Dr. Marjorie Faulstich Orellana, a professor of education at UCLA, offers insight: "Children in multicultural families often develop a unique transcultural identity. The key is to help them see this as a strength, not a source of confusion" (Orellana, 2020). Sophia's parents encouraged her to create a personal culture map, visually representing how her different cultural identities intersect and complement each other. "It helped me see that I'm not divided," Sophia reflects. "I'm multiplied."

4. Addressing Cultural Stereotypes and Biases

Confronting cultural stereotypes and biases can feel like battling mythical monsters—they're pervasive, often invisible, and can be deeply entrenched in society. For families embracing cultural literacy, combating these misconceptions is an ongoing challenge. The Jackson family faced this head-on when their son, Jamal, came home upset after a classmate told him he "didn't act Black enough" because he loved reading and classical music. "It was heartbreaking," Mrs. Jackson shares. "We had to help Jamal understand that his interests don't define his racial identity, and that diversity exists within every culture."

They turned this painful experience into a learning opportunity, creating a family project to research and celebrate Black authors, musicians, and scientists throughout history. "It became a journey of cultural pride for all of us," Mr. Jackson beams. Navigating these challenges requires open communication, creativity, and resilience. Dr. Geneva Gay, a leader in culturally responsive teaching, emphasizes: "The goal is not to erase differences, but to celebrate them. Cultural literacy is about adding to one's identity, not subtracting from it" (Gay, 2018).

Cultural literacy is like tending to a diverse garden. Each plant (or cultural aspect) needs specific care to thrive, but together, they create a beautiful, harmonious landscape. It's not about choosing one flower over another but nurturing a vibrant identity ecosystem. As you navigate these challenges, consider the words of Chimamanda Ngozi Adichie, a Nigerian writer, and public intellectual known for her impactful novels, essays, and talks that explore themes of identity, feminism, race, and politics: "The single story creates stereotypes, and the problem with stereotypes is not that they are untrue, but that they are incomplete. They make one story become the only story."

By embracing cultural literacy, you're helping your child write a rich, multifaceted story of their identity.

Conclusion

As we've explored in this chapter, cultural literacy is not an add-on to "regular" literacy; it's an integral part of what it means to be literate in our diverse, interconnected world. By honoring diverse cultural practices and languages, we enrich our children's literacy skills and their understanding of themselves and others.

Dr. Gay beautifully summarizes this idea: "Cultural literacy is about learning to read the world, not just the word" (Gay, 2018).

Key Takeaways:
1. Cultural and linguistic diversity are assets, not obstacles, in literacy development.
2. Honoring home languages and cultures strengthens overall literacy skills.
3. Translanguaging is a powerful tool for multilingual learners.
4. Educators play a crucial role in fostering cultural literacy in the classroom.
5. Cultural literacy is essential for success and understanding in our global world.

Supporting your child's literacy development includes embracing cultural practices, languages, and traditions. When we combine these elements, we strengthen children's learning and growth. This inclusive approach helps students develop confident identities while mastering essential literacy skills.

Reflection Question*:* Reflect on your cultural literacy journey. How has it shaped your approach to reading and understanding the world?

Further Reading

1. *The Dreamkeepers: Successful Teachers of African American Children* (2nd ed.). Ladson-Billings, G. (2009). Jossey-Bass. This seminal work explores culturally relevant pedagogy and its impact on student success.
2. *Translanguaging: Language, Bilingualism, and Education.* Palgrave Macmillan. García, O., and Wei, L. (2014). A comprehensive look at the theory and practice of translanguaging in educational settings.
3. *Language, Culture, and Teaching: Critical Perspectives* (3rd ed.). Nieto, S. (2018). Routledge. This book critically examines the intersection of language, culture, and education.
4. *Language, Power, and Pedagogy: Bilingual Children in the Crossfire.* Multilingual Matters. Cummins, J. (2000). An in-depth exploration of bilingual education and its sociopolitical contexts.
5. The National Association for Bilingual Education (NABE) - www.nabe.org This website offers a wealth of resources, research, and advocacy information related to bilingual education and cultural literacy.

Literacy Roots

Practical Exercises

1. **Family Language Map:** Create a visual representation of your family's linguistic heritage. Draw a family tree and label each person with the languages they speak. Include dialects and even phrases unique to your family. Discuss how languages have been passed down or acquired across generations.
   Learning Outcome: This activity helps visualize the linguistic diversity within families and promotes discussion about language heritage.
2. **Cultural Storytelling Night**: Organize a weekly storytelling night where family members take turns sharing stories from their cultural backgrounds. These could be folktales, personal anecdotes, or historical events. If possible, tell the stories in the heritage language with translations.
   Learning Outcome: This exercise promotes intergenerational communication, preserves cultural narratives, and enhances language skills.
3. **Multilingual Scavenger Hunt:** Create a scavenger hunt around your home or neighborhood using clues in different languages.
   Learning Outcome: This activity makes language learning interactive and fun while reinforcing vocabulary and comprehension in multiple languages.
4. **Cultural Literacy Journal:** Start a family journal where members can write or draw about their experiences with different cultures. This could include reflections on cultural events, new words

learned in different languages, or observations about cultural practices.

Learning Outcome: This exercise encourages regular reflection on cultural experiences and promotes metalinguistic awareness.

5. **Community Cultural Exchange:** Organize a cultural exchange event in your community or school. Families can share aspects of their cultural heritage through food, music, dance, or storytelling. Encourage participants to learn and use greetings or simple phrases in each other's languages.

   Learning Outcome: This activity promotes cultural awareness, community building, and practical application of language skills in a social context.

Chapter 8: Digital Literacy: Navigating the Online World

Overview

"Digital literacy is no longer a luxury; it is a necessity for full participation in our society," asserts Dr. Kristen Hawley Turner, a professor and Director of Teacher Education at Drew University in New Jersey. As parents and educators, we find ourselves at the frontier of a new literacy landscape where the written word intertwines with multimedia, social networks, and virtual realities. Our children are digital natives, born into this world of touchscreens and Wi-Fi, but navigating it successfully requires more than just intuitive tech skills—it demands a nuanced understanding of how to engage with digital information and tools critically.

In this chapter, we'll embark on a journey through the digital literacy ecosystem. We will explore the essential skills that make up digital literacy, from basic device navigation to complex content creation. You'll learn strategies to foster safe and responsible internet use, discover ways to evaluate quality digital content, and understand how to balance screen time with other important activities. Through case studies and expert advice, we'll tackle the challenges and seize the opportunities that digital literacy presents, preparing our children to survive and thrive in the digital age.

Defining Digital Literacy

What exactly is digital literacy? It is more than just knowing how to use a computer or smartphone. Digital literacy encompasses a range of skills that allow individuals to find, evaluate, create, and communicate information effectively in a digital environment. This includes:

1. Basic digital skills (using devices and software)
2. Information literacy (finding and evaluating online information)
3. Media literacy (understanding various digital media forms)
4. Communication and collaboration skills in digital spaces
5. Digital citizenship and online safety awareness

As we dive into each of these areas, remember that digital literacy, like traditional literacy, is a journey rather than a destination. Our goal is to equip our children with the skills to navigate this ever-evolving digital landscape confidently and responsibly.

Reflection Question: Think about your digital literacy journey. What skills have you had to learn as an adult that seems second nature to children today? How might this generational difference impact how we approach teaching digital literacy?

Age-Appropriate Digital Literacy Skills

Just as we scaffold traditional literacy skills, we must introduce digital literacy skills in age-appropriate ways. Understanding when and how to introduce different digital tools helps children use technology confidently and responsibly. Here's a general framework for developing these skills:

Early Childhood (Ages 2-5):
- Basic device navigation (with supervision)
- Introduction to educational apps and games
- Understanding the difference between real and digital worlds

Elementary (Ages 6-11):
- Basic internet navigation and search skills
- Introduction to digital communication (e.g., email, video calls)
- Understanding online safety basics

Middle School (Ages 12-14):
- Advanced search strategies
- Critical evaluation of online information
- Responsible social media use

High School (Ages 15-18):
- Complex digital content creation
- Understanding digital footprints and online reputation
- Advanced information literacy and fact-checking skills

These are guidelines. Every child develops at their own pace, and individual readiness should always be considered.

Sarah, a mother of three from Oregon, shared her experience: "I was worried about introducing my 5-year-old to tablets, thinking it might be too early. But we started with simple educational games, and I was amazed at how quickly he learned to navigate the device.

More importantly, it sparked his curiosity about letters and numbers in a way traditional methods hadn't."

Children today grow up surrounded by technology. Common Sense Media's 2023 survey reveals that 98% of children under eight access mobile devices at home, while 45% use tablets. These numbers show why we must teach digital literacy skills early, guiding children to use technology effectively and responsibly.

Impact of Digital Media on Early Childhood Development (Under 5)

The impact of digital media on early childhood development is a complex and evolving topic. There are potential benefits and risks, especially for children under five. Their activities are like a balanced diet. A mix of digital and traditional experiences is vital for their growth.

Digital media offers valuable educational opportunities through interactive content that supports early literacy, numeracy, and problem-solving skills. These complement traditional learning methods like storybooks and puzzles. Certain digital activities can boost skills like visual attention and spatial reasoning. However, traditional activities, like building blocks and imaginative play, are also vital for developing these skills.

Early tech exposure can build digital skills. It prepares kids for a tech-driven future. Yet, as mentioned earlier, this should complement rather than replace traditional activities like crafting and physical play, which establish fundamental problem-solving and critical-thinking skills. Creative expression flourishes through both digital means—via age-appropriate apps and software—and traditional outlets such as arts, crafts, and musical instruments. Digital tools improve social connections, especially video calls with distant family. Military families navigate the challenges of deployment and separation. Through these virtual connections, a deployed parent can still join family dinner discussions, help with homework, or share in daily moments that they would otherwise miss. Technology proves equally valuable for maintaining extended family relationships. Grandparents can watch their grandkids' school performances in real-time. Aunts and cousins can join family celebrations despite living in different states or countries. These digital interactions can't replace the warmth of physical presence, but they create chances for emotional connections and shared experiences. This tech helps preserve family ties despite the distance. It keeps strong bonds that support kids' identities and well-being.

However, parents and caregivers should be mindful of potential risks. Excessive screen time may delay language development by reducing crucial face-to-face interactions. Blue light and stimulating content before bed can disrupt sleep. Frequent exposure to fast-paced media might hurt attention spans and slow engagement. Increased sedentary time may cause obesity and poor posture. Social-emotional development may suffer if screen time creates a substantial barrier to in-person social interactions. Additionally, children risk accessing inappropriate content without proper supervision.

Parents and caregivers can create a rich childhood, but they must balance the benefits and risks of digital media. By blending screen-based activities with traditional play, they create an ideal environment. Children can enjoy hands-on experiences, like building blocks, outdoor play, and face-to-face interactions. They can also enjoy technology's educational potential. This balanced strategy helps kids develop skills for the digital age and the real world. It supports their physical, social, emotional, and cognitive growth.

Here are some guidelines for Screen Time and Content Selection (Under 5):
1. **Screen Time Limits:**
    - **Under 18 months:** Avoid screen media other than video chatting
    - **18-24 months:** Limited high-quality programming with adult interaction
    - **2-5 years:** No more than 1 hour per day of high-quality programming
2. **Content Selection:**
    - Choose age-appropriate, educational content from reputable sources
    - Prioritize slow-paced, interactive programs that encourage problem-solving
    - Avoid content with violence, strong language, or mature themes
    - Select apps and games that are specifically designed for early learners
3. **Parental Involvement:**
    - Co-view and co-play with your child to enhance learning and discussion
    - Use parental controls and safe search settings on devices

        o   Create tech-free zones and times, especially during meals and before bedtime
4. **Balance:**
        o   Ensure plenty of time for hands-on, creative play and physical activity
        o   Maintain a 5:1 ratio of real-world to digital activities
5. **Quality over Quantity:**
        o   Focus on the quality of digital experiences rather than just limiting time
        o   Use technology to supplement, not replace, important developmental activities
6. **Modeling:**
        o   Demonstrate healthy digital habits yourself
        o   Show how technology can be a tool for learning and creativity

These guidelines are general recommendations. Each child's needs may vary, and it's important to consult with pediatricians or child development specialists for personalized advice. As digital technology evolves, ongoing research will help refine our understanding of its impact on early childhood development. Parents and educators should stay informed about the latest findings and recommendations to make the best decisions for their young children's digital experiences. Just like a balanced diet is crucial for physical health, a balanced mix of digital and traditional activities is essential for holistic child development.

How digital media affects children's physical and mental health

Digital media affects children's development, both physically and mentally. Parents and caregivers must pay close attention to this. Research shows that blue light from screens disrupts sleep. It reduces melatonin production, as noted by Hale et al. (2019). Frequent exposure to fast-paced digital content can hurt kids' attention spans. Some interactive activities may boost skills like visual attention and task-switching.

The relationship between digital media and social development is complex. While technology can facilitate peer connections, excessive use may limit essential face-to-face interactions. Twenge and Campbell's 2018 study found that high digital media use lowers adolescents' well-being. To promote healthy digital habits, parents should establish clear boundaries following expert guidelines. The American Academy of Pediatrics advises against screen time for kids under 18 months, except for video chats. For ages 2-5, limit high-quality programming to one hour a day. Tech-free zones in bedrooms and dining areas boost real connections and sleep.

Parents play a crucial role in modeling responsible device habits. They should also ensure digital activities don't replace exercise. The WHO recommends that children aged 5-17 do at least 60 minutes of moderate to vigorous activity daily. Teaching digital literacy helps kids evaluate online content and understand the risks and benefits.

Use age-appropriate content filters. Set digital curfews. Choose educational content that fosters learning and creativity. Experts suggest avoiding screens at least an hour before bedtime to maintain sleep quality. It's essential to balance screen time with offline activities, which should boost creativity, social interaction, and physical movement. All things in moderation!

Regular, open talks about digital media use help. They address concerns and promote responsible online behavior. If parents use these approaches early, they can guide their children and help them develop healthy digital habits and well-being.

Evaluating and Selecting Quality Digital Content

In the sea of digital content, we must help children find quality educational resources. This requires careful thought. Parents and educators can start with Khan Academy, Highlights for Kids, and Duolingo—reputable sites with engaging, age-appropriate materials on various subjects. Common Sense Media, which reviews apps, games, and websites, is a valuable resource. The reviews evaluate their educational value, ease of use, and age-appropriateness.

When choosing digital content, prioritize resources that:
1. Encourage active participation, not passive consumption
2. Provide immediate feedback
3. Adapt to individual skill levels
4. Offer meaningful rewards for learning

The design and content must suit the child's development. It should be intuitive and have strong safety features to block inappropriate content. As Dr. Katie Davis emphasizes, quality digital content "invites exploration, creativity, and critical thinking." Look for platforms that let children create their own stories and artwork as well as solve open-ended problems while collaborating with peers.

Digital resources should boost traditional literacy skills through features like e-books with built-in dictionaries, writing apps with grammar feedback, and storytelling platforms that foster narrative development. Content that meets educational standards or was created with educators is sound and age-appropriate. Data privacy and security matter. Review privacy policies. Ensure strong protections for children's personal info and seek diverse and inclusive content that represents various cultures, backgrounds, and perspectives to broaden children's worldviews.

Before committing long-term, use free trials to assess the content's quality and fit. Consider platforms that use adaptive learning, which personalize the experience to each child's pace and style. Content providers' updates show a commitment to up-to-date practices and fixing bugs.

The most effective digital resources spark curiosity while promoting critical-thinking skills. They should be tools for exploration and creativity, and they should complement, not replace, traditional learning methods. When we carefully evaluate these aspects, parents and educators can help kids find engaging and enriching digital content. This will set them up for success in an increasingly digital world.

Strategies for Safe and Responsible Internet Use

As we open the digital world to our children, it's imperative to establish guidelines for safe and responsible use. Parents should start by setting clear rules and expectations for device use and online behavior. It's also vital to use parental controls and safe search settings for younger kids and to teach them about online privacy and the permanence of digital actions. Talking about cyberbullying and how to fight it helps kids by preparing them for tough online situations. Parents should also model good digital citizenship in their own online behavior. As Devorah Heitner, author of *Growing Up in Public*, says, "The goal isn't to be your child's surveillance system, but to be their mentor in the digital world."

Remember to review and update these settings as your child grows and platforms update their features. Also, it's crucial to talk with your children about online safety and responsible digital citizenship. Always check the official support docs for the latest platform instructions, as interfaces and settings can change over time.

Balancing Screen Time with Other Literacy Activities

While digital literacy is important, it shouldn't come at the expense of traditional literacy activities. Families should set and stick to screen time limits. They should also create tech-free zones or times, like during meals and before bedtime. It's valuable to encourage both digital and print reading. Use tech to enhance, not replace, hands-on learning. Parents can also engage in digital activities together with their children, turning screen time into family time. Dr. Jenny Radesky, a pediatrician, reminds us: "It's not just about screen time, but its quality and fit in a child's development."

Here are some concrete examples of age-appropriate activities that parents can do with their young children to develop digital literacy skills, organized by age group:

Preschool (Ages 3-5):
1. Interactive Storytelling:
    - Use apps like Toontastic 3D or Puppet Pals to create simple animated stories.
    - Read interactive e-books that allow children to touch elements on the screen to trigger animations or sounds.

2. Basic Coding Concepts:
    - Try the Kodable or Daisy the Dinosaur apps to introduce simple coding logic through games.
    - Use Code-a-pillar toys to teach sequencing and problem-solving.

3. Digital Art:
    - Explore drawing apps like Drawing Pad or Doodle Buddy to create digital artwork.
    - Take photos together and use simple editing tools to enhance them.

4. Educational Games:
    - Play alphabet and number recognition games like Endless Alphabet or Monkey Math School Sunshine.
    - Use pattern recognition apps like Shape Gurus to develop cognitive skills.

Early Elementary (Ages 6-8):
1. Guided Internet Exploration:
    - Use kid-friendly search engines like Kiddle or KidzSearch to look up information on topics of interest.
    - Teach basic internet safety rules while exploring together.

2. Digital Scavenger Hunts:
    - Create simple scavenger hunts where children need to find specific information or images online, with parental guidance.

3. Intermediate Coding:
    - Introduce block-based coding with ScratchJr or Code.org's Hour of Code activities.
    - Try programming toys like Sphero or Dash and Dot robots.

4. Digital Storytelling:
    - Use tools like Book Creator or StoryJumper to write and illustrate digital books together.

5. Basic Video Creation:
    - Make simple stop-motion videos using apps like Stop Motion Studio.
    - Record and edit short videos using kid-friendly video editors like Adobe Spark Video.

6. Online Communication:
    - Practice writing emails to family members or friends under supervision.
    - Have supervised video calls with relatives to practice digital communication skills.

7. Digital Citizenship:
    - Play online games that teach digital citizenship, like Digital Compass or Interland.

8. Virtual Field Trips:
    - Explore museums, zoos, or historical sites virtually using platforms like Google Arts & Culture.

Parents play a crucial role in guiding their children's digital education journey. Before introducing new apps or games, you must preview them to make sure they align with your family's values and your child's development. The preview must include: 1. Understanding the content. 2. Finding learning opportunities. 3. Checking for safety concerns. Setting appropriate time limits helps maintain a healthy balance between screen time and other activities. These limits should be flexible enough to accommodate meaningful learning experiences while ensuring children have plenty of time for physical play, socializing, and rest. Consider using a timer or schedule that is simple for children to understand and follow.

Parents should join their children as they explore online content, asking questions and discussing discoveries. This teamwork helps kids build critical thinking skills and allows parents to clarify misunderstandings right away. Digital activities can inspire real-life adventures. For instance, if a child enjoys a nature app, plan a hike or start a garden together. When kids learn new concepts online, it connects them to real experiences in their lives. Talk regularly about online safety and responsible behavior, and these talks should evolve as kids grow, tackling relevant issues and building strong digital citizenship skills. Encourage kids to think critically. Prompt them to question online info, assess sources, and consider what they share.

Being adaptable and following children's interests can enhance digital learning. When kids are curious, use digital tools to explore topics but set proper boundaries. Parents should also practice healthy digital habits, showing how technology can support learning and connecting with others. The aim is to introduce digital literacy skills gradually, complementing traditional learning. Parents can foster a balanced tech relationship for kids by curating appropriate content and blending screen time with offline pursuits. This approach nurtures curiosity and promotes healthy digital habits in children.

Reflection Question: What strategies have you found effective in balancing screen time with other activities?

How might you involve your children in creating and keeping this balance?

Using Technology to Enhance Traditional Literacy Skills

Digital tools can be powerful allies in developing traditional literacy skills. When used with care, technology improves literacy education. It increases student interest and strengthens reading and writing abilities. Interactive tools enhance understanding by working alongside proven techniques. This combination creates engaging learning experiences, empowering students on their literacy path.

Here's a look at how to leverage technology:

1. E-readers with built-in dictionaries:
   E-readers like Kindle or Nook offer instant access to word definitions, helping children expand their vocabulary in context. Many e-readers also allow highlighting and note-taking, encouraging active reading and comprehension strategies.
2. Audiobooks paired with print books:
   This combination, often called "immersion reading," can significantly improve reading fluency and comprehension. Services like Audible's Whispersync allow seamless switching between audio and text, catering to different learning styles.
3. Writing apps with immediate feedback:
   Tools like Grammarly and Hemingway Editor provide real-time grammar, style, and clarity feedback. This immediate response can help children develop vital writing skills and encourage self-editing.

4. Digital storytelling tools:
   Platforms like Storybird, Toontastic, and Book Creator allow children to create multimedia stories, enhancing narrative skills and creativity. These tools often include features like text-to-speech, further supporting literacy development.
5. Video chat for remote reading sessions:
   Applications like Zoom and FaceTime can connect children with family members or tutors for reading practice, expanding their support network and making reading a social activity.
6. Adaptive reading programs:
   Software like Lexia Core5 and Reading Eggs adapt to a child's reading level, providing personalized instruction and practice.
7. Interactive vocabulary games:
   Apps like Vocabulary.com and Vocab Genius turn vocabulary learning into an engaging game, reinforcing word knowledge through repetition and context.
8. Speech-to-text technology:
   Tools like Dragon Dictation can help children who struggle with writing to express their ideas more freely, focusing on content rather than mechanics.
9. Digital book clubs:
   Platforms like Goodreads and Biblionasium allow children to connect with peers over shared reading experiences, fostering a love of reading and critical-thinking skills.
10. Augmented Reality (AR) books:
    AR-enhanced books, such as those from companies

like Wonderscope, bring stories to life, increasing engagement and comprehension through interactive elements.

A 2022 study in the *Journal of Computer-Assisted Learning* highlights the potential of interactive e-books. This aligns with earlier research (2015) by Takacs et al., which found that multimedia features in digital books can support story comprehension and vocabulary learning, especially for children with language difficulties.

Research demonstrates how educational technology can significantly boost reading confidence and motivation among students. This is supported by Jones and Brown's 2011 study, which found that e-books can increase reading motivation, particularly for reluctant readers. However, it's important to note that technology should accompany, not replace, traditional literacy instruction. As Neumann and Neumann (2014) point out, the most effective approach is often balanced, combining digital and traditional literacy practices.

Reflection Question: Think about a recent experience where technology enhanced your child's literacy skills. How did this digital tool support or extend traditional literacy practices? What challenges, if any, did you meet, and how did you address them?

Bridging a Digital Divide

Bridging the digital divide is crucial for ensuring that all children have access to digital literacy education. A comprehensive approach includes leveraging various community resources. Public libraries offer free computer and internet access alongside digital literacy classes. Community centers often provide technology access and educational programs. Schools also extend support through after-hours computer lab access or device loan programs.

Several affordable internet options exist for families with limited means. Organizations like EveryoneOn help locate low-cost internet service and computers in specific areas, while the Lifeline Program offers discounted phone and internet service to eligible low-income consumers. Programs like Internet Essentials by Comcast provide budget-friendly internet options to qualifying households. For families needing devices, refurbished computer programs offer viable solutions. Organizations such as PCs for People and The On It Foundation provide refurbished or free computers to eligible low-income individuals and families with students. When traditional computer access isn't available, mobile-first strategies can be employed, such as utilizing smartphones for educational apps and internet access and focusing on mobile-friendly educational resources and websites.

Offline learning tools remain valuable alternatives, including downloadable educational content for offline use, educational TV programs, and DVDs from libraries, along with print materials that teach digital concepts without requiring devices. Community partnerships play a vital role, with local businesses often offering free Wi-Fi or sponsoring technology access programs, while churches and nonprofits frequently provide technology resources or classes. Government and nonprofit initiatives further expand access through programs like Connect2Compete, which partners with internet service providers to offer low-cost internet to eligible families. The National Digital Inclusion Alliance provides essential resources and advocacy for digital inclusion, and schools often implement solutions through device lending programs, extended computer lab hours, and partnerships with local businesses to provide internet access for students.

Creative community solutions have emerged, including community Wi-Fi projects establishing free public networks and mobile technology labs equipped with computers and internet access that visit underserved areas. Digital literacy workshops, available through libraries, community colleges, or nonprofit organizations, provide essential training, while online resources like GCFLearnFree.org offer free technology tutorials. Advocacy and support efforts continue to grow, with local groups forming to advocate for better internet access and participate in digital inclusion initiatives at local and state levels. Alternative learning approaches emphasize using analog methods to teach digital concepts and focusing on developing underlying skills like critical thinking and problem-solving that translate to digital contexts. For those with limited access, maximizing available resources becomes crucial. This includes prioritizing essential online activities during available internet time and using offline time to prepare for online sessions efficiently. Corporate programs often provide additional support, with many tech companies offering initiatives to increase digital access in underserved communities.

While access to technology is essential, many digital literacy skills can be taught conceptually without constant access to devices. The focus should remain on understanding core concepts, critical thinking, and responsible digital citizenship, which can be applied when technology is available. It's also crucial to stay informed about local and national initiatives to bridge the digital divide, as new programs and resources are continually being developed to address this important issue.

Digital Storytelling and Content Creation

One of the most thrilling developments in digital literacy is the shift from passive consumption to active creation. In today's digital age, children have the tools and platforms to not just consume content but to be at the forefront of its creation. This transition is empowering and essential for developing a deeper, more critical understanding of the media and information they interact with daily.

Digital storytelling platforms like Storybird and Canva have revolutionized how children engage with content. These tools allow them to go beyond traditional storytelling by integrating various media elements—text, images, audio, and video—into cohesive, dynamic narratives. For instance, a child can craft a story using a combination of their writing, illustrations they create or select, and voiceovers that add another layer of meaning to the text. This multimodal approach to storytelling caters to different learning styles and encourages children to experiment with various forms of expression.

The collaborative aspects of digital creation are particularly powerful. Children can work together on shared narratives in the same physical space or virtually from different locations, mirroring the teamwork and communication skills essential in today's globalized world.

Through this process, they learn valuable lessons in cooperation, problem-solving, and constructive feedback as they negotiate plot points, edit each other's work, and combine their creative talents. Such collaboration fosters a sense of community and shared purpose, making the creative process more enjoyable and meaningful.

Publishing and sharing work with a broader audience adds another dimension to the learning experience. When children see their stories published online, whether on a platform like Storybird or shared with family and friends via social media, it gives them a sense of accomplishment and pride. This public recognition can boost their confidence and inspire them to keep creating. Additionally, knowing that others will see their work encourages them to think critically about their content, ensuring it is polished and well-considered, enhancing their writing and storytelling skills.

Through digital creation, children develop multimodal literacy skills, learning to think about how different modes of communication—visual, auditory, and textual—can be combined to convey a message more effectively. They begin to understand that each mode has its strengths and can be used strategically to enhance the overall narrative. This skill is increasingly important in our media-saturated world, where the ability to analyze and create complex multimodal texts is essential.

Digital storytelling also provides children with a safe space to explore new forms of self-expression. Through their stories, they can express their thoughts, feelings, and experiences in ways that might be difficult to articulate through words alone. A child might create a digital story about their experience moving to a new school, using images and music to convey the emotions they felt during that time. This kind of creative exploration can be therapeutic and help children make sense of their experiences.

As literacy researcher Ernest Morrell notes, "Digital storytelling allows children to become producers of knowledge, not just consumers. It's a powerful tool for developing critical literacy skills."

Indeed, by creating digital content, children engage in critical thinking, creativity, and self-expression, deepening their understanding of the world around them. They learn to question the media they consume, recognize the power of storytelling, and develop the skills necessary to communicate effectively in a digital landscape.

Reflection Question: How might you encourage your child to move from being a digital content consumer to a creator? What stories or ideas might he or she be excited to share through digital media?

Critical Thinking Skills for Online Information

In our digital age, where information flows like a torrential river, equipping children with robust critical-thinking skills has become paramount. Think of it as providing them with a state-of-the-art vessel and a precision-engineered compass to navigate the often-tumultuous seas of online information.

The CRAAP test—Currency, Relevance, Authority, Accuracy, and Purpose—is a sophisticated filtration system for young minds. Dr. Megan Oakleaf, associate professor at the University of Syracuse iSchool, explains: "This heuristic helps students systematically evaluate information, much like scientists use criteria to assess the validity of experimental results" (Oakleaf, 2018). Consider 12-year-old Alex, who encountered a questionable health article on social media. Applying the CRAAP test, he astutely identified the article's outdated nature and lack of credible sources, prompting him to seek more reliable information from authoritative websites.

Cross-referencing information across multiple sources is akin to triangulating one's position using various celestial bodies. Emily, a high school student researching climate change, exemplifies this approach. She constructed a comprehensive understanding of the topic by synthesizing data from peer-reviewed scientific journals, reputable news outlets, and government reports. Dr. John Cook, a cognitive scientist specializing in misinformation, notes: "This multi-source approach helps build cognitive resilience against misinformation" (Cook, 2020).

Distinguishing fact from opinion is a vital skill in the digital landscape. It's comparable to differentiating between objective measurements and subjective interpretations in scientific experiments. The Parker family's experience with their son Jake, who inadvertently quoted blog opinions as facts, illustrates the importance of this skill. Dr. Sam Wineburg, a Stanford professor studying how people judge online information, emphasizes: "The internet is a powerful tool, but it requires a new set of skills to use it effectively. We need to teach our children to be critical consumers of information" (Wineburg, 2019).

Recognizing bias and propaganda is like a historian's work. They must conduct a thorough examination of primary sources. The Martinez family analyzes documentaries for bias, which aligns with Dr. Renee Hobbs, author of *Mind Over Media: Propaganda Education for a Digital Age*. She calls it "reading between the lines." It's a crucial skill in our media-saturated world (Hobbs, 2021).

Encouraging healthy skepticism and questioning is fundamental to scientific inquiry and critical thinking. This approach is supported by alarming findings from a 2023 Stanford History Education Group report, which revealed that 82% of middle school students struggled to distinguish between sponsored content and genuine news stories online. One of the researchers, Dr. Sarah McGrew, states: "These findings underscore the urgent need for explicit instruction in online civic reasoning" (McGrew et al., 2023).

Two key benefits emerge when we practice these strategies each day: We teach digital literacy and foster analytical inquiry. Dr. Claire Wardle, co-founder and former Executive Director of First Draft, aptly summarizes: "In this information ecosystem, critical thinking isn't just an academic skill—it's a survival skill" (Wardle, 2022).

Reflection Question: Considering the multifaceted nature of digital literacy, how might you create a comprehensive approach to integrating these critical thinking strategies into your family's routine? What potential barriers do you foresee, and how could you leverage available resources to overcome them?

The Role of Social Media in Modern Literacy

Social media has become an integral part of modern communication. It is a virtual public square where ideas are exchanged, debates unfold, and social norms are negotiated. This digital landscape presents unprecedented opportunities and unique challenges for literacy development. When exploring this terrain, it's essential to consider both the advantages and the potential drawbacks.

Concise Writing: The Art of Digital Brevity

Platforms like Twitter, with their character limitations, have ushered in a new era of concise communication. Dr. Bronwyn Clare Williams, a professor of English at the University of Louisville, observes: "These constraints can foster creativity and precision in expression. It's like the digital equivalent of writing haiku" (Williams, 2019).

Consider 15-year-old Zoe, who initially struggled with wordy essays. Her English teacher encouraged her to practice summarizing her arguments on Twitter. "It was challenging at first," Zoe reflects, "but it taught me to cut through the fluff and get to the heart of my ideas quickly."

Audience Awareness: The Global Stage of Social Media

Social media provides a real-time laboratory for understanding audience and context. Dr. Danah Boyd, a principal researcher at Microsoft Research, notes: "Teens on social media are constantly negotiating complex social situations, adjusting their communication style based on their audience. It's a sophisticated form of code-switching" (Boyd, 2018).

The Chen family witnessed this firsthand when their son, Alex, carefully crafted different posts for his Instagram (primarily friends) and LinkedIn (professional contacts) accounts. "It's fascinating to watch him contemplate his audience," Mrs. Chen remarks. "He's learning valuable communication skills that will serve him well in the future."

Visual Literacy: The Rise of the Image
In our increasingly visual culture, platforms like Instagram and TikTok are developing new forms of literacy. Dr. Kristin Fontichiaro, a clinical associate professor of information at the University of Michigan, explains: "Visual literacy—the ability to interpret, negotiate, and make meaning from information presented in the form of an image—is becoming as crucial as traditional text-based literacy" (Fontichiaro, 2021).

High school art teacher Mr. Raj Patel leverages this in his classroom: "I have students analyze social media images, discussing composition, color theory, and implicit messaging. Then, they create their own visual stories. It's remarkable how sophisticated their visual communication skills have become."

Digital Citizenship: Practicing Ethical Online Behavior
Social media serves as a training ground for digital citizenship. Dr. Mike Ribble, author of *Raising a Digital Child*, defines this as "the norms of appropriate, responsible behavior concerning technology use" (Ribble, 2020). The Johnson family implements a think before you post rule. "We discuss potential consequences of online actions," Mr.

Johnson explains. "When our daughter wanted to post about a disagreement with a friend, we discussed how that might impact their relationship. It led to a valuable discussion about online ethics."

Global Awareness: Windows to the World

Social media can be a powerful tool for developing global consciousness. Dr. Renee Hobbs, professor of communication studies at the University of Rhode Island, posits: "Social media can expose children to diverse perspectives and cultures, fostering empathy and global understanding" (Hobbs, 2022). Sixteen-year-old Maya's experience exemplifies this: "Through a school project, I connected with students from five different countries on Instagram. Seeing their daily lives and hearing their perspectives on global issues completely changed my worldview. It made the world feel both bigger and smaller at the same time."

Navigating the Challenges

While acknowledging these benefits, it's crucial to address social media's potential pitfalls. Issues like misinformation, cyberbullying, and privacy concerns necessitate careful guidance and open dialogue. Alec Couros, a distinguished professor of Educational Technology and Media at the University of Regina, Canada, aptly advises: "We need to help our children understand that their digital actions have real-world consequences."

This sentiment is echoed by Dr. Sonia Livingstone, a professor of social psychology at the London School of Economics: "Rather than restricting access, we should focus on developing children's critical digital literacy skills, enabling them to navigate online spaces safely and productively" (Livingstone, 2021).

The Martin family illustrates this balanced strategy. They have regular digital roundtable discussions where family members share their online experiences, both positive and negative. "It is not about policing their use," Mrs. Martin explains, "but about fostering open communication and critical thinking about their digital lives."

Social media literacy stands as an essential component of modern education in our digital world. Thoughtful engagement with online platforms helps children build crucial skills while learning digital ethics and responsible online behavior. Students develop into informed digital citizens who can navigate social media with confidence and understanding.

Reflection Question: How do you currently navigate social media use in your family? What positive aspects of social media might you highlight while also addressing potential risks?

Future Trends in Digital Literacy Education

As we look to the future, several emerging trends are actively reshaping the landscape of digital literacy. These innovations are not just changing how we teach and learn but fundamentally altering our understanding of what it means to be literate in an increasingly digital world. The convergence of artificial intelligence, virtual reality, and adaptive learning technologies is creating unprecedented opportunities for personalized, immersive education.

Artificial Intelligence is revolutionizing education through AI-powered tools that offer personalized learning experiences. AI tutors and chatbots provide students with instant feedback and support, helping them understand complex topics through platforms like Duolingo for language learning and Carnegie Learning's MATHia for mathematics. Adaptive learning platforms such as DreamBox, Knewton, and Smart Sparrow employ sophisticated AI algorithms to adjust the content and pace of lessons based on student performance, ensuring a truly personalized learning journey. These systems can analyze a student's learning history and preferences to recommend additional resources and materials that match their specific learning needs.

Virtual and augmented reality technologies are transforming traditional education by offering immersive learning experiences that enhance comprehension and engagement. Virtual field trips through platforms like Google Expeditions and Nearpod VR enable students to visit places they otherwise couldn't access, from historical sites to outer space or inside the human body, enriching subjects like geography, history, and science. In the realm of hands-on learning, VR provides realistic simulations for subjects like biology, chemistry, and physics, where students can safely conduct experiments in virtual labs through platforms like Labster and VictoryXR.

The understanding of basic programming concepts is increasingly viewed as a fundamental literacy skill, while data literacy has become crucial in our data-driven world. Adaptive learning technologies continue to evolve, providing real-time adjustments to meet individual learner needs and creating more effective educational experiences. The integration of AI and VR/AR into education offers considerable benefits. These technologies significantly boost student engagement through interactive and personalized learning experiences. AI provides tailored support for students with diverse learning needs, while VR democratizes access to rare experiences. Together, these tools help develop essential 21st-century skills, including problem-solving, critical thinking, and digital literacy.

However, implementing these technologies in educational settings comes with notable challenges. The substantial costs associated with VR equipment and AI software can be prohibitive for many educational institutions. Teachers require comprehensive training to effectively integrate these technologies into their teaching practices. Additionally, the use of AI raises significant concerns about privacy and data security, particularly regarding the collection and analysis of student data.

The fundamental goal of literacy remains steady: understanding and communicating meaning in powerful ways. Modern tools and contexts may shift, but these core skills serve as the foundation for all learning and connection. Teaching must adapt to emerging trends while keeping this essential purpose at its heart. The key lies in thoughtfully integrating these technologies while maintaining focus on core educational objectives and ensuring equitable access for all learners.

Conclusion: Empowering Digital Citizens

Digital literacy is an essential skill set for the 21st century. When we understand its components and guide age-appropriate skill development, our children become confident, responsible digital citizens. Technology enhances traditional literacy skills, creating new opportunities for learning and growth. Remember, your role as a parent is not to be a technology expert but a guide and mentor in the digital world. Stay involved, ask questions, and learn alongside your children as they navigate the digital landscape safely and effectively.

Key Takeaways:
1. Digital literacy is a crucial 21st-century skill encompassing more than technical ability.
2. With guidance and supervision, age-appropriate digital skills should be introduced early.
3. Quality digital content should engage, not just entertain, and complement traditional literacy skills.
4. Safe and responsible internet use requires clear guidelines and open communication.
5. Digital tools can enhance traditional literacy skills when used thoughtfully.
6. Critical thinking skills are essential for navigating online information.
7. Digital literacy education is evolving with technologies like AI and VR, offering new opportunities and challenges.

As we move forward in our literacy journey, we will explore how these digital skills intersect with the broader landscape of 21st-century skills.

Reflection Question: Considering the digital literacy skills discussed in this chapter, what areas do you feel most excited about exploring with your children?

Further Reading

1. *Digital Citizenship in Schools: Nine Elements All Students Should Know* (4th ed.). International Society for Technology in Education. Ribble, M. (2021). A comprehensive guide to teaching digital citizenship in educational settings.
2. *Create to Learn: Introduction to Digital Literacy.* Hobbs, R. (2017). Wiley-Blackwell. An in-depth exploration of digital literacy through project-based learning.
3. *Screenwise: Helping Kids Thrive (and Survive) in Their Digital World.* Heitner, D. (2016). Routledge. Practical advice for parents on guiding children through the digital landscape.
4. Common Sense Media (www.commonsensemedia.org) *is a nonprofit organization that provides education and advocacy to families to promote safe technology and media for children.*
5. Digital Literacy Resource Platform (https://digitalliteracy.gov/) *A U.S. government initiative offering resources and curricula for digital literacy education.*

Practical Exercises

1. **Digital Scavenger Hunt:** Create a list of age-appropriate information for your child to find online. Guide them through the process of using search engines effectively, evaluating sources, and cross-referencing information. Learning Outcome: Develop search skills, information evaluation, and critical thinking.
2. **Family Digital Citizenship Agreement:** Work together as a family to create a set of guidelines for responsible internet use. Include rules about screen time, online behavior, and privacy protection. Learning Outcome: Promotes understanding of digital citizenship and responsible online behavior.
3. **Multimedia Story Creation:** Use a digital storytelling tool (e.g., Storybird, Book Creator) to create a story together. Incorporate text, images, and possibly audio or video. Learning Outcome: Enhances digital content creation skills and multimodal literacy.
4. **Fake News Detective:** Present your child with a mix of real and fake news stories. Guide them through the process of fact-checking and identifying credible sources. Learning Outcome: Develop critical thinking skills and the ability to evaluate online information.
5. **Digital Literacy Time Capsule:** Create a digital time capsule using various media (photos, videos, text documents). Discuss how to organize and store digital information securely. Learning Outcome:

Improves understanding of digital organization and data management.

Chapter 9: Literacy for Life: Developing 21st Century Skills

Overview

"The new literacies almost all involve social skills developed through collaboration and networking. These skills build on the foundation of traditional literacy, research, technical, and critical analysis skills taught in the classroom." Media scholar Dr. Henry Jenkins highlights a crucial truth: In the 21st century, literacy has evolved into a complex web of competencies that intertwine with every aspect of our lives. Literacy is a vibrant, ever-expanding universe. At its core, we find the fundamental skills of reading and writing—the basic building blocks of traditional education. In today's rapidly changing world, literacy has become so much more. It's not just about decoding words on a page or crafting well-structured sentences; it's a gateway to many interconnected skills essential for success in the 21st century.

Consider how reading a news article online differs from reading a printed newspaper. Today's reader might fact-check claims in real-time, compare multiple sources, engage in online discussions, or create and share their response through social media. Each of these actions requires a blend of traditional literacy skills with newer competencies like digital, media, and information literacy.

In this chapter, we will explore how literacy serves as a launchpad for developing crucial life skills. Our focus shifts to the connections between reading and critical thinking, writing and creativity, and how digital literacy shapes our interaction with information. Expert insights and practical examples show how strong literacy skills create effective communicators, innovative problem-solvers, and empathetic global citizens. Technological advancements like artificial intelligence and virtual reality reshape how we interact with information and each other. Parents and educators must prepare children for both today's world and tomorrow's evolving landscape. By the end of this chapter, you'll have a roadmap for nurturing proficient readers, writers, and lifelong learners who are equipped to thrive in our complex, ever-evolving world.

Defining 21st-Century Skills

Before we plunge into the intricate connections between literacy and 21st-century skills, it's important to establish a clear understanding of what we mean by this oft-used term. While there's no universally accepted definition of "21st-century skills," education experts and industry leaders have reached a consensus on a core set of competencies that are essential for success in our rapidly evolving world. These skills are not entirely new; many have been valuable throughout human history. However, the digital age has increased their importance and changed the contexts in which they are applied.

Let me walk you through these essential skills for today's world: Think of critical thinking and problem-solving as your mental tool kit for navigating our complex world. Looking at situations from all angles and figuring out what information you can trust becomes vital when we are bombarded with content 24/7, right? Creativity brings fresh solutions and different thinking when faced with challenges. In today's fast-paced tech world, coming up with innovative solutions proves pure gold.

Now, communication changes everything. Whether crafting an email that gets results or giving a presentation that keeps everyone engaged, delivering your message effectively to different audiences makes all the difference. Working well with others defines true collaboration. These days, you might work with team members across different time zones and cultures, so listening, resolving conflicts, and solving problems together becomes key.

Information literacy might sound fancy, but understanding how to find, evaluate, and use information effectively creates your personal filter for the massive amount of data we encounter daily. Understanding media messages and how they shape our views reveals what lies beneath the surface of what you're watching, reading, or scrolling through. Tech literacy extends far beyond using a smartphone—being receptive to new technologies as they come and understanding how to use them responsibly matters most.

Being flexible and adaptable works like a superpower in today's world. Taking initiative and being self-directed lets you set goals, manage time, and keep learning without someone looking over your shoulder. Social and cross-cultural skills grow more important as our world gets more connected, building meaningful connections with people from all walks of life.

Getting things done efficiently and being someone people can count on makes all the difference. Leadership extends beyond being the boss to inspiring others, making ethical choices, and owning your actions and their impact.

These skills work together to help you thrive in our ever-changing world.

As we explore each of these skills, we will uncover how they are not isolated competencies but a web of interconnected abilities that build upon and reinforce each other. More importantly, we will explore how they are deeply intertwined with literacy development. Consider how reading a complex text exercises critical-thinking skills or how drafting a persuasive essay hones communication abilities. Alternatively, think about how researching a topic online simultaneously develops information, media, and technology literacy.

It is important to note that these skills are not meant to replace traditional academic knowledge but to complement and enhance it. Content knowledge remains vital; these skills provide the tools to apply that knowledge effectively in real-world contexts. Parents and educators, our challenge is to foster these skills alongside traditional literacy development. It is not about choosing one over the other but recognizing how they support and amplify each other.

Critical Thinking and Problem Solving: The Analytical Reader

Reading is far more than just decoding symbols on a page; it's an intricate dance of cognition, a fundamental act of thinking. When we truly engage with a text, we're not passive recipients of information but active participants in an intellectual journey. In many ways, reading critically mirrors the work of a detective—we gather clues (information from the text), analyze their significance, and piece them together to solve the mystery (comprehend the deeper meaning of the text). As children progress from basic literacy to more advanced reading skills, they're not just expanding their vocabulary or improving their reading speed. They're developing a crucial cognitive tool kit that extends far beyond literature. They are learning to think critically, question assumptions, consider multiple perspectives, and solve complex problems—skills that are invaluable in every aspect of life.

Dr. Patricia Alexander, co-author of the *Handbook of Educational Psychology*, beautifully captures this idea: "Deep reading is not just about decoding words, but about wrestling with ideas, considering alternative perspectives, and solving complex problems presented in text" (Alexander, 2012). This insight underscores the profound connection between literacy and critical thinking. When we engage in deep reading, we're absorbing information and grappling with concepts, questioning assumptions, and often reshaping our understanding of the world. Imagine a child engrossed in a story about a character grappling with a tough decision. As they progress through the narrative, they're not just following the plot; they are considering the character's motivations, predicting potential outcomes, evaluating the character's choices, and perhaps even imagining what they would do in a similar situation. This analysis, prediction, and evaluation process is critical thinking in action.

So, how can we, as parents and educators, foster this connection between reading and critical thinking? Here are some strategies:

1. Engage in meaningful discussions about books: Instead of simply asking, "Did you like the story?" dive deeper into open-ended questions that encourage analysis and interpretation. For example:
   - "Why do you think the character made that decision?"
   - "How might the story have been different if...?"
   - "What do you think the author was trying to say about...?"
2. Introduce texts with conflicting viewpoints: Expose children to diverse perspectives on the same topic. This could be through nonfiction articles presenting different sides of an issue or fiction stories that present moral dilemmas. Encourage your child to evaluate the arguments and evidence and form their opinions.
3. Use real-world problems as a springboard for research and reading: Connect reading to current events or issues relevant to your child's life. For instance, if your community is debating a new policy, encourage your child to research and read about it. This not only develops critical thinking skills but fosters civic engagement.
4. Encourage prediction and hypothesis-forming: Before finishing a story, ask your child to predict what might happen next and why. This develops both critical thinking and creativity.
5. Practice summarizing and synthesizing information: After reading a text, ask your child to summarize the main points in their own words. This requires

them to identify and express key information concisely, a valuable critical-thinking skill.
6. Explore the "why" behind facts: When reading nonfiction, focus on why it happened, not just what happened. This develops causal reasoning skills.
7. Compare and contrast different texts: If you have read multiple books by the same author or on the same topic, discuss their similarities or differences. This will develop your analytical skills and a deeper understanding of style and perspective.

The goal isn't to turn every reading session into a formal analysis. This approach's beauty is that it can be incorporated naturally into everyday reading habits, turning story time into an opportunity for rich, engaging discussions that develop critical thinking skills.

Reflection Question: What questions can you ask your child to help them think more deeply about the story they are reading?

This question invites us to consider how to tailor our approach to each unique story and child. Some potential questions might include:
- "How do you think [the character] felt when [that event] happened? Why?"
- "If you were in [the character's] situation, what would you have done differently? Why?"
- "What do you think is the most important lesson from this story? Why?"
- "How does this story relate to your own life or experiences?"

- "What do you think the author wants us to think about after reading this story?"

Thoughtful questions invite children to explore texts more deeply and discover hidden meanings. Students learn to analyze character choices, connect stories to their lives, and think critically about important themes. These discussions transform children into strong readers and critical thinkers who can tackle challenges across all subjects and life experiences.

Our exploration of literacy and 21st-century skills reveals how critical thinking ignites and amplifies other essential competencies. Strong analytical readers move beyond mere comprehension; they interrogate texts, challenge assumptions, forge connections across ideas, and launch their own innovative thoughts from what they read. When we cultivate this deep engagement with reading, we equip our children not just for academic achievement but for a lifetime of dynamic learning, creative problem-solving, and intellectual discovery.

Creativity and Innovation: The Imaginative Writer

Writing is a creative act. Whether crafting a story, developing an argument, or even composing an email, writing engages the imagination and fosters original thinking. As children hone their writing skills, they simultaneously nurture their creative capacities and innovative potential. Sir Ken Robinson, best known for his 2006 TED Talk "Do Schools Kill Creativity?" emphasizes this connection: "Creativity is as important in education as literacy, and we should treat it with the same status" (Robinson, 2006).

Creative writing serves as a foundation for innovation across various disciplines. Imaginative writing develops essential skills like generating original ideas, making unexpected connections, and thinking flexibly. These skills transfer powerfully to fields like science, technology, and business. The creative writers of today could become tomorrow's innovative entrepreneurs and visionary artists.

To foster this connection between writing and innovation, parents can:

- Encourage diverse creative writing projects: Beyond traditional short stories, explore formats like podcasts, blogs, graphic novels, or even augmented-reality narratives. These varied mediums can spark excitement and push creative boundaries.
- Use thought-provoking writing prompts: Offer prompts that challenge conventional thinking, such as "Write a story from the perspective of a household object" or "Describe a world where gravity works differently."
- Celebrate unique ideas and approaches: Praise your child's original concepts and unconventional storytelling techniques. This reinforces the value of innovative thinking.
- Collaborate on family writing projects: Create a shared story in which each family member contributes a chapter, fostering a collaborative, creative environment.

- Explore interdisciplinary writing: Encourage writing combining different subjects, like a science-fiction story incorporating actual scientific concepts.
- Engage with local writing communities: Participate in young writer's workshops or book clubs to expose your child to diverse creative perspectives.

Reflection Question: Can you think of a fun writing project that would spark your child's imagination while also encouraging them to think innovatively about a real-world issue?

Every time we nurture creativity and innovation through writing, we open new doors for children's expression and understanding. These essential skills empower them to navigate and shape our complex, rapidly evolving world. As they develop their creative writing abilities, children become better writers and more imaginative thinkers, problem solvers, and innovators in all aspects of their lives.

Communication and Collaboration: The Articulate Conversationalist

In the 21st century, literacy extends far beyond the solitary acts of reading and writing. It encompasses effective communication and collaboration skills, which are increasingly crucial in our interconnected world. As children develop their literacy skills, they also cultivate their abilities to articulate ideas, work with others, and navigate complex social interactions.

Dr. Karen R. Harris, best known for developing the Self-Regulated Strategy Development (SRSD) model of strategy instruction, emphasizes this connection: "Collaborative writing activities not only improve literacy skills but also foster communication, negotiation, and teamwork abilities essential for the modern workplace" (Harris, 2006). This insight highlights how literacy practices can serve as a foundation for developing broader social and professional competencies. Communicating effectively through spoken and written language is a cornerstone of academic, professional, and personal success. Similarly, collaboration has become indispensable in our increasingly interconnected and complex world. Strong literacy skills prepare children to work well with others and make meaningful contributions to group projects. Students learn to share ideas clearly while developing the collaboration skills needed for success. Their growing abilities to read, write, and communicate transform them into valuable team members who can tackle challenges together.

Here are a few strategies to foster these connections:
1. Encourage group reading and writing projects:
    • Organize book clubs where children can discuss their readings, share interpretations, and learn to articulate their thoughts.
    • Facilitate collaborative storytelling exercises where each child contributes to a shared narrative, promoting creativity and teamwork.
    • Engage in family reading activities, taking turns reading aloud and discussing the content.

2. Practice giving and receiving constructive feedback on writing:
   • Teach children how to provide specific, actionable feedback on their peers' writing.
   • Model how to receive criticism graciously and use it to improve one's work.
   • Organize peer-review sessions for writing projects, emphasizing respectful communication and constructive suggestions.
3. Use digital tools for collaborative storytelling or research projects:
   • Explore online platforms that allow for real-time collaborative writing.
   • Engage in digital pen pal programs to practice written communication with peers from diverse backgrounds.
   • Use shared online documents for group research projects, teaching digital collaboration skills.
4. Develop presentation skills:
   • Encourage children to present their written work orally, helping them translate written ideas into spoken communication.
   • Practice creating visual aids (like posters or slides) to accompany presentations, integrating multiple forms of communication.
5. Engage in debate and discussion activities:
   • Organize structured debates on age-appropriate topics, teaching children to articulate arguments and respond to counterpoints.
   • Hold family discussions on books or current events, encouraging a respectful exchange of ideas.

6. Explore multicultural communication:
   • Read stories from different cultures and discuss how communication styles might vary across contexts.
   • If possible, engage in language-exchange activities to appreciate diverse forms of communication.
7. Practice active listening:
   • Teach children the importance of listening carefully to the ideas of others before responding.
   • Play listening games that require careful attention to details in spoken narratives.

Strong literacy skills give children more than the ability to read and write. They learn to express themselves, collaborate, and engage in their communities, skills that boost academic and career success and enrich personal and social connections. Teaching strong literacy early will anchor communication skills, preparing children to adapt and thrive in our connected, changing world.

Information, Media, and Technology Literacy: The Digital Navigator

Navigating and using the vast information at our fingertips is a critical skill. These skills, called information, media, and technology literacy, build on basic literacy and add new complexities and opportunities.

Dr. Donald J. Leu has influenced how we think about reading in the digital era. As the John and Maria Neag Endowed Chair in Literacy and Technology at the University of Connecticut and director of the New Literacies Research Lab, he has found key differences between traditional and digital reading. What makes his work particularly compelling is his discovery that reading online actually demands different skills than reading print. As he puts it, "Online reading comprehension is not isomorphic with offline reading comprehension; additional skills and strategies are required." A strong traditional reader is not, by default, a skilled digital reader. These are distinct skill sets that deserve their own attention and development.

The digital world our children navigate today is a double-edged sword. While they enjoy unprecedented access to information and diverse perspectives, they must also learn to wade through potential misinformation, biased content, and an overwhelming volume of data. As parents and educators, we have the important task of nurturing their critical-thinking abilities to help them flourish in this information-rich environment.

Let's explore some effective approaches to building these essential skills: When teaching online research strategies, we can start by introducing the power of well-chosen keywords and advanced search features. Students need to understand the importance of cross-referencing information and recognize the unique value of academic databases compared to general web searches. Source evaluation has become particularly essential in the digital age. The CRAAP test offers a practical framework for assessing sources based on Currency, Relevance, Authority, Accuracy, and Purpose. Students benefit from understanding the distinction between primary and secondary sources in digital contexts, as well as grasping the significance of peer review in academic publications.

Media literacy deserves special attention in our digital landscape. By analyzing advertisements and news articles together, students learn to identify persuasive techniques and understand how different media formats can shape the same message. Discussions about filter bubbles and echo chambers in social media help them recognize how their online environment might limit their exposure to diverse perspectives.

Digital citizenship forms another crucial component of modern literacy. Students need guidance in protecting their privacy, understanding their digital footprint, and fostering positive online interactions. This knowledge helps them navigate social media and online communities more responsibly.

Critical consumption of digital media involves identifying bias in online content and distinguishing between fact and opinion. Understanding how algorithms influence our online experiences helps students become more conscious consumers of digital information, and creative and ethical use of digital tools empowers students to move beyond passive consumption. Introducing basic coding concepts and discussing copyright principles helps them become responsible digital creators. Projects that blend traditional and digital literacy skills often yield particularly engaging learning experiences.

Balanced technology use remains essential amid these digital literacy efforts. Students need strategies for managing digital distractions and maintaining healthy screen time habits alongside their other activities. This comprehensive approach to digital literacy doesn't aim to shield children from the digital world but equips them with tools for confident, responsible navigation. As they develop these skills, they're better positioned to harness digital resources for learning, creativity, and problem-solving.

Moving beyond pure academics, these competencies form the foundation for success in our digital world. Helping students excel with information, media, and technology prepares tomorrow's leaders to become active citizens, sharp thinkers, and powerful voices for positive change.

Reflection Question: Which digital literacy skills do you see as most vital for learners today?

Flexibility, Adaptability, and Self-Direction: The Lifelong Learner

The ability to adapt and take charge of your own learning is essential for success. Literacy plays a key role in building these skills, as it provides the foundation for lifelong learning and personal growth. Carol Dweck's concept of a "growth mindset" is particularly relevant here, as it emphasizes viewing challenges as opportunities rather than threats. As Dweck puts it, "In a growth mindset, challenges are exciting rather than threatening. So rather than thinking, oh, I'm going to reveal my weaknesses, you say, wow, here's a chance to grow."

Children who view reading challenges as opportunities to tackle harder books with confidence and determination. Their positive mindset helps them push through difficult writing projects, leading to greater success and growth. Children develop lasting resilience when they see each reading and writing challenge as a step toward improvement.

Literacy is about more than just reading and writing—it fosters flexibility, adaptability, and self-direction. Here's how: When encouraged to read different types of books and subjects, kids learn to think in different ways. You might try a monthly reading challenge with different kinds of books, like sci-fi novels, memoirs, or poetry. Reading also helps solve problems. When children use books to learn new things or find answers, they discover they can find information on their own.

It's important to celebrate when kids tackle challenging reading or writing projects. This supports Dweck's idea that effort matters more than natural ability. Try picking a slightly harder book or writing task each week and talking about ways to handle the challenge. Think about how you learn—keeping a journal about what you've read, writing down questions, and connecting stories to your own life can help.

Finally, working on reading and writing projects about things you love can make learning more interesting. You might start a blog about your favorite topic or write and illustrate your own story. This helps you learn to guide your own education.

When we blend reading and writing skills with the ability to adapt and learn independently, we prepare students for more than just success in school; we set them up to thrive in life and their future careers. Our role as teachers and parents extends beyond developing reading and writing abilities. We're shaping curious minds who bounce back from challenges and stay excited about learning as they grow and face new experiences.

Social and Cross-Cultural Skills: The Empathetic Reader

Understanding and caring about different viewpoints has become valuable. Books are a fantastic way to develop these social skills, giving us glimpses into lives, cultures, and experiences different from our own. As Chimamanda Ngozi Adichie wisely points out, "The single story creates stereotypes, and the problem with stereotypes is not that they are untrue, but that they are incomplete. They make one story become the only story" (Adichie, 2009). That's why it's so important to read many different stories to better understand the world around us.

Research shows that reading stories helps us understand others better. Dr. Keith Oatley, who studies how our minds work, found that reading fiction improves our ability to understand and connect with others. He notes, "Fiction is a beneficial simulation because negotiating the social world effectively is extremely tricky, requiring us to weigh up myriad interacting instances of cause and effect" (Oatley, 2011). This makes sense because dealing with social situations can be tricky, and we need to understand how different actions affect people.

How can we use reading to build these important social skills? Start by reading books by authors with different backgrounds and cultures. You can mix it up with stories about various social issues, different time periods, and places around the world. Include both new and classic books to see how views have changed over time.

When reading, compare the characters' lives with your own. Think about how their culture affects their choices and how they see the world. It's interesting to consider how different characters might handle the same situation based on their backgrounds. Take some time to learn about the cultural and historical setting of the stories you read and think about how the author's own background might influence how he or she tells the story. Try stepping into the characters' shoes, maybe write a diary entry pretending to be them, or think about how the story would change if told from another character's point of view. Look for common themes like love, growing up, or dealing with loss across different cultural stories. It's fascinating to see how these universal experiences show up differently (or similarly) in various cultures.

Don't just stick to books. Compare stories to their movie versions and discuss how different cultures are depicted. Watch documentaries or read news articles about the cultures you're learning about in books. Even better, try connecting with real people from different backgrounds through pen pals or attending cultural events in your community. Make reading diverse stories a family activity and encourage everyone to read books that challenge their usual perspectives. As Dr. Rudine Sims Bishop says, "Books are sometimes windows, offering views of worlds that may be real or imagined, familiar or strange. These windows are also sliding glass doors, and readers only have to walk through in imagination to become part of whatever world the author has created or re-created" (Bishop, 1990). Through exploring diverse stories and experiences in books, we develop more than just reading skills—we learn to connect with and appreciate people from all walks of life in our worldwide community.

Productivity, Accountability, and Leadership: The Engaged Citizen

Engaged citizenship and leadership indeed rely on fundamental literacy skills. These skills help individuals to articulate ideas clearly, comprehend complex issues, and inspire others. These are all essential for effective leadership. John F. Kennedy, the 35th president of the United States, said, "Leadership and learning are indispensable to each other" (Kennedy, 1963). This highlights the link between leadership and literacy.

Fostering Connections Between Literacy and Leadership

To encourage the connections between literacy and leadership, it is important to engage in activities that promote related skills:

- **Encourage Active Participation**: Encourage children and young adults to write letters to local leaders about issues they care about. This not only improves their writing skills but teaches them how to engage with civic processes and express their concerns effectively.
- **Support Debate and Student Government**: Participation in debate clubs or student government can significantly enhance critical thinking and public speaking skills. These platforms provide opportunities to practice articulating arguments and

understanding diverse perspectives, which are key aspects of leadership.
- **Discuss Language and Persuasion**: Engage in discussions about how leaders use language to inspire and persuade. Analyzing speeches and writings of influential leaders can help individuals understand the power of words and how to use them effectively to mobilize and motivate others.

Expanding Engagement through Civic Involvement
Engaged citizenship extends beyond literacy and involves active participation in community and civic life. Here are additional ways to enhance civic engagement:
- **Stay Informed**: It is vital to keep up with local politics and understand who has decision-making power in the community. This knowledge empowers citizens to make informed decisions and hold leaders accountable.
- **Volunteer and Participate**: Volunteering in community activities fosters a sense of belonging and responsibility. Whether it's participating in local clean-up drives or supporting community events, these activities build community spirit and demonstrate the impact of collective action.
- **Engage in Dialogue**: Platforms for digital citizen participation allow individuals to share ideas and voice concerns from the comfort of their homes. This engagement promotes transparency and allows citizens to contribute to shaping their communities.
- **Exercise Your Right to Vote**: Voting is a fundamental way to participate in democracy. It

enables citizens to influence policy direction and hold elected officials accountable for their actions.

Reflection Question: Reflect on the role of literacy in your civic engagement. How can improving your literacy skills enhance your ability to participate in and contribute to your community and its leadership?

Diverse Perspectives: 21st Century Literacy in Action

Literacy extends far beyond the traditional abilities to read and write. Modern students need to navigate an increasingly complex digital landscape while developing critical thinking skills that bridge cultural and technological divides. These multifaceted literacy skills are not just academic requirements—they are essential tools for success in a rapidly evolving global society.

Let's look at how these skills might play out in the lives of different students:

Zoe, 16, United States- 7:30 a.m.: Zoe starts her day by checking a news app and evaluating headlines and sources (Information Literacy, Critical Thinking). 9:00 a.m.: In English class, she participates in a group discussion about *To Kill a Mockingbird*, relating themes to current events (Communication, Social, and Cross-Cultural Skills). 3:00 p.m.: After school, Zoe works on her blog about environmental issues, researching and writing a post about local sustainability efforts (Creativity, Media Literacy, Leadership).

Ahmed, 16, Egypt- 8:00 a.m.: Ahmed reads a bilingual newspaper, comparing Arabic and English coverage of world events (Information Literacy, Cross-Cultural Skills). 11:00 a.m.: In a coding class, Ahmed collaborates with classmates on a mobile app project (Technology et al.). 6:00 p.m.: He participates in an online creative writing workshop with peers worldwide (Creativity, Communication, Cross-Cultural Skills).

Mei, 15, China- 7:00 a.m.: Mei practices English by watching and analyzing TED Talks (Communication, Critical Thinking). 2:00 p.m.: Mei leads a discussion in a literature class comparing Chinese and Western fairy tales (Leadership, Cross-Cultural Skills). 8:00 p.m.: She works on a digital storytelling project, blending traditional Chinese art with modern animation techniques (Creativity, Technology Literacy).

Challenges and Pitfalls in Developing 21st Century Skills

While developing these modern literacy skills offers clear advantages, we must recognize several key challenges. The digital divide remains a significant barrier, with recent studies showing that some Americans, particularly older adults and children in low-income households, still lack basic internet access. Though communities are working to bridge this gap through programs providing devices and internet access to students in need, the disparity persists.

Students today also face an overwhelming amount of information, making it difficult to sort through and evaluate content effectively. Teachers and parents often struggle to help young people find reliable sources while managing the sheer volume of available information. Another challenge is striking the right balance between traditional and new literacy skills. While digital competency is increasingly important, core reading and writing abilities remain essential. Schools must find ways to develop both sets of skills without sacrificing either.

As students spend more time online, protecting their privacy and safety has become a crucial concern. Additionally, keeping up with rapidly changing technology requires ongoing adaptation—what's current today may be outdated tomorrow, demanding continuous learning from both students and educators. These challenges are significant but not unassailable. With proper support and resources, students can develop the comprehensive literacy skills needed for success in today's world.

Recent Research and Job Market Relevance

Today's job market is changing fast, and employers want workers with modern skills more than ever before. Research shows that being creative, working well with others, and adapting to change are crucial abilities that go hand-in-hand with reading and writing skills. As businesses change and new technology appears, companies look for people who can handle lots of information and communicate well in different ways. The most successful workers understand that reading and writing aren't just basic skills; they're tools that help you keep learning and growing throughout your career.

Recent research and industry reports consistently highlight this evolving landscape, demonstrating how literacy skills intersect with workplace demands:

- **World Economic Forum Report (2021)**: This report predicts that by 2025, 50% of all employees

will need reskilling due to the increasing adoption of technology. This underscores the necessity for continuous learning and adaptability, skills rooted in literacy practices such as critical thinking and problem-solving.
- **LinkedIn's Workplace Learning Report (2020)**: The top three skills that companies most need are creativity, persuasion, and collaboration. These skills are cultivated through literacy activities that encourage innovative thinking, effective communication, and teamwork.
- **Society for Human Resource Management Study (2019)**: This study found that 75% of HR professionals report skill gaps in job applicants, particularly in data analysis, critical thinking, and communication. These areas of deficiency highlight the need for literacy education emphasizing analytical skills and effective communication.
- **National Association of Colleges and Employers Survey (2022)**: Employers identified problem-solving skills, teamwork, and communication skills as the top attributes they seek on a candidate's resume. These skills are nurtured through literacy activities that involve collaborative projects and critical discussions.

Satya Nadella, CEO of Microsoft, captures the essence of lifelong learning with his statement: "The learn-it-all does better than the know-it-all."

To build these important connections between learning and success, we can take several practical steps. First, students should explore different types of reading and writing, from scientific papers to creative stories. This variety helps develop a wide range of skills that can be useful in many situations.

Teachers and parents play a crucial role by showing how they use reading and learning in their own lives. When adults share their own learning challenges and victories, it helps students understand that learning is a lifelong journey, not just something that happens in school. It's also important to celebrate both effort and achievement. When students tackle difficult texts or writing projects, recognizing their hard work—even if the results aren't perfect—encourages them to keep trying. Technology can support this learning process through online research tools and writing platforms that make collaboration easier.

Perhaps most importantly, we need to help students develop a "growth mindset"—the belief that they can improve through effort and practice. Learning about those who persevered through setbacks helps students reframe their own struggles as necessary steps toward mastery. Focusing on these strategies can help parents and educators provide children with the skills necessary to thrive in the modern workforce. Literacy is not just about reading and writing; it's about preparing for a future where adaptability, creativity, and effective communication are paramount.

Reflection Question: How can you incorporate opportunities for developing 21st-century skills into your child's daily routine, and what role can literacy play in this process?

Conclusion: Literacy as a Launchpad

As we have explored in this chapter, literacy is far more than the ability to read and write. It serves as the foundation upon which a whole array of pivotal 21st-century skills is constructed. By building strong literacy skills and linking them to broader skills, parents can help their children succeed in school and life. Dr. Maryanne Wolf, a cognitive neuroscientist, summarizes this idea: "The reading brain circuit is a testament to the human brain's protean capacity to make new connections among its existing structures. This capacity allows us to learn to adapt to an ever-changing world" (Wolf, 2018).

Key Takeaways:
1. 21st-century skills are deeply interconnected with literacy development.
2. Critical thinking, creativity, communication, and collaboration are fundamental skills built on a foundation of literacy.
3. Digital, information, and media literacy are increasingly crucial in our technology-driven world.
4. Developing empathy and cross-cultural understanding through diverse reading is essential in our global society.
5. Literacy skills are essential to engage citizenship and leadership.
6. While developing these skills can be challenging, their importance in the job market and for lifelong success is clear.
7. Parents and educators play a crucial role in fostering the connections between literacy and 21st-century skills.

Books, pens, and conversations spark a child's journey into literacy, and our communities offer vital resources to nurture these skills. As young minds explore stories, craft words, and share ideas, they build more than reading and writing abilities. They cultivate the foundation for lifelong learning and success in today's world. Every interaction fuels their growth, shaping future achievers one page, sentence, and dialogue at a time.

Further Reading

1. *Confronting the Challenges of Participatory Culture: Media Education for the 21st Century.* The MIT Press. Jenkins, H., Clinton, K., Purushotma, R., Robison, A. J., & Weigel, M. (2009). A comprehensive exploration of the skills needed to participate fully in today's media-rich culture.
2. *Four-Dimensional Education: The Competencies Learners Need to Succeed.* Center for Curriculum Redesign. Fadel, C., Bialik, M., & Trilling, B. (2015). Provides a framework for understanding the competencies needed in the 21st century, including knowledge, skills, character, and meta-learning.
3. *The New Education: How to Revolutionize the University to Prepare Students for a World in Flux.* Basic Books. Davidson, C. N. (2017). This book examines how education needs to evolve to prepare students for a rapidly changing world, with a focus on developing adaptable, lifelong learners.
4. Common Sense Education (https://www.commonsense.org/education/): A comprehensive resource for educators and parents, offering lesson plans, articles, and tools for developing digital literacy and 21st-century skills.
5. P21 Partnership for 21st Century Learning (http://www.battelleforkids.org/networks/p21) A coalition of education, business, and government leaders focused on developing frameworks and resources for 21st-century skills education.

Practical Exercises

1. **Digital Storytelling Project:** Create a multimedia story using a platform like Storybird or Adobe Spark. Incorporate text, images, and possibly audio or video to tell a personal story or explore a topic of interest. Learning Outcome: Develop digital literacy, creativity, and multimodal communication skills.
2. **Cross-Cultural Book Club:** Form a family or community book club that reads diverse literature from various cultures. After each book, discuss the story and the cultural context and how it compares to your own experiences. Learning Outcome: Enhances cross-cultural understanding, critical thinking, and communication skills.
3. **Fact-Checking Challenge:** Choose a current news topic and compare how it's reported across different media outlets. Fact-check claims using reputable sources and discuss how different perspectives are presented. Learning Outcome: Develops information literacy, critical thinking, and media-analysis skills.
4. **Collaborative Problem-Solving Activity** Identify a local community issue (e.g., recycling, public spaces, youth programs) and research it using various sources. Brainstorm solutions and create a proposal to address the problem. Present your findings and proposal to family members or local community leaders. Learning Outcome: This activity fosters research skills, critical thinking, collaboration, and civic engagement.

5. **Technology Trends Presentation** Research an emerging technology (e.g., artificial intelligence, augmented reality, blockchain) and create a presentation explaining how it works and its potential impact on society. Present your findings to family members or peers, encouraging questions and discussion. Learning Outcome: Enhances technology literacy, research skills, and the ability to explain complex concepts.

Chapter 10: Community Matters: Leveraging Local Resources

Overview

The African proverb "It takes a village to raise a child" rings especially true regarding literacy. Our modern literacy "villages" now stretch across continents and cultures, weaving together diverse perspectives, shared wisdom, and rich resources that amplify how children learn and flourish. This expanded village now encompasses teachers, librarians, authors, digital creators, and countless others who enrich our children's literacy journeys. Together, these diverse voices and perspectives weave a strong foundation for lifelong learning and growth.

As we have journeyed through the landscape of literacy development, we've explored the vital roles that parents, schools, and technology play in nurturing a child's reading and writing skills. Let's widen our lens to encompass the broader community and its wealth of resources that can enhance your family's literacy journey. This expansion of focus is not just beneficial—it's essential in our interconnected world. We will explore how to tap into your community's rich tapestry of resources to create a vibrant, supportive environment for literacy growth. We will discover how local libraries, community centers, businesses, and online platforms can become powerful allies in your journey. Communities unite for literacy in countless ways, from local bookstore story times to global virtual reading circles, and you can tap into and strengthen these vibrant networks.

This chapter invites you to reimagine your place in our shared literacy landscape. Every family that engages with community literacy initiatives helps create a richer learning environment for all. As a literacy advocate ready to spark change, you will discover practical strategies to amplify community impact. Together, we'll explore how our "village" nurtures not just individual readers and writers but cultivates a generation of confident, curious learners.

The Power of Community in Literacy Development

Dr. Susan B. Neuman, a professor of childhood and literacy education at New York University, emphasizes the importance of community involvement: "When communities rally around literacy, they create a culture of reading that benefits all children, regardless of their socioeconomic background" (Neuman, 2016). Communities that embrace literacy create lasting transformation for our children. It creates a supportive ecosystem that extends far beyond the confines of home and school. This collective approach can lead to what researchers call a "literacy-rich environment"—a setting where reading and writing are valued, visible, and integrated into daily life.

Children internalize literacy's value when they witness adults reading in public spaces, discover literary snippets on park benches and bus stops, and see community leaders champion the transformative power of books. These seemingly minor encounters shape their perception of reading as both vital and joyful. Communities that unite around literacy generate extraordinary possibilities. Their collective expertise and resources spark innovative initiatives that transcend what individual families or schools could achieve alone, from citywide reading challenges to vibrant book festivals to mobile libraries serving marginalized neighborhoods.

Community-driven literacy initiatives dissolve societal barriers, transforming reading into a unifying force that bridges socioeconomic divides. This democratization of literacy opportunities aligns with Dr. Stephen Krashen's 2004 research demonstrating how access to books and rich literary environments correlates directly with reading achievement. Each community resource we explore weaves into a larger tapestry of literacy support. When you engage with these initiatives, you strengthen not just your child's reading journey but energize an entire culture of literacy that elevates our community.

Reflection Question: Think about your community. How could you contribute to strengthening the literacy culture in your neighborhood or town?

Building a Network of Literacy-Minded Families

When families who value literacy connect, they create powerful momentum for each other. These relationships spark shared reading adventures, writing projects, and ongoing encouragement. As Dr. Catherine Snow from Harvard's Graduate School of Education explains, "When families come together around literacy, they create a powerful support system that reinforces the importance of reading and writing" (Snow, 2017). Her research illuminates how social connections amplify learning—our shared goals and encouragement multiply the impact of our individual efforts. Here are some practical ways to build and nurture this network:

1. Organize Book Swaps: Book swaps offer an excellent opportunity to affordably refresh home libraries while fostering a sense of community. These events can be as simple as a neighborhood gathering or as structured as a school-wide initiative. Beyond the practical benefit of accessing new reading material, book swaps encourage discussions about books, expose children to diverse reading choices, and model the value of sharing resources.
2. Create Literacy Playgroups: Combining playdates with literacy activities creates a dynamic environment where children associate reading and writing with fun and social interaction. These playgroups might involve shared reading sessions, storytelling circles, or even creative writing activities appropriate for the children's ages. Research shows that peer-to-peer learning can be highly effective, and these playgroups provide a natural setting for such interactions (Topping, 2005).
3. Share Resources: Creating a community newsletter or social-media group dedicated to sharing literacy events and tips can be a game-changer. This ongoing exchange of information keeps literacy at the forefront of families' minds and provides a

wealth of ideas and opportunities. It might include updates on local author visits, reviews of new children's books, or strategies for encouraging reluctant readers.
4. Family Literacy Nights: Organize regular gatherings where families come together to engage in literacy activities. This might involve group reading sessions, writing workshops, or even literacy-themed game nights. These events provide a structured yet social environment for literacy engagement.
5. Intergenerational Literacy Programs: Partner with local senior centers or retirement communities to create programs where children read to or with older adults. This not only supports literacy development but fosters valuable intergenerational connections and empathy.

The power of these networks lies in their ability to normalize and celebrate literacy as a core family and community value. When children see their peers and other adults actively engaged in and excited about reading and writing, it reinforces the importance and enjoyment of these skills. Networks create what sociologists call "social capital"—the benefits that come from our social connections. In the context of literacy, this social capital can translate into increased access to resources, shared knowledge about effective strategies, and a support system for overcoming challenges.

The African proverb "If you want to go fast, go alone. If you want to go far, go together" illuminates our literacy journey perfectly. Your networks do not need to be large or formal to create lasting change. Even a small circle of dedicated families can transform how children embrace reading and writing. Regular connection and mutual encouragement build sustainable literacy practices that ripple beyond our individual homes. When you engage with these literacy-minded networks, you strengthen your children's growth and your community's culture of learning. Together, we venture farther than any single family could travel alone.

Libraries: The Heart of Community Literacy

Imagine a place where knowledge flows as freely as water from a fountain, stories sprout like seeds in a garden, and curiosity is cultivated like a precious crop. This place exists in every community—your local library. Far more than mere repositories of books, libraries are vibrant hubs of literacy, learning, and community engagement.

Personal Connections: A librarian recalled a touching moment when a young girl returned a book late and expressed guilt over it. The librarian reassured her, saying, "Books are meant to be enjoyed, not just returned on time." This simple interaction encouraged the girl to continue reading without fear of making mistakes. The librarian later received a heartfelt letter from the girl, thanking her for understanding and support, reinforcing empathy's importance in literacy development.

1. **Public Libraries**: Libraries enrich literacy in countless powerful ways. They offer a cornucopia of story times tailored to different age groups, from "Wiggle and Giggle" sessions for toddlers to more

sophisticated book discussions for older children. These events are like fertile soil for young minds, helping literacy take root and flourish. Maria, a librarian in Boston, shares: "I've seen shy toddlers blossom into confident preschoolers through our weekly story times. It's not just about reading books; we sing, dance, and craft—all while building crucial pre-literacy skills."

2. **Summer Reading Programs—Preventing the Summer Slide:** The "summer slide" in reading skills is like a slippery slope many children unknowingly descend during their vacation. Libraries offer a safety net in the form of summer reading programs. These initiatives transform reading from a chore into an adventure, complete with challenges, rewards, and a sense of community. Jake, a 10-year-old from Portland, exclaims: "I read 20 books last summer! The library had this cool space theme; every book I read was like a new planet I discovered. I even won a telescope!"

   A community center staff member shared how a summer reading program transformed the lives of local children. Many participants came from low-income families and lacked access to books at home. The staff organized engaging activities encouraging reading, such as themed story hours and book-related crafts. Initially reluctant to read, one child blossomed into an enthusiastic participant, stating, "I never knew reading could be this fun!"

This change improved literacy skills and fostered a love for reading.

3. **Access to Diverse Reading Materials—A Buffet of Books:** Libraries are like literary buffets, offering an array of reading materials to suit every taste and need. From picture books to young adult novels, from magazines to e-books, variety ensures every child can find something that whets their reading appetite. Dr. Lina Chen, a literacy researcher, notes: "Exposure to diverse reading materials is crucial for developing well-rounded literacy skills. Libraries provide this exposure at no cost, leveling the playing field for children from all socioeconomic backgrounds."

   Creating Lifelong Readers: Another librarian shared her experience with a young boy who struggled with reading. She helped him discover his passion for graphic novels through personalized book recommendations and one-on-one reading sessions. Over time, he improved his reading skills and became a regular visitor to the library, often volunteering to help younger children with their reading. The librarian remarked, "Seeing him grow from a hesitant reader to a confident one was one of the most rewarding experiences of my career."

4. **Literacy Workshops—Empowering Parents as First Teachers:** Recognizing that parents are a child's first and most influential teachers, many libraries host workshops to equip parents with tools to support literacy at home. These sessions are like

literacy boot camps for parents, arming them with strategies to make reading a natural and enjoyable part of family life. Tom, a father of three in Chicago, recalls: "I was at a loss on how to help my dyslexic daughter. The library's workshop on supporting diverse learners was a game-changer. Now, we have a tool kit of strategies that have boosted her confidence and skills."

5. **Technology Access—Bridging the Digital Divide:** Libraries serve as bridges across the digital divide. By providing free access to computers and the internet, libraries ensure that all children can develop the digital literacy skills essential for 21st-century success. Aisha, a high school student, shares: "I don't have a computer at home, but I can always count on the library. I've written all my essays and applied to colleges using their computers. The librarians even helped me navigate online research databases!"

6. **Community Programs—Literacy Beyond Books:** Libraries often host programs that promote literacy in its broader sense: the ability to understand and engage with the world. From coding classes to financial literacy workshops for teens, these programs expand the definition of what it means to be literate in today's world.

These are just some of the threads in the rich tapestry of experiences that libraries weave in communities. Libraries are not just buildings filled with books; they are living, breathing organisms that adapt to the needs of their communities, nurturing literacy in all of their forms. Author Neil Gaiman once said, "Google can bring you back 100,000 answers. A librarian can bring you back the right one." In the quest for literacy, libraries and their dedicated staff are the unsung heroes, guiding lights illuminating the path to knowledge, imagination, and lifelong learning.

Case Study: The Salinas Family
The Salinas family's journey to literacy exemplifies how community resources and personal initiative can transform a family's educational landscape. As recent Latino immigrants, the Salinas family faced common challenges: language barriers, limited access to literacy resources, and socioeconomic constraints. Mrs. Salinas, with only a second-grade education, initially felt ill-equipped to support her child's literacy development. However, her determination to provide her family with a better future actively led her to seek community resources.

Mrs. Salinas's turning point came when she volunteered for a Partners in Print school program. This involvement opened doors to valuable training sessions, equipping her with skills to read effectively with children at school and home. The program also provided access to books she could bring home, significantly enriching their home literacy environment. Mrs. Salinas embraced this opportunity, establishing regular reading sessions with her child and frequently purchasing books at her child's request, further nurturing a love for reading.

Despite facing obstacles such as the distance to local libraries, Mrs. Salinas demonstrated remarkable resilience. She maximized the resources available through the school, proving that families can overcome environmental constraints with creativity and determination. Her proactive approach paid off, as teachers soon noticed her child's increased reading confidence and participation in school activities, contributing to overall academic success.

The Salinas family's story is a testament to the power of community engagement in literacy development. Mrs. Salinas improved her child's literacy skills and enhanced her understanding of the educational system, enabling her to better support her child's learning journey. Their experience invites us to reflect on the resources available in our communities and how we might leverage them to support literacy development in our families, overcome barriers, and create a supportive literacy environment at home.

Community Literacy Programs and Initiatives: Weaving a Tapestry of Learning

Picture literacy as a vibrant tapestry, with schools forming the primary threads. Community literacy programs are intricate embellishments that add depth, texture, and color to this tapestry. These initiatives extend learning beyond the classroom, creating a rich, immersive environment where literacy thrives. Let's explore the diverse landscape of community literacy programs:

1. Tutoring Programs: Personalized Pathways to Literacy. Community centers and nonprofit organizations often run tutoring programs, providing one-on-one or small-group support. These programs are like literary lighthouses, guiding

struggling readers through the sometimes turbulent waters of learning to read. Maria Rodriguez, a volunteer tutor in San Antonio, shares: "I've been tutoring Jamal, a third-grader, for six months. When we started, he could barely read a simple sentence. Now, he's devouring chapter books! The look of pride on his face when he finishes a book is priceless."

2. Book Clubs: Cultivating a Community of Readers. Book clubs for children and parents are like literary gardens where ideas bloom and perspectives flourish. They foster a love of reading, critical thinking, and communication skills. Twelve-year-old Zoe from Minneapolis enthuses: "I love my kids' book club! We read *Wonder* last month, and our discussion about kindness and acceptance was deep. I never knew books could make you think so much about real life!"

3. Literacy Fairs: Carnival of Words. Community literacy fairs transform reading and writing into a carnival of fun. These events are like literacy amusement parks, with each activity a new ride into the world of words. James Chen, organizer of the annual WordFest in Seattle, explains: "Our fair has everything from storytelling tents to alphabet scavenger hunts. Last year, we even had a 'human library' where kids could 'check out' experts in different fields for short conversations. It's about showing kids that literacy is a ticket to endless adventures."

4. Intergenerational and multilingual literacy programs: These programs create bridges across ages, languages, and cultures. Senior citizens pair with young readers, while multilingual initiatives celebrate diverse linguistic traditions. These programs weave rich tapestries of connection. For example, eighty-year-old Margaret, whose animated storytelling sessions with young Sophie spark joy across generations, or Li Wei's Chinese-English bilingual program in San Francisco that nurtures both language skills and cultural understanding. "Our program celebrates the cultural wealth these children possess," Wei explains. "We're not just raising readers; we are nurturing global citizens." These initiatives transform simple reading sessions into powerful exchanges that keep minds sharp, hearts young, and communities connected across all boundaries.
5. Literacy-Focused Family Events and Activities: Making Words Come Alive. Community events incorporating literacy in engaging ways are like bringing books to life. They transform reading from a solitary activity into a shared, vibrant experience.

    a) Author Visits: Meeting the Wizards Behind the Words- When authors visit bookstores and libraries, it is like children getting to meet the wizards who conjure their favorite story worlds. Nine-year-old Aisha recounts: "Meeting Rick Riordan was amazing! He told us how he came up with his mythological adventures. When I read his books, I feel like I'm in on a secret."

b) Storytelling Festivals: Oral Traditions in the Digital Age- These events are like time machines, connecting children to literacy's ancient, oral roots. They remind us that before words were written, they were spoken and heard. Professional storyteller Jack Thompson muses: "In our digital age, there's something magical about seeing a crowd of children spellbound by a spoken story. It uniquely awakens their imagination."

c) Poetry Slams: Words as Performance Art- For older children and teens, poetry slams turn language into thrilling performance art. These events are like verbal gymnastics, showcasing the power and flexibility of words. High school English teacher Samantha Lee observes: "I've seen shy students transform on the poetry slam stage. It gives them a powerful voice and a new appreciation for the impact of words."

Dr. Timothy Shanahan's observation about the value of community literacy programs rings true across these diverse initiatives: They provide additional support and motivation, often that crucial spark igniting a lifelong love of reading and learning.

Dr. Maryanne Wolf, author of *Proust and the Squid: The Story and Science of the Reading Brain*, says, "We are not born to read. We are born with the potential to read." Community literacy programs help realize this potential, creating a rich ecosystem where literacy can flourish in all of its forms. These programs and events form a vibrant constellation of literacy opportunities, each star illuminating a different facet of language and learning. Together, they create a community where words are celebrated, stories are shared, and every child can become a reader and lover of words and ideas.

Reflection Question: What unique literacy resources does your community offer that you haven't explored?

Cultivating a Literacy Ecosystem: When Communities Come Together

Communities nurture literacy through countless interconnected efforts. While schools anchor literacy development, local businesses, volunteer programs, book clubs, and community centers amplify their impact. These diverse elements fuel a thriving culture of literacy that enriches every learner. Let's see how each part of our community strengthens literacy growth.

Partnering with Local Businesses

Local businesses often infuse literacy into their spaces. For example, independent bookstores double as vibrant literacy hubs. "We don't just sell books; we cultivate readers," explains Sarah, owner of Turning Pages in Austin, Texas. "Our weekly story time has grown so popular that we've moved it to the park next door. Last week, over 100 kids and parents sprawled on picnic blankets, entranced by *Where the Wild Things Are*."

Cafés create unique spaces where reading and community converge, brewing both coffee and literacy. Some cafés have found a perfect blend: combining the comfort of a warm drink with the joy of reading. They're like cozy reading nooks that smell of freshly brewed coffee. At Bookmark Cafe in Seattle, barista James notes: "Our monthly 'Cocoa and Chapters' event for middle-grade readers stays packed. Kids sip hot chocolate while passionately debating the latest Rick Riordan book."

Local newspapers connect children's growing literacy skills with community engagement. Fifteen-year-old Lacy from Rosepine, Louisiana, shares: "I love reading my school's paper. Last month, they featured the recycling project we have been working on. Seeing my quotes in print made me realize the power of words!"

Dr. Ernest Morrel's research affirms how these business partnerships strengthen literacy beyond classroom walls, creating dynamic spaces where reading and community life naturally intersect.

Volunteer Opportunities
Reading and literacy help build stronger communities and brighter futures. When people volunteer their time to teach others to read, they make positive changes that last for generations. There are many volunteer opportunities you can take advantage of in your community. For example:

Reading to Seniors: Bridging Generations Through Stories. This intergenerational activity connects the wisdom of the past with the curiosity of the future. Eighty-five-year-old Margaret shares: "When little Tommy reads to me, it's not just the story in the book that unfolds. We share our own stories, too. Last week, his book about space travel led me to tell him about watching the moon landing."

Classroom Reading Volunteers: Parents Supporting Young Readers. When parents volunteer to read in classrooms, they enrich the learning environment and demonstrate the importance of literacy. Parent volunteer James notes: "Reading to my daughter's first-grade class has become a weekly highlight. The children's enthusiasm is contagious and seeing them engage with stories shows how reading brings people together."

Literacy Tutoring: Readers Teaching Readers. When older children tutor younger ones, it creates ongoing literacy development across generations. High school junior Samantha reflects: "Tutoring Emma in reading has taught me so much. Explaining phonics rules made me appreciate how complex English is. Seeing her face light up when she read a whole page by herself? Priceless."

Creating Neighborhood Book Clubs: Growing a Community of Readers

Reading groups bring people together to share stories and discover new ideas. These gatherings build lasting friendships and create readers who love books for life. Through discussion and sharing different views, reading becomes an activity that strengthens community bonds and opens minds to fresh perspectives.

Parent-Child Book Clubs: Bonding Through Books. These clubs connect generations through shared stories. Tom, a father of two, shares: "Our parent-child book club has become a monthly highlight. Discussing *Bridge to Terabithia* with my daughter opened conversations about friendship and loss that I never expected. It's brought us closer in ways I couldn't have imagined."

Genre-Specific Clubs: Diving Deep into Literary Worlds. These specialized groups explore specific types of books in detail. Fourteen-year-old Aisha gushes: "Our sci-fi book club broadens our thinking. Last month, we compared Asimov's predictions in *I, Robot* to today's AI. Mind-blowing!"

Multilingual Reading Groups: Celebrating Linguistic Diversity. These groups support multiple languages and traditions in diverse communities. Maria, who runs a Spanish-English reading group, notes: "We are not just reading; we are celebrating our heritage and building cross-cultural understanding. Watching kids switch effortlessly between languages as they discuss books is truly remarkable."

Utilizing Community Centers and After-School Programs

Community centers and libraries actively support literacy and education, welcoming everyone seeking to learn and grow. These spaces create opportunities for success beyond regular school hours. Some of these programs include:

1. Homework Help programs give students the extra guidance they need to understand challenging material and excel in their studies. Many students who struggled initially have improved their grades and confidence through this focused support.
2. Digital Literacy Support programs help community members develop essential computer skills. Library staff assist with job applications, résumé writing, and technology training, helping people gain employment and independence in our digital world.

3. Creative Writing Workshops foster young talent by providing spaces where new authors can develop their skills. Students write original stories, poems, and plays, building confidence and creativity while strengthening their writing abilities.
4. Drama clubs bring literature to life through performance. Students who may find reading challenging often connect with texts in new ways when acting them out, making complex works like Shakespeare more accessible and enjoyable.

These community-based learning programs create a welcoming environment where education feels more like an adventure than a chore. Unlike traditional tutoring, they blend learning with social interaction, creative expression, and hands-on activities. Students build confidence alongside friendships while developing essential skills for success. The variety of programs ensures everyone finds their perfect fit, whether through group discussions, creative writing, drama, or technology workshops.

Accessing Literacy Support for English Language Learners

Families navigating multiple languages and community resources need essential support for literacy development. ESL classes empower parents to participate in their children's education, from reading bedtime stories to helping with homework. Libraries host bilingual story times that celebrate linguistic diversity and help children move confidently between languages. Cultural literacy events showcase different traditions through storytelling, creating spaces where families see their experiences reflected and learn about other cultures. Through these programs, families build stronger connections to both their heritage language and English, while children develop pride in their cultural identity and curiosity about other cultures. These community resources create an inclusive environment where multilingual literacy flourishes, strengthening family bonds and fostering cross-cultural understanding.

The Impact of Community-Wide Reading Initiatives

Large-scale reading initiatives transform individual reading experiences into shared community adventures. When a city comes together around a single book, it creates connections across neighborhoods, ages, and backgrounds. These programs spark conversations in coffee shops, libraries, and homes, bringing literature into everyday life.

1. One Book, One City: A Literary Common Ground. These programs are like community-wide book clubs, creating a shared literary experience that spans neighborhoods and generations. Mayor Johnson of Millbrook, NY, shares: "When we chose *To Kill a Mockingbird* for our citywide read, it sparked conversations about justice and empathy across our entire community. I saw teenagers discussing the book with their grandparents in coffee shops. It was beautiful."

Literacy Roots

A notable success story that exemplifies the power of community-wide reading initiatives is the One Book, One Freeport program in Freeport, Illinois. Launched in 2011, this innovative initiative set out to unite the entire community through a shared reading experience, weaving a tapestry of literacy and dialogue that crossed all social and cultural boundaries. The program's impact was profound and far-reaching. It brought together residents of all ages and backgrounds, creating a common ground where diverse voices could mingle and share perspectives. As participants delved into the same book, they built unexpected connections, broke down long-standing social barriers, and engaged in rich discussions about the themes presented in their shared read.

One Book, One Freeport did more than just promote reading; it sparked a cultural renaissance in the community. The initiative catalyzed a surge in participation at related events such as book discussions, author visits, and cultural activities. These gatherings provided fertile ground for participants to dig deeper into the book's themes and forge stronger bonds with their fellow readers, elevating the entire reading experience to new heights. The program's influence extended far beyond its official run. Many participants reported a rekindled passion for reading, continuing to actively engage with the library and other community resources long after the last page was turned. The initiative's success rippled outward, inspiring neighboring communities to launch their reading programs and cementing its legacy as a powerful force for promoting literacy and community engagement.

The One Book, One Freeport initiative stands as a testament to the transformative power of community-wide reading programs. It demonstrates how a single book can become a bridge, connecting diverse individuals, fostering a sense of community, and igniting a lifelong love of reading that continues to burn bright long after the final chapter is closed.

2. Little Free Libraries: These neighborhood book exchanges are like literary lemonade stands, offering refreshments for the mind on every corner. Eight-year-old Emma bubbles: "I love our Little Free Library! Last week, I left my favorite Roald Dahl book and found a cool book about space. It's like Christmas every time I open it!"
3. Community Reading Challenges: These friendly competitions transform reading into a community-wide adventure. Librarian Mr. Thompson chuckles: "Our summer reading challenge turned into a delightful citywide obsession. We had grandparents competing with their grandkids to log the most reading hours. In the end, our whole community won."

These community initiatives form a rich, interconnected web of literacy support. They transform reading from a solitary activity into a shared journey of discovery. As Dr. Morrell suggested, these efforts not only bolster literacy skills but strengthen the very fabric of our communities. It's a beautiful reminder that literacy, at its heart, is not just about reading words but about connecting lives.

Reflection Question: Imagine your community started a One Book, One Community program. What book would you recommend, and how do you think it could bring different groups together or spark important conversations? Consider the potential impact on various age groups, cultural backgrounds, and social issues in your area.

Conclusion

Communities offer valuable resources to support family literacy. Local libraries, community programs, businesses, and neighborhood initiatives give children access to diverse reading materials and experiences. These resources create a network of support that strengthens reading skills and builds a community where literacy thrives. Key takeaways from this chapter include:

1. Libraries offer a wealth of free resources and programs.
2. Community events and initiatives can make literacy engaging and fun.
3. Local businesses can be valuable literacy partners.
4. Volunteering and creating reading groups strengthen community bonds.
5. Diverse families can find tailored support within the community.
6. Digital resources complement in-person community offerings.
7. Challenges in accessing resources can be overcome with creative solutions.

Call to Action: This week, commit to exploring at least one new community resource for literacy. Whether it's attending a library event, joining an online reading group, or volunteering for a literacy program, every interaction with community literacy resources sends a powerful message to your child about the value and joy of reading and writing. As you move forward, consider how you can not only use these resources but contribute to them, helping to strengthen the literacy support in your community.

In our next chapter, we will look to the future, exploring emerging trends and innovations in family literacy. Combining the community support we have discussed here with cutting-edge approaches ensures that our children are well-prepared for tomorrow's literacy challenges and opportunities.

Further Reading

1. *Giving Our Children a Fighting Chance: Poverty, Literacy, and the Development of Information Capital. Teachers College Press.* Neuman, S. B., & Celano, D. (2012). An in-depth look at how community resources can impact literacy development, especially in underserved areas.
2. *Handbook of Family Literacy* (2nd ed.). Routledge. Wasik, B. H. (Ed.). (2012). A comprehensive resource on family literacy, including chapters on community partnerships and resources.
3. *Literacy Research: Theory, Method, and Practice, Vol. 68.* SAGE Publications. Compton-Lilly, C., Rogers, R., & Lewis Ellison, T. (2019). This volume includes several articles on community literacy initiatives and their impact.
4. National Center for Families Learning (https://www.familieslearning.org/): A website offering resources, research, and program ideas for family and community literacy.
5. Little Free Library (https://littlefreelibrary.org/) The official website of the Little Free Library movement, with resources for starting and maintaining community book exchanges.

Practical Exercises

1. **Community Literacy Resource Map:** Create a visual map of literacy resources in your community. Including libraries, bookstores, community centers, and businesses or organizations offering literacy-related programs. Use different colors or symbols to categorize the resources. Learning Outcome: Develops awareness of available community resources and spatial thinking skills.
2. **Family Literacy Challenge:** Design a month-long family literacy challenge. Include activities like visiting the library, attending a community story time, writing a letter to a local leader, or starting a mini book club with neighbors. Track your progress and celebrate your achievements. Learning Outcome: Encourages active engagement with community literacy resources and family bonding through literacy activities.
3. **Little Free Library Project:** If your community doesn't have one, plan a Little Free Library for your neighborhood. Design the structure, decide on its location, and create a plan for stocking and maintaining it. If you already have one nearby, organize a book drive to keep it well-stocked. Learning Outcome: Promotes community engagement and understanding of grassroots literacy initiatives.
4. **Literacy Volunteer Experience:** Volunteer for a local literacy program or create your own, such as reading to seniors at a retirement home or helping with an after-school homework club. Reflect on

your experience in a journal or blog post. Learning Outcome: Develop empathy, communication skills, and a deeper understanding of community literacy needs.
5. **Community Literacy Event Proposal:** Design a proposal for a community-wide literacy event. This could be a book festival, a One Book, One Community program, or a series of author talks. Include potential partners, a budget, and a marketing plan. Learning Outcome: Enhances planning skills and understanding of large-scale community literacy initiatives.

Chapter 11: The Future of Family Literacy: Innovations and Trends

Overview

"The future belongs to those who learn more skills and combine them in creative ways," says Robert Greene, author of *Mastery*. In the realm of family literacy, this future is arriving faster than we might imagine. As we stand on the brink of a new era in literacy education, driven by technological advancements and groundbreaking research, how can we prepare our children to thrive in a world where the very definition of literacy is constantly evolving?

Our exploration of family literacy concludes with a forward-looking perspective. The literacy landscape continues to evolve rapidly through technological advances, new research findings, and shifting societal norms. This chapter will explore emerging trends and innovations shaping family literacy, preparing you for upcoming challenges and opportunities. We will examine:

- The impact of AI and machine learning on personalized learning and tutoring
- Virtual and augmented reality in creating immersive reading experiences
- The ongoing debate between print and digital reading formats
- Neuroscience insights into literacy development
- Future workplace literacy requirements
- Adapting literacy practices for diverse family structures

- Global trends in literacy education
- The role of gaming and gamification in literacy

While discussing futuristic scenarios like holographic storytelling and AI tutors, we'll also cover more immediate innovations. Throughout, we'll emphasize that, despite changing tools and contexts, the core goal remains nurturing a lifelong love of reading and writing. By the chapter's end, you will understand the possibilities and challenges ahead in family literacy, equipping you to guide your child's literacy journey in our evolving world.

The Literacy Landscape of Tomorrow

Imagine stepping into a child's bedroom in the near future. Instead of a traditional bookshelf, you see a sleek device that projects a three-dimensional hologram of a lush forest with a simple voice command. The child excitedly says, "Let's read *The Enchanted Woods*!" Suddenly, the room transforms into a vibrant, immersive woodland scene. As the story unfolds, characters materialize as if by magic, moving and interacting with the young reader.

This isn't a scene from a sci-fi movie, it's a glimpse into the future of storytelling and literacy education. While holographic books might still be a few years away, many groundbreaking innovations are already reshaping how we approach reading and writing.

Take, for instance, the case of Emma, a 7-year-old struggling reader from London. Emma's parents were concerned about her progress until they enrolled her in a pilot program using AI-powered tutoring. The AI tutor, adapting to Emma's unique learning style and pace, provided personalized instruction that transformed her reading experience. Within months, Emma's reading fluency improved dramatically, and more importantly, she developed a newfound love for books.

"It was like having a patient, always-available reading buddy," Emma's mother shared. "The AI tutor knew exactly when to challenge Emma and when to offer support. It made all the difference."

The future of literacy goes beyond individual experiences. Imagine a global tapestry of readers and writers connected across vast distances by technology. This isn't just a fanciful idea, it's beginning to take shape through platforms like Global Stories, a project that connects classrooms across continents. Students in New York, Lagos, and Tokyo collaborate to write stories, sharing their diverse perspectives and cultures. It's as if the classroom walls have dissolved, replaced by windows to the world.

Dr. Aisha Patel, an education researcher involved in the project, explains: "What we're seeing is the emergence of truly global literacy communities. Children are not just learning to read and write—they're learning to be global citizens, understanding diverse viewpoints from an early age."

However, as we marvel at these technological wonders, it's imperative to remember that they are tools, not ends in themselves. Like a master craftsman who knows when to use a power tool and when to rely on their hands, educators and parents must learn to balance these new technologies with time-honored literacy practices.

Consider the story of the Johnson family in rural Minnesota. Despite having access to the latest educational apps and online resources, they found that their most treasured literacy ritual was their nightly "story circle." Each family member, from 6-year-old Zoe to 70-year-old Grandpa Joe, takes turns reading aloud or telling a story. This simple practice has improved everyone's literacy skills, strengthened family bonds, and fostered a deep love of storytelling.

"In our high-tech world, there's something magical about sitting together and sharing stories," says Sarah Johnson, the family matriarch. "It reminds us that literacy is about human connection at its heart."

This blend of high-tech innovation and timeless human practices will likely define tomorrow's literacy landscape. It's as if we are building a bridge between the island of technological advancement and the island of traditional literacy practices. This bridge allows us to move freely between both realms, taking the best from each to create rich, engaging literacy experiences.

The exploration of these innovations continues, from AI tutors to global writing communities, from holographic books to family story circles, with our core goal remaining in focus. Our guiding compass through these uncharted waters should be this essential purpose: nurturing a love of reading and writing that will serve your child throughout their life. This beacon steers our course through the exciting but sometimes overwhelming sea of new literacy technologies. The literacy landscape of tomorrow is not a distant shore but a horizon we're actively sailing toward. We can harness these innovative tools while preserving the timeless value of human connection and storytelling, ensuring this new world of literacy becomes one where every child can thrive, discover, and fall in love with the written word.

The Impact of AI and Machine Learning on Literacy Education

Imagine a world where every child has a personal literacy coach, available day and night, tirelessly adapting to their unique needs and learning style. This isn't a far-fetched dream but a glimpse into the rapidly evolving landscape of literacy education, shaped by the transformative power of artificial intelligence (AI) and machine learning.

Personalized Learning

AI-powered platforms are revolutionizing personalized learning, much like a master tailor crafting a bespoke suit. These systems meticulously measure a child's learning "dimensions"—their pace, style, strengths, and challenges—and create a custom-fit educational experience.

Miguel is a 9-year-old with dyslexia from Phoenix, Arizona. Traditional one-size-fits-all reading programs left him frustrated and discouraged. However, when his school introduced an AI-powered reading platform, everything changed. The system quickly identified Miguel's specific challenges and adjusted accordingly, presenting texts with specialized fonts, breaking down complex words, and providing extra practice in areas where he struggled. "It was like the program really understood Miguel," his teacher, Ms. Rodriguez, shared. "It knew when to push him and when to offer support. We saw improvements not just in his reading skills but also in his confidence."

Intelligent Tutoring Systems
What if you had Ernest Hemingway or Jane Austen as a personal writing coach, providing immediate feedback on your prose? While AI cannot quite replicate these literary giants, intelligent tutoring systems are bringing us closer to this ideal. These systems act like a vigilant writing companion, offering real-time grammar, style, and structure suggestions. It's just like having a seasoned editor looking over your shoulder, gently guiding your pen (or keystrokes) toward clearer, more effective communication.

Dr. Emily Chen, an educational technologist, conducted a study with high school students using an AI writing tutor. "The results were remarkable," she notes. "Students who used the AI tutor significantly improved their writing clarity and structure. However, what struck me was how it boosted their confidence. They felt more comfortable experimenting with language because they had immediate, nonjudgmental feedback."

One student in Dr. Chen's study, 16-year-old Jamal, put it succinctly: "It's like having a super-smart friend who's always there to help with my essays. It doesn't just correct my mistakes; it helps me understand why something is wrong and how to fix it."

Predictive Analytics: The Early Warning System
Like a device that detects early warning signs of earthquakes, AI can spot reading problems in students before teachers or parents notice them. This new

technology isn't just a better way to test reading skills; it's completely changing how we help struggling readers by catching and fixing problems early instead of waiting until students fall behind.

Sophie entered kindergarten as a bright-eyed 5-year-old with natural curiosity and engagement. While her teachers noted her enthusiasm, the school's AI-powered assessment tool revealed something deeper; subtle patterns in Sophie's phonological awareness tasks pointed to potential dyslexia risk factors. The school acted immediately on this early warning signal, implementing targeted interventions that might have taken months or years to initiate through traditional observation alone.

"It's like having a crystal ball," said Sophie's mother, Lisa. "Instead of waiting for Sophie to fall behind, we were able to give her the support she needed right from the start. It has made all the difference in her confidence and love for reading."

Dr. Rose Luckin's observation that AI has the potential to provide every child with a personal tutor, available 24/7 and adapting to their individual needs and pace of learning is not just an academic statement—it's a reality unfolding in classrooms and homes around the world.

The Human Touch: Irreplaceable and Indispensable

While we marvel at these technological advances, we must remember that AI is a tool, not a replacement for human interaction in literacy development. Like a master musician with a finely tuned instrument, the real magic happens when skilled educators and involved parents use AI to enhance, not replace, their interactions with children. Dr. Marcus Lee, a child psychologist specializing in literacy development, emphasizes this point: "AI can provide incredible support, but it can't replace the warmth of a parent's lap during story time, the excitement of acting out a favorite book together, or the deep discussions that arise from shared reading experiences."

The Johnsons, a family from Portland, Oregon, embody this balanced approach. They use AI-powered reading apps to support their children's literacy development but maintain a strict "no screens" policy during their nightly family reading time. "The apps are great for practice," says Mr. Johnson, "but nothing beats the connection we feel when we're all huddled together, lost in a good book."

We need balance as we navigate this brave new world of AI-enhanced literacy education. AI and machine learning offer unprecedented opportunities to personalize learning, provide immediate feedback, and identify potential challenges early. Yet, the role of parents and educators remains irreplaceable. Your engagement, emotional support, and shared excitement about stories and ideas are the fertile soil in which the seeds of literacy, planted and nurtured by both human and artificial intelligence, can truly flourish.

AI is not replacing the human element in literacy education; it's augmenting our abilities, allowing us to support each child's literacy journey with unprecedented precision and adaptability. It's an exciting time to be a parent or educator, as we have more tools than ever to help every child discover the joy and power of reading and writing.

Virtual and Augmented Reality in Reading and Storytelling

Imagine if, instead of just reading about Alice's adventures in Wonderland, you could shrink down and join her at the Mad Hatter's tea party or if you could walk alongside Frodo and Sam on their journey through Middle earth. This is the transformative power that virtual reality (VR) and augmented reality (AR) bring to the world of reading and storytelling. The power of these technologies stretches beyond new ways to read—it is revolutionizing storytelling at its core.

Immersive Reading: From Spectator to Participant

VR has the potential to transform readers from passive spectators into active participants in the stories they read. It's like the difference between watching a travel documentary about ancient Egypt and standing in the shadow of the Great Pyramid of Giza. This level of immersion can make abstract or complex concepts tangible and more accessible to grasp.

Jenny is a 12-year-old struggling with her history lessons about ancient Rome. Reading about the Colosseum in a textbook left her unengaged and struggling to remember key facts. However, when her class used VR headsets to virtually explore the Colosseum, walking through its corridors and standing in the arena, Jenny's understanding was transformed. "It was like I was there," Jenny exclaimed. "I could see how massive it was and hear the crowd roar. When I read about gladiator battles, I can picture exactly where they happened. It's not just words on a page anymore."

Interactive Storytelling: When Books Come Alive

VR transports readers to new worlds, and AR brings those worlds into our reality. Imagine reading a pop-up book in which the characters don't just pop up but walk across your coffee table, interact with each other, and respond to your touch. This is the promise of AR in storytelling.

The Johnson family's experience with AR storybooks illustrates this potential. Seven-year-old Ethan, a reluctant reader, was given an AR-enhanced version of *The Little Prince* for his birthday. As he read the book, pointing his tablet at the pages, the characters appeared in 3D, moving and speaking. The little prince walked across the pages, the fox darted between real-world objects in their living room, and stars twinkled above their couch. "It was magical," Ethan's mother shared. "For the first time, Ethan was excited about reading. He wanted to read the book over and over, discovering new interactive elements each time. It sparked his imagination in a way traditional books hadn't."

This fusion of physical books with digital elements bridges the tangible comfort of traditional reading and the engaging interactivity of digital media. It's like having a master storyteller bring the tale to life right before your eyes.

Language Learning: A Passport to New Worlds

VR and AR are like linguistic teleportation devices in language learning, immersing learners in authentic language environments without leaving their homes. Imagine learning Spanish by virtually strolling through the streets of Barcelona, ordering coffee in a Parisian café to practice your French, or discussing kabuki with a virtual guide at a Japanese theater.

According to new research, virtual-reality technology shows promising results for adult language learners, too. Students made faster progress with vocabulary and pronunciation compared to standard teaching methods. Their confidence grew dramatically as they practiced in virtual environments. Total immersion helps language skills develop naturally, whether in virtual or real-world settings. While classroom learning builds crucial foundations, students need chances to practice their skills regularly. Active use of the language prevents learned skills from slipping away over time.

One participant, 45-year-old Michael, was learning Italian for an upcoming trip. "With VR, I wasn't just memorizing phrases from a book," he explained. "I was using them in context—ordering food in a virtual trattoria and asking for directions on a simulated street in Rome. When I went to Italy, I felt like I'd already been there. The language felt natural, not something I struggled to remember from a textbook."

The Balancing Act: High-Tech and High-Touch

While VR and AR's potential in reading and storytelling is immense, it's important to maintain a balance. These technologies should enhance, not replace, traditional reading experiences and real-world interactions. It's like adding spice to a well-loved recipe—it can enhance the flavor, but too much can overpower the original dish. Dr. Mina Johnson-Glenberg's insight into VR and AR, which creates embodied learning experiences that enhance comprehension and retention, is key. These technologies can make the abstract concrete, the complex simple, and the distant immediate.

The Zhang family's experience illustrates this balance. They incorporate AR storybooks and VR language learning into their children's routines but maintain a strict policy of traditional bedtime stories. "The tech is great for engagement and making difficult concepts clearer," Mr. Zhang explains. "But there's something irreplaceable about snuggling up with a physical book, using our imaginations to bring the story to life. We want our kids to experience both."

These new technologies serve as tools for reading, imagining, and connecting through stories. Our goal focuses on using VR and AR to ignite a love for reading and learning that extends beyond the virtual world and into the real one. Through immersive experiences, students can step onto the pages of a book, walk alongside characters, and discover new worlds in ways previous generations could only dream about.

Reflection Question: How might you incorporate VR or AR experiences into your family's reading routine to enhance, rather than replace, traditional reading practices?

What potential benefits and challenges do you foresee in striking this balance?

The Evolution of Print Books vs. Digital Reading

Modern literacy thrives in its diversity. Print books deliver lasting, proven foundations, while digital platforms contribute evolving innovations and fresh possibilities. The challenge lies not in choosing between them but in weaving their distinct strengths together to create dynamic literacy environments.

The Enduring Power of Print

Print books continue to hold their ground despite the digital revolution, especially regarding deep reading and comprehension. The physical act of turning pages and the tactile experience of holding a book create a kind of cognitive map, helping readers navigate complex ideas and retain information. Dr. Maria Chen, a cognitive psychologist specializing in reading, explains: "Print books engage our senses in a way that supports focus and deep processing. It's like the difference between hiking a trail and flying over it—both have their place, but the ground-level experience often leads to a deeper connection and understanding."

This advantage is particularly pronounced for younger children. The Johnson family's experience illustrates this point beautifully. When 7-year-old Zoe struggled with reading comprehension, her parents decided to limit screen time and increase physical book reading. "The change was remarkable," shares Zoe's mother,

Samantha. "Zoe often got distracted by notifications or the urge to switch apps when reading on a tablet. With print books, she seemed more immersed in the story. She started asking deeper questions about the characters and plot. It was like a physical book created a sacred space for reading."

The Digital Frontier
While print books offer depth, digital platforms bring breadth and accessibility to the table. It's like having an entire library at your fingertips, complete with a team of instant research assistants. Consider the case of Alex, a high school student with dyslexia. Traditional books often left him frustrated and discouraged. However, Alex's relationship with reading was transformed when his school introduced e-readers with customizable fonts, text-to-speech features, and built-in dictionaries. "It was like someone finally gave me the right pair of glasses," Alex explains. "I could adjust the text to what worked best for me, look up words instantly, and even have sections read aloud when I was struggling. I felt in control of my reading experience for the first time."

Digital platforms offer powerful advantages for students with different learning needs. Reading tools can adjust text size, spacing, and style to match each student's preferences and abilities. These customization features make books and articles more accessible, helping diverse learners tackle challenging material with confidence.

The Hybrid Approach: Best of Both Worlds

The argument about whether print or digital books are better has a simple answer: use both. Good readers can get comfortable with both regular books and digital devices, picking whichever works best at the time. I love using this mix-and-match approach—sometimes, a paper book works better, and sometimes, my tablet is the perfect choice. The Martinez family exemplifies this balanced approach. They maintain a home library of physical books and use e-readers and digital platforms. "We choose the format based on the purpose," explains Mr. Martinez. "For bedtime stories and deep reading, we prefer print books. For travel, research, or when we need quick access to a wide range of texts, we go digital."

This hybrid approach extends to educational settings as well. Ms. Thompson, a middle school English teacher in southern Maryland, has seen the benefits firsthand: "We use print books for our core novels, encouraging students to annotate and engage deeply with the text. Nevertheless, we use digital platforms for research projects, collaborative writing, and access to a broader range of supplementary texts. It's not an either/or situation—it is about using the right tool for the right task."

The Intentional Reader

Dr. Naomi Baron emphasizes the importance of intentional choices when using different reading formats in our evolving landscape. She encourages readers to become conscious consumers of literature, selecting formats with the precision of a chef choosing ingredients. "Think of different reading formats as tools in a tool kit," Dr. Baron explains. "A hammer and screwdriver have their uses, and the skilled craftsperson knows when to use each. The skilled reader should choose the most appropriate format for their current reading goal."

Families can teach and cultivate this intentional approach. The Hatler family holds regular "reading reflection" sessions where they discuss both content and format choices. "We talk about why we chose a particular format for a book and how it affected our reading experience," shares Mrs. Hatler. "This practice helps our kids become more conscious, intentional readers. They are learning to think about what they read and how they read."

The future holds rich possibilities in both print and digital reading. Understanding and leveraging the strengths of each format while making intentional choices creates diverse reading experiences that serve different needs, preferences, and learning styles. This metacognitive awareness, thinking deeply about how we think and learn, empowers readers to make strategic decisions about their reading formats. The ability to reflect on and adjust our reading approaches represents a higher level of literacy development essential for success in our digital age.

Reflection Question: Think about your reading habits or those of your family. How do you currently balance print and digital reading? Can you identify specific situations where one format might be more beneficial than the other?

Emerging Research in Neuroscience and Literacy Development: Unveiling the Brain's Literary Landscape

Picture the human brain as a vast, ever-changing cityscape, where skyscrapers of knowledge rise and new neural highways are constantly under construction. Recent advances in neuroscience are like sophisticated satellite imaging, allowing us to observe this bustling metropolis of the mind with unprecedented clarity. These discoveries are revolutionizing our understanding of acquiring and improving literacy skills, offering new hope for struggling readers and exciting possibilities for learners of all ages.

Brain Plasticity: The City That Never Sleeps

The concept of brain plasticity, our brain's remarkable ability to adapt and grow throughout life, is akin to a city that's always under renovation. Just as urban planners can redesign outdated infrastructure, our brains can forge new neural pathways at any age, challenging the old notion that cognitive development has a strict closing time. Modern reading interventions can help students of any age overcome long-term struggles.

One fifty-eight-year-old student with lifelong dyslexia experienced dramatic improvements through focused instruction. Four months of specialized training changed both her brain patterns and reading abilities. Her progress from simple children's books to complex novels proved that effective reading support can unlock potential at any stage of life. For parents and educators, this means maintaining a growth mindset about literacy skills. Whether nurturing a five-year-old's budding interest in letters or supporting a fifty-five-year-old's quest to enhance reading comprehension, remember that the brain's "Department of Literary Construction" is always open for business.

Multisensory Learning: Engaging the Brain's Symphony Orchestra

Neuroscience research increasingly shows that our brains don't process information in isolated chambers but as interconnected symphonies. Regarding literacy, engaging multiple senses can create a rich, harmonious neural concert, enhancing learning and retention. Consider the innovative approach of Mr. Sánchez, a third-grade teacher in Franklin, Kentucky. When introducing new vocabulary, he transforms his classroom into a multisensory playground. Students don't just read and write words; they sing them, sculpt them from clay, act them out in charades, and even create scented Play-Doh associated with each word's meaning.

"It's like we are composing a symphony with words," Mr. Sánchez explains. "Each sense adds a new instrument to the orchestra, making the melody of learning more complex and memorable. I've seen remarkable improvements in retention and enthusiasm since implementing this approach." This multisensory method is like giving the brain a variety of instruments to play the same tune. Each sensory experience—visual, auditory, tactile, olfactory, or gustatory—creates another neural pathway to the information, making it easier to recall and apply later.

Emotional Connections: The Heart of Literacy's Metropolis

Perhaps one of the most profound insights from neuroscience is the intricate dance between emotions and learning. The brain's emotional centers, particularly the amygdala, act like the central park in our cerebral city—a place where memories are formed, experiences are processed, and learning takes root.

Dr. Amelia Chang, an educational neuroscientist, conducted a groundbreaking study on the impact of emotional engagement on reading comprehension. "We discovered that when students formed positive emotional connections to the material through personal interest, enjoyment, or an engaging teaching style, their comprehension and retention improved by up to 40%," she reports. This finding underscores the importance of making reading and writing educational, enjoyable, and meaningful experiences. It's not about superficial "edutainment" but about creating genuine emotional resonance with literacy activities.

The Patel family's "Story Cuisine Nights" offers a heartwarming example of this principle in action. Every Sunday, they choose a book to read together and then prepare a meal inspired by the story. For *Around the World in 80 Days*, they had a globe-trotting feast with dishes from various countries. For *Charlie and the Chocolate Factory*, they turned their kitchen into Wonka's workshop, creating whimsical treats.

"At first, we just wanted to make reading more fun," shares Mrs. Patel. "But we have seen incredible changes. Our children's vocabulary has expanded, their comprehension has deepened, and most importantly, they've developed a genuine love for books. They see stories as gateways to new adventures on the page and in the kitchen."

Practical Applications: From Neural Neighborhoods to Literacy Landscapes
Dr. Stanislas Dehaene's statement about using our understanding of how the brain learns to read to design more effective teaching methods is not just theoretical; it's being implemented in classrooms and homes worldwide, transforming the landscape of literacy education. The Orton-Gillingham approach, widely used to help individuals with dyslexia, incorporates neuroscience principles like multisensory instruction and systematic phonics. This method provides a detailed map of the brain's "literacy district," guiding learners along the most efficient neural pathways to reading proficiency.

    For parents and educators, these neuroscience insights offer reassurance and direction. The brain's plasticity means constructing literacy skills, an ongoing project with room for improvement at any age. The power of multisensory learning encourages us to design rich, varied "literacy environments" that engage all the senses. The importance of emotional connections reminds us that fostering a love of reading and writing is as essential as teaching mechanics; it is about building a city of knowledge that people want to inhabit and explore.

Reflection Question: Considering the neuroscience principles we've discussed—brain plasticity, multisensory learning, and emotional connections—can you envision an activity that would engage multiple senses, create positive emotional associations, and capitalize on the brain's ability to form new connections? How might this approach differ from traditional literacy instruction methods?

Predictions for Workplace Literacy Requirements

The modern workplace demands an expanded understanding of literacy. Traditional reading and writing skills now serve as foundational elements in a much broader landscape of professional competencies. The 21st century continues to reshape the requirements for professional success, introducing new essential skills.

Digital literacy is fundamental to today's workplace and is an essential skill set for every professional. Reading and writing must now pair with technological fluency. Maria, a journalist with 20 years of experience in print media, encountered this shift when her newspaper transitioned to a digital-first model. "It was like I had been writing with a quill all my life, and suddenly, I was expected to use a spaceship," she recalls. Maria quickly adapted to writing for digital platforms, creating multimedia content, engaging with readers on social media, and using data analytics to inform her reporting. Her experience mirrors countless professionals across industries where digital literacy has become mandatory. From doctors navigating electronic health records to teachers creating online learning modules, confident use of digital tools represents a baseline expectation.

Digital literacy powers success in today's workplace, becoming as essential as basic reading and writing. Modern workers need skills beyond just operating technology. They must understand how digital tools shape communication, recognize online opportunities and risks, and adapt to rapid technological changes.

Data literacy forms another component of modern professional competency. The ability to interpret, analyze, and make data-based decisions proves essential across virtually all sectors. From marketing professionals tracking campaign metrics to healthcare workers monitoring patient outcomes, mastering data literacy enables professionals to extract meaningful insights and drive more informed decision-making.

Alex, a marketing manager at a mid-sized company, illustrates this evolution: "Five years ago, my job was all about creative campaigns and catchy slogans," Alex says. "Now, I spend as much time analyzing customer data and A/B testing results as I do brainstorming ideas. If you can't speak the language of data, you're at a significant disadvantage." This transformation extends beyond traditionally "technical" roles. HR professionals use data to inform hiring decisions and predict employee satisfaction. Teachers leverage learning analytics to personalize instruction. Small business owners rely on customer data analysis to maintain competitiveness.

Adaptive literacy represents the capacity to evolve and thrive amid change, a cornerstone skill in today's professional landscape. This competency proves especially vital in our shifting work environment. Consider James, a software developer with 15 years in the field, who exemplifies this principle: "When I started, I was coding in languages that are practically obsolete now," he reflects. "I've had to relearn my craft from the ground up at least three times. The most valuable skill I've developed is not proficiency in any particular language or framework—it is the ability to adapt quickly to new ones."

Rachel, an elementary school teacher from Montgomery, Alabama, demonstrates this need beyond tech: "When I started teaching 20 years ago, I thought I was set with my degree and teaching certificate," she recalls. "But in the last two decades, I've had to learn about digital education tools, new pedagogical approaches, social-emotional learning techniques, and post-pandemic hybrid teaching models. The content I teach hasn't changed much; the kids still need to learn reading, writing, and arithmetic. How I teach it constantly evolves."

Organizational psychologist Dr. Marcus Lee suggests viewing adaptive literacy as a meta-skill: "It's not about what you know, but how quickly and effectively you can know something new," he explains. "In a world where specific skills can become obsolete almost overnight, the ability to rapidly acquire new competencies is invaluable."

Professional literacy will continue evolving. Digital literacy, data literacy, and adaptive literacy represent current best practices in professional development. Don't think of these as separate skills to be acquired, but as interconnected competencies that reinforce each other. Digital literacy often involves data literacy, which requires adaptive literacy to keep up with new tools and techniques.

The goal is to develop a holistic approach to continuous learning.

Alvin Toffler's prediction rings true: Success in the 21st-century workplace depends not on specific competencies but on continuous adaptation and learning. Professional excellence requires mastering new skills while remaining prepared for future changes.

Reflection Question: Consider your current role or your aspiring career. How might the evolving literacy requirements we've discussed impact this field in the next 5-10 years? How might enhancing these skills benefit your career and influence other areas of your life?

The Evolution of Family Structures and Literacy Practices

Family literacy practices have evolved beyond traditional bedtime reading to reflect the complexity of modern family structures and learning approaches. Modern families incorporate diverse methods, including digital tools, cultural traditions, and multiple languages, into their daily literacy routines. These practices extend beyond books to include social media, video calls, and interactive learning apps, which create dynamic learning environments for all family members. The changing nature of literacy practices reflects broader societal shifts in how families communicate, learn, and share knowledge across generations.

Multiple languages shape literacy in our interconnected world. The Nguyen-Schmidt family demonstrates this multilingual reality. Mai Nguyen from

Vietnam and Klaus Schmidt from Germany raise their children in the United States, creating a home where Vietnamese, German, and English blend naturally. "At first, we worried about confusing the kids," Mai shares. "But we've found that our multilingual environment has enriched their literacy development. Our older daughter, Mia, seamlessly switches between writing stories in English for school, chatting with her Oma in German over video calls, and singing Vietnamese lullabies to her little brother."

Dr. Ilya Novodvorskiy, an American developer and father living in Prague, shares his research on cognitive development in multilingual children. He advocates for simple yet effective practices like reading bedtime stories in multiple languages, playing word games between languages, and labeling everyday items around the house in different languages. His insights led him to develop Readmio, an interactive reading app that bridges traditional storytelling with modern technology. The app combines classic stories in multiple languages with sound effects and music, creating an engaging reading experience. "We often hear that parents use it as a motivation for kids to start reading," Novodvorskiy said. "Children get excited because they know if they keep reading, then a sound will play. So, it's more of a learning tool for them."

Digital tools have fundamentally changed how families maintain literacy connections across distances. Parents working abroad can now participate in their children's reading development through various digital platforms. Readmio's recording feature allows parents to create story recordings their children can replay, maintaining the intimate connection of story time despite physical separation. These technological advances help preserve the emotional bonds of family reading while supporting multilingual literacy development.

Digital tools now expand family literacy beyond physical locations. Grandparents read e-books to grandchildren across countries, while siblings engage in competitive word games through educational apps. These digital literacy tools complement traditional reading experiences, enhancing rather than replacing the irreplaceable warmth of reading physical books together. The technological evolution of family literacy maintains meaningful connections while creating new opportunities for learning and interaction. Literacy development flows multidirectionally between generations in modern families.

The Martinez family represents this dynamic exchange. Grandmother Rosa shares Spanish stories and cultural literacy with her grandchildren while receiving technological literacy guidance from them. "It's a beautiful exchange," says Elena Martinez, Rosa's daughter. "Mom's stories spark the kids' imagination and connect them to their heritage. Furthermore, watching the kids patiently teach her to use a tablet or smartphone is heartwarming. Everyone is learning, everyone is teaching."

Dr. Catherine Compton-Lilly, author of *Reading Time: The Literate Lives of Urban Secondary Students and their Families*, emphasizes building on individual family strengths in literacy development. "Think of family literacy as a multigenerational treasure chest," she suggests. "Each generation contributes its unique gems of knowledge and experience. The key is to open this chest regularly, allowing all family members to contribute and benefit." Dr. Compton-Lilly emphasizes that family literacy practices exhibit as much diversity as families themselves. This diversity represents a strength to celebrate and leverage rather than a challenge to overcome.

The Thompson-Wongs, a blended family with a rich mix of cultural backgrounds, exemplify this concept through their "Family Literacy Festival" tradition. Each family member contributes a literacy practice from their background, creating a vibrant tapestry of learning experiences. Grandpa John might recite classic English poetry, while stepmom Liu Hui teaches Chinese calligraphy, and teenager Zack demonstrates the art of crafting compelling social media stories.

Embracing Diversity in Family Literacy Practices
Sarah Thompson-Wong reflects, "Our family's diversity initially seemed complicated. However, it has transformed into our greatest asset through its integration into our literacy practices. We are not merely teaching reading and writing; we are cultivating cultural understanding, creativity, and a passion for learning." This approach resonates strongly with Dr. Compton-Lilly's recommendation to identify and build upon each family's unique literacy strengths. The goal involves creating a literacy ecosystem where every family member, regardless of age, background, or physical location, can contribute to and benefit from a rich tapestry of literacy experiences.

Flexibility, inclusivity, and creativity remain paramount in navigating the evolving landscape of family structures and literacy practices. Families can weave their unique patterns into the grand tapestry of literacy through various means: multilingual storytelling, digital collaboration, or intergenerational knowledge exchange. These diverse approaches ensure that literacy practices remain relevant, engaging, and reflective of each family's unique composition and cultural heritage.

Reflection Question: Consider your family's literacy practices. Are there untapped resources within your family (e.g., languages, cultural traditions, technological skills) that could enrich your family's literacy experiences?

Global Trends in Literacy Education

Literacy education has evolved into a dynamic, global phenomenon in today's interconnected world. Ideas, practices, and challenges flow freely across cultures and continents, reshaping the educational landscape. UNESCO's Futures of Education initiative serves as a global navigation system for literacy, recognizing the need to prepare learners for an unpredictable future in our rapidly changing world.

Today's schools teach more than just reading and writing. Teachers help students learn to solve problems and adapt to new situations. Every lesson combines traditional learning with real problem-solving skills, preparing students for future challenges they might face. Students learn that success requires more than memorizing facts and figures.

Students tackle real-world problems while learning their regular subjects. They practice planning ahead, making good choices, and finding creative solutions. These projects help students see how their school lessons connect to solving actual community problems. Each project builds confidence and shows students the real value of their education.

A student created a reading program to help people deal with climate change problems. She discovered that reading skills help people understand and handle real-life challenges. The project showed her how reading and writing connect to solving problems in her community, and through this work, she learned that good communication skills can help create positive changes in the world.

These kinds of projects help students learn both basic skills and ways to handle future challenges. Students figure out how to study problems, make smart choices, and find solutions. This helps them become better learners who can deal with changes throughout their lives. Most importantly, students discover that learning never stops and that every new skill makes them better prepared for tomorrow's challenges.

Critical literacy has become essential in our information-saturated world. Educators now focus on teaching students how to navigate, evaluate, and utilize the vast amount of information available. Javier, a high school teacher in Mexico City, notes, "I used to focus on teaching my students to find information. Now, I spend more time teaching them how to evaluate it. With so much misinformation out there, critical literacy isn't just an academic skill; it's a survival skill."

In Estonian schools, media literacy education begins as early as kindergarten and continues through high school. A mandatory 35-hour "media and influence" course is required for 10th-grade students, focusing on the role of media and journalism in society, including social media dynamics, bot and troll functions, and online security. Liisa Koik, a high school media literacy teacher in Lähte, Estonia, notes that many elective courses involve students creating their own media content. This hands-on approach helps them understand how various forms of content are created and can be used to persuade or manipulate.

Maria Murumaa-Menge, a lecturer at the University of Tartu in Estonia and a former high school media literacy teacher, emphasizes the importance of making lessons relevant to students' interests. Teachers use memes, social media posts, videos, and animations to illustrate key concepts about evaluating information. Her innovative approach encourages students to analyze trending content from platforms like TikTok and Instagram, teaching critical thinking through familiar digital media formats. Students learn to identify reliable sources, fact-check viral content, and understand how algorithms influence their daily information consumption.

Literacy educators are forming worldwide communities of practice, sharing ideas and best practices across cultures and contexts. The Global Literacy Exchange Program (GLEP) exemplifies this trend, connecting classrooms worldwide for collaborative literacy projects. Teachers from diverse backgrounds participate in virtual workshops and mentorship programs, developing innovative approaches to literacy instruction that blend traditional and digital methods. Educational technology platforms facilitate these cross-cultural exchanges, enabling real-time collaboration on projects ranging from digital storytelling to multilingual reading initiatives.

Maria, a teacher from Brazil who is participating in GLEP, shares her experience: "Last year, my students collaborated with a class in Japan on a digital storytelling project. They improved their English skills and gained a deeper understanding of each other's cultures. It broadened their perspective on what literacy means in different contexts." The project culminated in a virtual showcase where students presented their stories to families and educators from both countries, demonstrating how digital tools can transform traditional storytelling into an interactive, cross-cultural learning experience. These global communities demonstrate significant value in enriching literacy education worldwide. Such initiatives foster cultural exchange, broaden perspectives, and enhance literacy skills in diverse contexts, preparing students for a globally interconnected future.

The Power of Global Perspective in Local Contexts
While global trends shape literacy education worldwide, their implementation often takes on unique forms in local contexts. In rural India, Barefoot College exemplifies this approach by respecting and incorporating local knowledge while aligning with UNESCO's future-focused initiatives. Barefoot College's "Solar Mamas" program is a prime example of this localized approach. The program trains illiterate or semi-literate middle-aged women, often grandmothers, to become solar engineers. These women develop functional literacy that combines traditional

wisdom with new technological skills as part of their training.

The program's methodology is particularly noteworthy. As Bunker Roy, the founder of Barefoot College, explains, "When women are trained, they train others. We will make the role of grandmothers more visible in society and show that they can be leaders." This approach not only empowers individual women but contributes to community development. The impact of this program is significant. Since 1990, more than 1,750 women from 96 countries in the Global South have been trained as solar engineers.

These "Solar Mamas" have brought solar electrification to their villages, improving the quality of life for their communities. The experiences of many women in the program reflect similar sentiments of empowerment and community development. The program demonstrates that literacy, in this context, extends beyond reading and writing to include technical skills and the ability to contribute meaningfully to one's community.

Global literacy education is shifting beneath our feet, moving us toward something more interconnected, critical, and adaptive. Look at Barefoot College; its approach speaks volumes about where we are headed. It shows us what is possible when we honor local wisdom while embracing new technologies. Its learners engage critically with our rapidly changing world, adapting to and shaping it in real time. The future of literacy education stands right here, at this intersection of tradition and innovation.

Reflection Question: Consider your literacy education experience or that of your children/students. What aspects of global literacy education could be most beneficial in your community, and how might they be adapted to fit local needs and cultural contexts?

The Role of Gaming and Gamification in Literacy

Imagine a world where learning to read is as engaging as defeating the final boss in a video game, writing stories is as thrilling as exploring a vast open-world adventure, and mastering grammar is as satisfying as earning a high score. This is the promise of gaming and gamification in literacy education—a world where the power of play meets the pursuit of knowledge. Educational games are transforming the landscape of literacy instruction, turning what might once have been seen as tedious drills into exciting adventures. It's as if we've found a way to coat the sometimes-bitter pill of learning with a layer of pure fun.

Take Tyler, a nine-year-old who struggled with reading and writing. Traditional methods left him frustrated and disengaged. Then, his teacher introduced Word Quest, a role-playing game where players advance by decoding words, crafting sentences, and weaving narratives. The transformation was remarkable. Tyler began begging for more reading time, excitedly sharing stories about the new powers (words) he had learned and the quests (writing assignments) he had completed. His reading level jumped two grades in just one semester.

Games tap into our intrinsic motivation systems, providing clear goals, immediate feedback, and a sense of progress—all key elements in effective learning. It's like hijacking the brain's reward system for educational purposes. Gamification applies these engaging principles to non-game contexts. In literacy instruction, this might mean turning a writing class into a season-long story championship or transforming vocabulary learning into a word-collecting expedition.

Consider Ms. Johnson's high school English classroom in Chicago. She implemented a gamified approach where students became master wordsmiths who could level up their characters (writing skills) by completing various quests (assignments). They earned experience points for good work, unlocked new abilities (writing techniques), and faced boss battles (major essays) at the end of each unit. The results spoke for themselves: Attendance improved, participation skyrocketed, and work quality noticeably increased.

Narrative-based games are particularly powerful tools for enhancing storytelling skills and reading comprehension. They immerse players in rich, interactive narratives, requiring deep engagement with the text, critical decision-making, and often the creation of narrative branches. The Martínez family discovered this when their fourteen-year-old daughter Sophia, an avid gamer showing little interest in traditional literature, began playing Inkle's 80 Days, a narrative game based on Jules Verne's classic novel. Soon, she read extensively within the game, exploring the original novel for secrets and optimal paths and creating her own interactive stories, practicing complex writing skills without even realizing it.

These games teach a new form of literacy: interactive, nonlinear, and deeply engaging. Players become active participants in story creation and interpretation, like actors in a play rather than mere spectators.

The success of gaming in literacy education rests on several cognitive science principles:

1. Active, Critical Learning: Games encourage players to approach problems actively and critically, much like good readers approach texts.
2. Risk-Taking in Safe Environments: Games allow for experimentation and failure without severe consequences, encouraging essential learning risks.
3. Just-in-Time Information: Games provide information when needed and can be applied immediately, enhancing retention and understanding.
4. Performance Before Competence: Games allow players to perform before they're fully competent, with scaffolding and support, much like learning to read and write.

However, gaming and gamification should be seen as powerful tools in a diverse pedagogical toolkit, not replacements for other forms of instruction. Think of them as spices in the meal of literacy education—they can make the experience more flavorful and enjoyable, but you still need the substantive ingredients of good curriculum design, skilled teaching, and meaningful content. The intersection of gaming and literacy reveals new horizons in education, where reading and writing become not just educational but engaging and enjoyable. When we tap into the power of play, we open pathways to literacy that reach learners who might otherwise struggle or disengage.

Reflection Question: Think about your own experiences with learning or teaching literacy skills. What potential benefits and challenges do you foresee in using games or gamification for literacy development in your context?

Preparing for Unknown Future Literacy Challenges

The future of reading and writing skills keeps changing in both expected and surprising ways. This means teachers and students need to prepare carefully. Today's education system values flexibility more than any other skill. Students and teachers need to solve problems in ways that work for many different situations, not just one specific challenge.

The COVID pandemic showed why being flexible matters so much. Mr. Thompson, who taught for thirty years in White Plains, Maryland, proved this point. Though he had decades of teaching experience, switching to online classes made him completely rethink how he taught. This change turned his class into a place where everyone, including himself, learned new ways to teach and study together.

Nonetheless, basic literacy skills remain essential for learning. Critical thinking helps students solve complex problems. Good communication lets them share ideas clearly in different ways. The ability to combine information helps them understand complicated topics. Julia, who recently graduated from college with a liberal arts degree, found these skills valuable in her tech job.

Even when she had to learn new computer programs often, her basic skills helped her adjust quickly.

The Global Literacy Network (GLN) helps teachers prepare for future challenges through worldwide teamwork. Teachers share new ideas and learning trends on this platform. Maria, who teaches in Brazil, used advice from teachers worldwide to bring augmented reality (AR) reading apps into her classroom, showing how international connections can improve local teaching.

The Martinez family takes a complete approach to modern literacy. They mix traditional reading with digital tools, talk about news, and practice coding. This variety helps their daughter Sophia feel confident trying new things, especially when working with AI writing assignments. She succeeds because she knows how to analyze problems and ask important questions.

An individual's success in future literacy depends on three things: strong basic skills, knowledge of new developments, and flexibility with new challenges. Students today must handle complicated learning while keeping their core abilities strong. This mix creates students who can handle future learning challenges well. Teachers need to keep learning and developing their skills while maintaining what works from traditional teaching. Schools must provide support for both old and new teaching methods. Parents play a big role, too, in helping their children to continue learning at home.

Technology keeps adding new tools and ways to learn. Digital skills work together with traditional reading and writing. Students need to think carefully about online information while understanding content in all formats, and schools must find ways to combine these different types of learning effectively.

Future literacy education needs to balance new ideas with proven methods. Teachers must keep learning the essential basics while using new teaching approaches and technology. This combination helps students develop lasting skills alongside modern abilities, preparing them for school and work success.

Reflection Question: Think about a recent change or challenge you've encountered in your own literacy practices or teaching literacy to others. What steps can you take to stay informed about emerging literacy trends and research in your context?

Conclusion: Embracing the Future of Family Literacy

Modern tools like AI systems and virtual reality reshape how families learn together. Workplaces demand new skills, transforming literacy education at an incredible speed. However, the basic elements of literacy remain strong through these changes. People need connection while learning and sharing stories stay central to family education. Digital technology opens new paths for family learning. Parents explore interactive stories with their children, while grandparents connect through video calls. Traditional bedtime stories now feature digital elements that bring characters to life. Busy families adapt reading time to their schedules: Single parents include stories in daily routines, mixed families share tales from different cultures, and working parents use technology to stay involved.

Today's jobs require strong literacy skills, and workers need to understand complex information and write clearly for various audiences. Family reading habits build these important abilities early. Children from reading-rich homes typically perform better in school and work. Traditional methods such as face-to-face book discussions remain valuable, as they develop critical thinking, journal writing encourages self-expression, and physical books provide unique learning experiences. The future of literacy balances innovation with proven practices. New tools enhance learning while maintaining human connections. Families discover meaningful ways to blend traditional and digital approaches, creating strong foundations for success in an evolving world.

Key Takeaways from this chapter:
1. **Technological Integration:** AI, VR, and AR are reshaping literacy education, offering personalized learning experiences and new ways to engage with text.
2. **Evolving Workplace Literacy:** Digital literacy, data literacy, and adaptive learning skills are becoming crucial in the modern workplace.
3. **Diverse Family Structures:** Multilingual literacy, digital family literacy, and intergenerational approaches are adapting to changing family dynamics.
4. **Global Perspective:** Literacy is increasingly viewed as a global issue, with critical literacy skills essential for navigating our information-rich world.

5. **Gamification in Learning:** Game-based learning and gamification techniques are powerful tools for enhancing engagement in literacy education.
6. **Preparation for the Unknown:** Fostering adaptability, emphasizing core skills, and staying informed are crucial strategies for future challenges.

Parents remain the most influential force in their child's literacy development. Staying informed about emerging trends, embracing innovations, and nurturing a love of reading and writing create a foundation for academic success and lifelong learning. Be a parent who is a curious, adaptable co-learner alongside their children. You don't need to understand every new technology perfectly. A strong belief in basic reading and writing skills leads to better success for children.

The creation of a rich literacy culture requires understanding key principles from early childhood through school years. Good reading and writing habits start early in childhood and grow through the school years. Parents who mix old and new ways of teaching keep their kids interested in learning. This helps children handle school challenges better and brings families closer through learning together.

In our final chapter, we will bring together all we've explored, providing you with a roadmap for creating a rich, enduring culture of literacy in your family. We'll synthesize the insights gained from early childhood through the school years and beyond, focusing on how you can apply these principles to foster a lasting love for literacy. Armed with knowledge of timeless principles and cutting-edge innovations, you will be well-prepared to guide your child's literacy journey, no matter what the future holds.

Further Reading

1. *Come Home: The Reading Brain in a Digital World. Harper.* Wolf, M. (2018). Reader. An exploration of how digital technology is changing the way we read and process information.
2. *The Anti-Education Era: Creating Smarter Students through Digital Learning.* Palgrave Macmillan. Gee, J. P. (2013). Discusses how digital media and technology can be leveraged to enhance learning and literacy.
3. *Translanguaging: Language, Bilingualism, and Education. Palgrave Macmillan.* García, O., & Li, W. (2014). Explores the concept of translanguaging and its implications for multilingual literacy practices.
4. Future of Education and Skills 2030 - OECD (https://www.oecd.org/education/2030-project/). An ongoing OECD project examines future education needs, including evolving literacy requirements.
5. Common Sense Media: Digital Literacy Resources (https://www.commonsense.org/education/digital-literacy) offers educators and parents a wealth of resources on digital literacy and citizenship.

Practical Exercises

1. **Tech-Enhanced Storytelling:** Create a multimedia story using a digital platform (e.g., Storybird, Adobe Spark). Incorporate text, images, and possibly audio or video. Involve family members in creating different parts of the story. Learning Outcome: Develop digital literacy skills while fostering creativity and family collaboration.
2. **Family Data Detective Challenge:** Choose a topic of family interest (e.g., local weather patterns, family spending habits). Collect relevant data over a week, then use free online tools to create visualizations. Discuss insights as a family. Learning Outcome: Enhances data literacy skills and critical thinking in a family context.
3. **Multilingual Family Book Club:** Select a book available in multiple languages spoken in your family or community. Read it together, comparing versions and discussing cultural nuances. Learning Outcome: Promotes multilingual literacy and cross-cultural understanding.
4. **Future Literacy Scenario Planning:** As a family, brainstorm potential future scenarios (e.g., In 2040, all books are holographic). Discuss how literacy skills might need to be adapted and create a plan to develop those skills. Learning Outcome: This activity encourages adaptive thinking and long-term planning for literacy development.
5. **Gamify a Literacy Challenge:** Take a current family literacy goal (e.g., reading for 20 minutes daily) and turn it into a game. Create a point system,

levels, and rewards. Implement it for a month and discuss the results. Learning Outcome: Applies gamification principles to literacy practices, potentially increasing engagement.

Chapter 12: Empowered Parents, Lifelong Readers

Overview
As we reach the final chapter of our journey through the landscape of family literacy, it's time to gather all we have learned and look toward the future. Throughout this book, we have explored parents' crucial role in nurturing literacy from early childhood through the school years and beyond. Now, let's focus on how you can synthesize these insights to create a lasting culture of literacy in your family.

In this final chapter, we will provide you with the tools, strategies, and inspiration to turn this vision into reality. We will guide you through creating a family literacy action plan, offering practical tips for overcoming common obstacles and celebrating milestones along the way. You will learn to model effective literacy behaviors, extend learning beyond reading, and foster critical-thinking skills. Through real-life examples and expert insights, we'll explore how to create a lasting literacy legacy that will shape your children's academic success and their approach to life. By the end of this chapter, you'll be equipped to transform your home into a vibrant literacy ecosystem, nurturing curious, engaged, and empowered lifelong learners.

The Power of Parental Influence: Nurturing the Roots of Literacy
Picture reading and writing skills as a towering, robust oak. While teachers, peers, and society may shape its branches,

parents nurture its roots, providing the foundation for all future growth. As Dr. Catherine Snow so aptly puts it, "Parents are a child's first and most enduring teachers. The habits, attitudes, and skills they foster in the early years have lifelong impacts" (Snow, 2017). This profound truth has been the North Star guiding our journey through the landscape of family literacy. Like skilled gardeners tending to a precious sapling, parents have the unique power to cultivate a love for reading and writing that can flourish for a lifetime.

When Priya and Raj Patel emigrated from India to the United States, they were determined to give their children the best possible start in life. Despite working long hours at their small business, they made literacy a cornerstone of their family culture. "We didn't have much when we first arrived," Priya recalls, "but we always had books. We read together every night in both English and Hindi. It wasn't just about learning to read; it was our way of connecting as a family and exploring our new world together."

Years later, their children credit this early emphasis on literacy for their academic success and enduring love of learning. Their daughter, Anjali, now a pediatrician, shares: "Those nightly reading sessions were not just about stories; they taught us curiosity, critical thinking, and the joy of discovery. It's a gift I'm now passing on to my children."

The Patel family's story beautifully illustrates the enduring impact of parental influence on literacy development. Creating an environment that values reading and writing enriches daily family life. Literacy becomes a natural part of everyday activities, building enjoyment and confidence over time. Children thrive when reading and storytelling blend seamlessly into regular routines.

Recap of Key Strategies: A Tool Kit for Literacy Success

Let's revisit the key strategies we have explored. These strategies are essential tools in a parent's literacy tool kit. Parents who master these strategies can guide their child's literacy journey with precision and care.

1. Early language exposure and interaction (Chapter 2)- Children's linguistic development thrives on rich, consistent interaction from the beginning. The Martinez family turned everyday activities into language-learning opportunities. "We narrated everything," laughs Maria Martinez. "Grocery shopping became a vocabulary lesson, bath time a sing-along. Our neighbors probably thought we were a bit odd, but our kids eagerly absorbed every new word!"

2. Creating a literacy-rich home environment (Chapter 3)- A strong literacy environment provides the foundation for learning. The Johnsons transformed their tiny apartment into an educational space. "Books in every room, labels on everything, magnetic letters on the fridge," describes Tom Johnson. "Our home centered around reading and writing at every turn."

3. Developing comprehensive literacy skills (Chapter 4)- Comprehensive literacy involves developing multiple interconnected skills together. The Wong family worked on all these skills as part of their

daily life. "We played word games at dinner, wrote family newsletters, and even turned grocery lists into poetry," shares Lisa Wong. "It made literacy feel less like a chore and more like a family adventure."

4. Building strong school/home partnerships (Chapter 5)- Strong connections between home and school accelerate literacy progress. Mr. Thompson, a single father, found this particularly crucial. "I made sure my daughter's teachers knew me. We were a team, all pulling in the same direction. It made a world of difference."

5. Addressing literacy challenges (Chapter 6)- Parents must be ready to tackle literacy challenges head-on when they arise. The Smiths faced this when their son was diagnosed with dyslexia. "It was tough," admits Sarah Smith, "but we educated ourselves, worked closely with specialists, and never gave up. Seeing Jake now, confidently reading aloud in his school play, makes all that effort worthwhile."

6. Honoring cultural diversity in literacy practices (Chapter 7)- This is about recognizing that literacy manifests differently across various cultural contexts. The Nguyens celebrated their Vietnamese heritage through literacy. "We read Vietnamese folktales, wrote letters to relatives in Hanoi, and created bilingual family cookbooks," shares Linh Nguyen. "It made literacy a bridge between cultures for our children."

7. Navigating digital literacy (Chapter 8)- This requires mastering both traditional and digital

reading practices. The Garcias found a balance that worked for their family. "We have 'unplugged' reading time and 'connected' reading time," explains Carlos Garcia. "It is about using technology as a tool and not letting it take over."

8. Fostering 21st-century literacy skills (Chapter 9)- This involves adapting literacy education for an evolving future. The Changs are focused on critical thinking and creativity alongside traditional reading skills. "We analyze the news as we read it. We don't just consume stories; we create them," says Michael Chang. "We're preparing our kids to be literate in a world we can't even imagine yet."

9. Leveraging community resources (Chapter 10)- This involves extending literacy learning beyond the home environment. The Robinsons became regulars at their local library. "Storytimes, writing workshops, coding classes, we tried it all," shares Emma Robinson. "It showed our kids that literacy isn't just a family value; it's a community treasure."

10. Preparing for future literacy trends (Chapter 11)- This focuses on adapting literacy practices for emerging technologies and approaches. The Taylors embraced this with enthusiasm. "We are always exploring new ways to engage with text," says David Taylor. "VR storytelling, interactive e-books, coding, we see it all as part of the evolving literacy landscape."

Each of these strategies represents a vital tool in developing lifelong readers. As many of our families have discovered, the key is to integrate them into daily life in a natural and enjoyable way. It's not about perfection but creating a diverse and engaging environment where reading and writing skills can develop naturally.

Creating a Family Literacy Action Plan

Creating a structured approach to your family's literacy development is essential. You now have strategies and knowledge from this book, but success requires a well-designed implementation plan. This is where your Family Literacy Action Plan becomes essential. You will need to evaluate your current situation, establish goals, select appropriate methods, and maintain flexibility.

Dr. Laura Justice, a professor of early childhood education, emphasizes the importance of this systematic approach: "Intentionality in literacy support makes a significant difference. When parents have a clear plan, they're more likely to engage in literacy-promoting activities consistently" (Justice, 2019). Strategic engagement with literacy activities leads to better outcomes than unstructured approaches, though both can be rewarding.

Let's break down the steps to create your Family Literacy Action Plan:

Step 1: Assess Your Current Literacy Environment
Think of this as surveying your base camp before embarking on your expedition. What supplies (literacy practices) do you already have? Which ones are working well? Where might you need to acquire new tools or skills?

The Thompson family found this step eye-opening. "We realized we were great at bedtime reading, but we weren't doing much to encourage writing," shares Mrs. Thompson. "It was like we had packed plenty of food for our journey but forgotten the water!"

Action Step: Take a week to observe your family's interactions with literacy. Keep a log of reading times, writing activities, conversations about books, or the use of digital literacy tools. This will give you a clear picture of your starting point.

Step 2: Set Realistic Goals

Now that you know where you're starting from, it's time to choose your destination. But remember, like any journey, it's often better to plan several shorter trips rather than one marathon expedition.

The Garcias found this approach helpful. "We were tempted to set a goal of reading for an hour daily," Mr. Garcia admits. "But with our busy schedules, that just wasn't realistic. Instead, we set a goal of 15 minutes of family reading time each evening and two monthly library visits. It was ambitious but achievable."

When setting goals, make them SMART: Specific, Measurable, Achievable, Relevant, and Time-bound. Instead of "read more," try "Read together for 15 minutes every evening" or "Write and mail a letter to grandma every Sunday."

Step 3: Choose Specific Strategies

This is like choosing which paths you'll take on your journey. Select strategies from the book that align with your goals and fit your family's interests and dynamics.

The Poole family turned this into a collaborative activity. "We had a family meeting, and everyone chose a strategy they wanted to try," explains Mrs. Poole. "Our teenager picked creating a family blog, our 10-year-old wanted to start a comic book club, and our 6-year-old was excited about alphabet scavenger hunts. It gave everyone a stake in our literacy journey." Include a mix of activities that target different literacy skills: reading, writing, speaking, listening, and critical thinking.

Step 4: Create a Schedule
Now, it's time to plot your route. Decide when and how you'll implement these strategies. Like any successful expedition, consistency and routine are key.

The Robinsons found that linking literacy activities to existing routines worked best for them. "We started playing word games at dinner, reading aloud during breakfast on weekends, and having a family 'book club' discussion every Friday night," shares Mr. Robinson. "By piggybacking on routines we already had, it was easier to make literacy a consistent part of our day."

Action Step: Create a visual schedule or calendar to keep everyone on track. You might even create a family literacy map to mark your progress and celebrate milestones.

Step 5: Review and Adjust
Every good expedition leader knows the importance of regularly checking the map and being willing to adjust the route if needed. Plan to review your progress regularly and be prepared to modify your plan.

The Lee family found this step crucial. "After a month, we realized our writing activities weren't engaging our youngest," Mrs. Lee recalls. "So, we switched from journal writing to creating picture books together. The flexibility kept everyone motivated and involved."

Set regular check-in points, perhaps monthly, to discuss what's working, what's challenging, and how you might need to adjust your plan. Remember, the goal is progress, not perfection. Creating and following a Family Literacy Action Plan prevents you from leaving your literacy journey to chance. You're setting a clear course, equipping yourself with the right tools, and preparing to navigate whatever challenges you encounter. The journey, daily interactions, shared stories, and collective growth are just as important as the destination.

Reflection Questions: Consider your family's current literacy practices and goals. What would be the first step in your Family Literacy Action Plan? What potential challenges do you foresee and how might you address them proactively?

Overcoming Common Obstacles: Navigating the Hurdles on Your Literacy Journey

When families begin their literacy journey, they often create detailed plans and set enthusiastic goals. However, real-world challenges emerge that require practical solutions to maintain momentum. Let's explore some common obstacles and how to navigate them, keeping your literacy adventure on track.

- **Time Constraints**: Finding Literacy in the Nooks and Crannies of Life

Modern families face significant time constraints daily. It takes some strategic planning and observation, but numerous opportunities can be found to incorporate literacy into daily routines. Parents and caregivers can identify and maximize brief periods throughout their day during meals, commutes, bedtime routines, and waiting times to engage in meaningful literacy activities. These small but consistent moments accumulate to create a substantial impact on literacy development.

The Martinez family, always on the go with three active children, found creative ways to infuse literacy into their hectic schedule. "We turned our car into a rolling library," laughs Mrs. Martinez. "Audiobooks during commutes, word games while waiting in lines, and reading road signs became fun activities. We realized we didn't need to find time for literacy; we needed to find literacy in our time."

Dr. Richard Allington, former president of the International Literacy Association, emphasizes this approach: "Literacy doesn't require long, uninterrupted blocks of time. Short, frequent engagements throughout the day can be just as effective, if not more so" (Allington, 2019).

Try this: Create a "literacy on the go" kit with small books, word game cards, or a notebook for collaborative storytelling. Keep it in your bag or car, ready to transform those in-between moments into literacy opportunities.

- **Resistance from Children**: Turning "Have to" into "Want to"

Trying to engage a reluctant reader sometimes feels like pushing a boulder uphill. The key is to shift the perspective from obligation to opportunity, from "have to" to "want to."

The Thompsons faced this challenge with their 10-year-old son, Jake. "He saw reading as a chore," Mr. Thompson recalls. "So, we decided to tap into his passion for basketball." They started with basketball player biographies, then moved to sports journalism, and even explored the physics of the perfect jump shot. "Suddenly, reading wasn't a chore; it was a way to fuel his passion."

Dr. Nell Duke's insight is spot on: "The most powerful motivator for reading is a child's curiosity and interests" (Duke, 2020). It's about building bridges between what they love and what they read.

Try this: Create a "Reading Wish List" with your child. Let them fill it with books, magazines, or curious topics. Make obtaining these materials a reward or a special treat.

- **Inconsistency**: The Power of "Getting Back on Track"

Life has a way of derailing even the best-laid plans. The secret is not never falling off the wagon but how quickly you climb back on it.

The Lee family's experience illustrates this perfectly. "We had a great literacy routine going," shares Mrs. Lee, "but then came a hectic month of work travel and school projects. Our reading time went out the window." Instead of getting discouraged, they treated it as a learning opportunity. "We had a family meeting and brainstormed how to get back on track. The kids came up with the idea of a 'literacy comeback challenge' with small rewards for consistent engagement."

Dr. Timothy Shanahan's words ring true here: "Consistency over time is more important than perfection at the moment" (Shanahan, 2018). It's the overall trend that matters, not the occasional dip.

Try this: Implement a "literacy streak" tracker. Celebrate small milestones of consistent engagement, and if the streak breaks, make starting a new one an exciting challenge rather than a disappointment.

- **Technology Distractions**: Balancing the Digital and the Tangible

In today's world, technology is like a powerful current in the river of daily life. The goal isn't to dam it up entirely but to learn to navigate it skillfully.

The Peterson family encountered challenges with technology balance in their household, particularly with their children's excessive screen time. Upon realizing that parental habits influenced their children's behavior, they developed a comprehensive family media strategy. Their approach included establishing designated screen-free periods and areas within their home while also exploring ways to integrate technology as a complement to traditional literacy practices rather than a replacement.

Dr. Lisa Guernsey, Director of Education Policy at New America and author of *Screen Time: How Electronic Media Affects Children from Birth to Age Five*, emphasizes the importance of intentional technology integration. Her research demonstrates that the key lies not in categorizing technology use as inherently positive or negative but in developing thoughtful approaches that align digital tools with established literacy objectives (Guernsey, 2021).

Try this: Create a "digital literacy challenge" where family members use technology to create rather than consume. This could involve writing a family blog, creating digital stories, or even coding simple games based on favorite books.

Overcoming these obstacles is part of the journey, not a detour from it. Each challenge you navigate strengthens your family's literacy muscles and deepens your commitment to the journey.

Your persistence and creativity in addressing literacy challenges teach children valuable lessons about literacy's importance and resilience's power. Finding innovative solutions to literacy obstacles promotes reading and writing skills while developing problem-solving abilities, adaptability, and a growth mindset. When families tackle these challenges together, they create a supportive environment where learning becomes a shared adventure rather than an isolated task.

Dr. Peter Johnston, author of *Opening Minds: Using Language to Change Lives* and researcher specializing in literacy development and educational psychology, emphasizes the transformative impact of our approach to literacy challenges. His research shows that discussions about overcoming literacy obstacles play a crucial role in shaping children's identities as learners and problem-solvers (Johnston, 2022). These challenges become integral parts of your family's unique literacy development, with each overcome obstacle strengthening your collective learning journey.

The Importance of Parental Modeling

Parental modeling shapes children's literacy development through consistent demonstration and engagement. When parents actively read, write, and engage with language, they establish these activities as valuable and meaningful pursuits. This direct influence creates the foundation for children's literacy growth. Parents who openly share their reading experiences and writing processes help children understand the practical applications of these skills in daily life. Children begin to view literacy as an essential tool for communication, learning, and personal expression. These early observations of parental literacy behaviors often develop into lifelong positive attitudes toward reading and writing.

Parents who read regularly inspire their children to become readers, too. Research consistently shows that children develop stronger reading habits when they see their family members enjoying books.

The Power of Example: More Than Words Can Say
Let's dissect the situation involving the Johnsons. Mark Johnson, a busy accountant, rarely had time for leisure reading. His 9-year-old daughter, Emma, showed little interest in books despite her parents' encouragement. Recognizing the disconnect, Mark made a conscious decision to change his habits. "I started reading for 30 minutes every evening, right in the living room where Emma could see me," Mark shares. "At first, she was puzzled. But soon, curiosity got the better of her. She'd ask what I was reading and why I was laughing or looking

serious. Before long, she was curling up next to me with her book."

This simple act of modeling had a transformative effect. Emma's reading scores improved, but more importantly, she discovered the joy of getting lost in a good book. Mark's example spoke louder than any lecture or mandate ever could. Dr. Laura Shapiro, a developmental psychologist specializing in literacy, explains this phenomenon: "Children are natural mimics. When they see their parents genuinely enjoying reading, it creates a powerful, often subconscious, desire to experience that enjoyment themselves. It's like lighting a candle from an already burning flame—the passion for reading spreads naturally."

Creating a Literacy Ecosystem: Beyond Books
Parental modeling extends beyond reading books alone. A strong literacy foundation comes from making text-based activities a fun daily habit and these practices foster lifelong learning and link literacy to daily life. Families actively build stronger reading and writing skills through everyday life. Kids learn the value of reading when parents discuss news at dinner, write about family adventures, and create plays together. Cooking, helping neighbors, and family projects naturally include reading activities. Regular reading and writing activities teach children these skills without making them feel like homework. They discover how reading and writing enhance their daily lives.

Following recipes, writing letters about local issues, and sharing stories strengthen reading and writing naturally. These daily activities keep families connected and improve community relationships. Kids understand the importance of literacy skills when they do different types of reading and writing and parents turn regular activities into fun practice opportunities. Small moments build strong reading and writing habits over time.

Reading and writing activities improve how kids share their thoughts. They discover how literacy helps them express ideas, tackle problems, and strengthen their community. Daily exposure to reading and writing creates lasting lessons. Kids realize reading and writing extend beyond school subjects into valuable life tools, and these skills empower them to connect with others and create positive change in their world.

Dr. Elizabeth Birr Moje, Dean of the University of Michigan School of Education, studies youth literacy and culture in and out of school. She developed the concept of "literacy sponsorship." Her research shows that parents who model diverse literacy practices do more than develop skills. They create a culture where literacy is key to daily life and personal growth. This approach turns literacy from an academic skill into a key tool and helps kids understand and engage with the world. It shapes how they see and value reading and writing.

The Ripple Effect: Beyond the Family
When the Thompsons launched their neighborhood "Parents Who Read" book club, they never expected it would revolutionize how local children viewed reading. What began as adults seeking their literary escape transformed into a powerful lesson about the ripple effects of community behavior. "We just wanted to reconnect with

books ourselves," Mrs. Thompson explains, her eyes lighting up. "Nobody anticipated how watching their parents get excited about reading would impact the kids. Suddenly, reading was not just homework; it became this cool activity that grown-ups chose to do."

The transformation in their community reveals a fundamental truth about literacy: It flourishes when embedded in social connection. The journey to literacy is as much about community as it is about capability. When children are surrounded by people who celebrate reading and writing, these skills transform from classroom requirements into cultural touchstones that help define who they are and how they relate to the world. The Thompsons' accidental experiment in social learning reveals that sometimes the most powerful teaching moments happen outside the classroom, around living room coffee tables where parents gather to share their latest reads.

Practical Steps: Kindling Your Literacy Flame
To effectively model literacy, consider these strategies:
- Make your reading visible: Read in common areas of your home, not just in private.
- Share your reading experiences: Discuss interesting things you've read, ask for book recommendations, and share your thoughts on current reads.
- Engage in visible writing: Keep a journal, write letters, or start a blog. Let your children see you in the act of writing.
- Use literacy skills in everyday life: Show how you use reading and writing for practical purposes, from following recipes to writing emails.

- Express enjoyment: Don't be afraid to laugh out loud at a funny passage or express emotion about what you're reading.
- Create family literacy traditions: Start a family book club, have poetry reading nights, or collaborate on writing projects.

Reading works best when families keep it natural and fun instead of trying to make it perfect. Kids develop good reading habits when they see their parents enjoying books, writing notes, or sharing interesting stories. When reading and writing feel like normal parts of daily life, kids want to join in without being pushed. They pick up these habits naturally just by watching their family.

Parents who read pass this good habit to their children, teaching them more than just reading skills. Kids who grow up with books and writing feel more confident sharing their ideas. They discover that reading helps them learn new things and have fun at the same time. These good feelings about reading stay with them as they grow up, helping them do better in school, work, and life.

Family reading creates special bonds and helps kids see themselves as readers. When parents share books they love, kids want to discover their own favorite stories, too. Simple moments like reading together or talking about books make a big difference. Kids learn that reading opens doors to new ideas and adventures, making them want to keep reading throughout their lives.

Reflection Questions: Think about your literacy habits. How visible are they to your children? How might you involve your children in your literacy practices, turning them into shared experiences?

Celebrating Literacy Milestones and Successes

Creating strong literacy skills requires more than teaching children to read and write. True success comes from three things: focused practice, daily involvement, and meaningful celebration of progress. When families create an environment that combines structured learning with real praise, children bond more with reading and writing. These skills and achievements make literacy a family affair, not just schoolwork.

Successful literacy environments carefully balance structured activities with sincere recognition of progress. Regular reading times, writing practice, and vocabulary building create essential foundations. Recognizing both small wins and big successes boosts motivation and confidence. Together, these elements create momentum, move children forward, and spark a love of learning.

Dr. Carol Dweck's research shows that praising natural talent can backfire despite good intentions. Her work shows that recognizing specific efforts and learning strategies improves results. Students build resilience and true enthusiasm when praise focuses on their process, not their abilities. Simple, meaningful celebrations tied to specific reading achievements create a lasting impact. Here are six proven approaches from families:

1. Book Bloom Wall: The Patel family adds paper flowers to their wall for each completed book.
2. Story and Snack: The Thompsons celebrate reading goals with café visits for book discussions.

3. Read and Pick: The Lee family rewards reading milestones with bookstore visits to choose new books.
4. Author Parties: The Robinsons host themed celebrations for completed book series.
5. Time Capsules: The Martinez family collects annual writing samples, book lists, and goals to track growth.
6. Reading Tree: The Wongs mark finished books with leaf tags and hold seasonal reflection celebrations.

Dr. Linda Gambrell's research on literacy motivation reveals that purposeful celebration creates a lasting impact beyond temporary encouragement. Her studies show that students read more with regular, meaningful recognition of their progress. They gravitate toward challenging texts and frequently choose to read for pleasure. They engage more with reading and stay enthusiastic about it and are more likely to share their reading. This creates a self-reinforcing cycle of literacy engagement.

Recognizing steady progress proves to be as imperative as celebrating major milestones. Research shows that students gain confidence and stay motivated when families and educators value their daily reading efforts. Small victories, like finishing a tough chapter or learning new words, deserve attention. So do larger achievements, like completing books or advancing reading levels. This balanced approach to recognition helps students and shows that growth happens gradually through sustained effort.

The Jones family discovered this through experience. They noticed their daughter comparing her reading level to her classmates and feeling discouraged. Their solution? They award effort stars for each 15 minutes of focused reading. This simple system shifted attention from comparison to personal improvement.

Dr. Peter Johnston's research in his book *Opening Minds* reinforces this approach. He found that our language around reading achievements shapes how students view learning itself. When we celebrate steady effort and specific strategies, students develop both resilience and genuine enjoyment of reading and writing.

This mindset extends beyond just reading levels. Students who receive recognition for their dedication tend to take on harder challenges, persist through difficulties, find more satisfaction in their progress, and develop stronger learning strategies.

Dr. Nell Duke found that celebrating reading and writing achievements matters more than we might think. Each recognized milestone opens doors to new ideas and deeper understanding. When families value both effort and success, reading and writing become more than school tasks. They become tools for lifelong learning. This creates confident learners who see literacy as a core part of their identity and their way of understanding the world.

Reflection Question: Think about your family's current approach to acknowledging literacy achievements. What's one new way you could celebrate literacy milestones that would be meaningful and motivating for your family?

Beyond Literacy: Fostering Lifelong Learning
The Foundation of Learning
Literacy serves as a fundamental starting point for broader educational development. While reading and writing form essential foundational skills, they represent the beginning rather than the end of educational growth. Dr. Dweck emphasizes that our goal must extend beyond creating proficient readers to developing children who embrace learning and welcome challenges. This broader vision of literacy recognizes that technical reading proficiency alone does not guarantee educational success.

Children need opportunities to apply these abilities across diverse learning contexts. They engage more readily with challenging material when they view reading and writing as pathways to exploration and understanding, which transforms reading and writing from academic requirements into powerful instruments for learning and discovery. Ultimately, this creates a self-reinforcing cycle in which improved literacy skills enable deeper learning, which in turn motivates further reading and writing development.

Those who view literacy as part of a larger learning journey show greater persistence when facing difficult texts or complex writing tasks. They approach these challenges with curiosity rather than frustration, understanding that struggle often precedes breakthrough moments in learning. Dr. Dweck's research particularly highlights how this mindset allows students to maintain motivation even when encountering advanced material that stretches their current abilities.

Creating an Environment for Learning
Successful learning environments integrate multiple elements beyond basic literacy, combining physical spaces designed for exploration with thoughtful adult facilitation. These environments require designated areas for reading, writing, and project work, with resources organized to promote self-directed learning. Adults enhance these spaces by asking open-ended questions, providing time for extended exploration, and modeling curiosity-driven, problem-solving behaviors.

The power of well-designed learning environments emerges from their ability to build on children's natural curiosity while maintaining a supportive structure. Dr. Sugata Mitra's research demonstrates that children naturally pursue deeper understanding when genuinely interested in a subject, often extending beyond initial material without prompting. This natural progression flourishes when children have autonomy in choosing learning directions, access to varied resources, and the freedom to explore questions without rigid time constraints.

Learning environments function best when they incorporate both individual and social learning opportunities. Through group discussions, collaborative projects, and peer teaching opportunities, children develop critical thinking skills alongside their literacy abilities. These social interactions, combined with technology integration and flexible assessment methods, create a comprehensive learning experience where success is measured by growth rather than standardized benchmarks, and multiple forms of expression are valued as evidence of learning.

Ways Families Make Learning Fun

The Space Explorer
Zoe is a 10-year-old who got hooked on sci-fi books. Instead of just letting her read solo, her family turned her space obsession into a whole adventure. They frequently visited the local planetarium, spent nights stargazing in the backyard, and even tackled building a telescope together. Pretty soon, their dinner conversations were bouncing from black holes to Greek myths about constellations. One book sparked a whole universe of learning!

The Dinner Detective Game
The Greers turned their regular family dinner into something special with their "Fact or Fiction" game. Everyone brings a cool fact they learned that week, and the rest of the family plays detective to figure out if it's true. Not only is it fun, but it helps develop critical evaluation skills for all the information they encounter.

The Challenge Champion
Alex used to struggle with writing; it just was not his thing. His family came up with this idea called the "Challenge Journal." Using different writing prompts, they treated each one like a puzzle to solve. They brainstormed ideas, tried different approaches, and tracked what worked. Before long, Alex went from dreading writing to seeing it as a challenge he could tackle.

The Question Board
Over at the Lees' house, they have a Question of the Week board where anyone can post whatever makes them wonder, whether it's "Why do cats purr?" or "How do planes stay up?" The whole family gets in on finding answers.

The Power of "Not Yet"
Here's what's cool about the way kids learn: When they start seeing tough stuff as challenges rather than roadblocks, everything changes. Instead of saying, "I can't do this," they start asking, "How can I figure this out?" It's amazing how a simple shift in thinking can make such a big difference.

Creating Your Family's Learning Vibe
Make learning a part of everyday family life. The most successful families don't treat learning as something that happens only at school. They weave it into regular conversations, family activities, and daily routines. When curiosity and questioning become as natural as breathing, the magic happens.

Practical Strategies for Fostering a Love of Learning
- Implement "Exploration Saturdays," where the family learns a new skill or explores a new topic together.
- Encourage children to teach something they've learned to the family, fostering more profound understanding and communication skills.

- Celebrate mistakes as learning opportunities, sharing your learning challenges and how you overcome them.
- Engage in community learning projects, volunteering, or citizen science initiatives to connect learning with real-world impact.

Dr. Alison Gopnik, a developmental psychologist, expresses this goal: "The point of parenting is not to create a particular kind of child. The point of parenting is to provide a protective environment within which a child can experience the world. We're not trying to shape them into a particular kind of adult. We're trying to give them the most robust, flexible, resilient ways of finding out about the world" (Gopnik, 2016).

Reflection Questions: Think about your family's approach to learning beyond reading and writing. What's one area of curiosity or interest that you could explore together as a family? How might you turn this exploration into an opportunity to foster critical thinking, embrace challenges, and celebrate the learning process?

Generational Impact of Family Literacy

Family literacy fundamentally shapes individual development while influencing broader societal change. Research demonstrates that children raised in literacy-rich environments become adults who focus on reading with their children. This creates multigenerational educational engagement and success patterns.

Maria Martinez grew up in a household where books were scarce, and reading received little emphasis.

She transformed this narrative by establishing literacy practices at the core of her family's daily routines. Despite initial challenges with her reading confidence, her persistence created lasting change. Her daughter Sofia now teaches her kids those practices. This shows that literacy habits, values, and engagement strategies pass naturally between generations.

This transformation of literacy practices often extends beyond individual families into broader communities. Military families on Fort Johnson demonstrate this evolution through their neighborhood book boxes. What began as a simple donation box grew into many community projects: a mini-library at the mailbox hub in each neighborhood, regular reading events at the education center for the homeschool community, and thriving book clubs for adults and children.

These initiatives strengthen the already tight-knit military community while building valuable social connections through shared learning experiences. Parents and children forge lasting friendships during book club discussions, sharing not just literary insights but the daily trials and triumphs of military life. The community's shared commitment to literacy has created unexpected support networks, with veteran families mentoring newer arrivals through both books and life experiences.

The impact of strong literacy foundations reaches even further into professional and economic success. The Johnson family illustrates this progression through three generations of readers. Their literacy-enriched home produced three successful professionals: an entrepreneur, a journalist, and a researcher. The entrepreneur crafts compelling business proposals. The journalist investigates complex social issues. The researcher publishes groundbreaking scientific papers. Their mother established daily reading routines, encouraged debate over dinner, and filled their home with diverse reading materials. The children grew up discussing news articles, analyzing story perspectives, and writing creative pieces for fun.

Each Johnson sibling credits their career achievements to these early literacy practices. Their ability to research thoroughly, think critically, and communicate stems from years of guided reading discussions and writing activities at home. These skills were especially valuable in their jobs. They helped them analyze market trends, investigate stories, and contribute to academic discourse. The family's focus on literacy created strong readers and confident pros who could process complex info and share their insights.

Contemporary research reinforces these real-world examples. Studies show that family literacy practices help acquire skills through regular reading and guided learning. Children in literacy-rich environments develop enhanced learning capabilities, improving comprehension and retention across all academic subjects. Critical thinking skills emerge through text analysis, discussion, and exploration of diverse reading materials. Literacy researchers highlight strong connections between early reading experiences and later life outcomes, including academic success, career achievement, and civic participation.

The ongoing evolution of family literacy practices shapes future generations while influencing community development and societal progress. Strong literacy foundations enhance educational outcomes and create academic and professional success opportunities. They expose readers to diverse literature, which builds cultural understanding. They also strengthen social networks through shared learning experiences. Literacy initiatives at the individual, family, and community levels create lasting change and show that early literacy leads to valuable contributions to society beyond personal success.

Reflection Questions: How have you seen the impact of your efforts extend beyond your immediate family? Can you envision ways to amplify this effect in your community?

Conclusion: Your Literacy Legacy

As we turn the final pages of this book, we find ourselves not at an ending but at the beginning of a remarkable journey. The path of family literacy you're embarking on or continuing is one of the most profound and impactful adventures you will ever undertake. Your commitment to fostering a culture of literacy in your family extends far beyond teaching basic skills. You are creating a transformative way of being in the world that will enrich your children's lives in countless ways.

Your family's literacy practices are seeds you're planting in fertile soil. Some will sprout quickly, bringing immediate joy and engagement. Others may take years to fully bloom, perhaps not revealing their full beauty until your children are adults themselves. Every story read, every word written, and each shared conversation about books and ideas nurtures these seeds, helping them grow strong and deep roots. As children's author Emilie Buchwald wisely noted, "Children are made readers on the laps of their parents" (Buchwald, 1992). This simple yet profound statement encapsulates the essence of family literacy. It's not just about the mechanics of reading or the skills of writing; it's about the warmth of connection, the spark of shared discovery, and the gentle guidance of a loving parent or caregiver.

Reading together with children creates powerful learning moments that go far beyond basic reading skills. These shared experiences build emotional bonds while expanding vocabulary and understanding of how stories work. Children learn to follow plot lines, predict what happens next, and understand different perspectives through story characters.

Daily reading together helps children discover new ideas and better understand the world. They learn to connect with different characters' feelings and situations, building empathy and social awareness. Each shared story adds to their knowledge while showing them that reading brings both joy and value to life. Most importantly, these cozy reading moments teach children that books offer endless adventures and discoveries.

Kids who read regularly with family members develop stronger language skills and a deeper understanding of stories. They learn to see reading as both fun and useful, building habits that help them succeed in school and life. These natural reading experiences shape children into confident readers who truly enjoy books and understand their power to teach and entertain.

Your literacy legacy is more than just the books on your shelves or the writing on your walls. It's the culture of curiosity, critical thinking, and love of learning that you're cultivating. It is the family traditions built around stories, the inside jokes referencing favorite characters, and the deep discussions sparked by shared reads. This legacy can shape not just your children's academic success but their worldview, relationships, and future contributions to society.

Nobody's reading journey is perfect, and you will face obstacles along the way. Sometimes, daily responsibilities will disrupt your reading plans, or you might lose your drive to keep going. When doubts creep in, consider what literacy expert Dr. Timothy Shanahan discovered: "The most powerful predictor of children's literacy is not the number of books in the home, or the amount of time spent reading. It is the parents' belief in literacy's importance and commitment to fostering it" (Shanahan, 2019). Your dedication to reading and your conviction that it matters will make the biggest difference. Trust in the cumulative effect of your efforts, knowing that each small act of literacy engagement contributes to a larger, life-changing whole.

Key Takeaways from this chapter:
- Family literacy efforts have far-reaching effects, impacting not just individual children but entire communities and future generations.
- Family literacy's effect extends to social, economic, and civic realms, contributing to a more informed and engaged society.

- Creating a literacy legacy is about more than teaching skills; it's about cultivating a love of learning and a way of engaging with the world.
- Consistency and commitment in family literacy practices are more important than perfection.
- Parents' belief in the importance of literacy is a powerful predictor of children's literacy success.

As you close this book and continue your family's literacy journey, may you be filled with excitement for the adventures that await. Your efforts are not just shaping your children's futures; they contribute to a more literate, thoughtful, and connected world. Here's to the stories you will share, the words you will write, and the lifelong readers and learners you are nurturing. Your literacy legacy starts now, and its impact is boundless!

Further Reading

1. *Come Home: The Reading Brain in a Digital World.* Harper. Wolf, M. (2018). Reader. An exploration of how digital technology is changing the way we read and its implications for child development.
2. *What To Read When: The Books and Stories To Read With Your Child.* Avery. Allyn, P. (2017). A guide to selecting appropriate books for children at different developmental stages.
3. *Raising Kids Who Read: What Parents and Teachers Can Do.* Jossey-Bass. Willingham, D. T. (2015). A research-based approach to fostering a love of reading in children.
4. National Center on Improving Literacy (https://improvingliteracy.org/): A comprehensive resource for parents and educators, offering evidence-based literacy strategies and information.
5. Reading Rockets (https://www.readingrockets.org/): A national multimedia project offering information and resources on how young kids learn to read, why so many struggle, and how caring adults can help.

Practical Exercises

1. **Family Literacy Vision Board:** Create a visual representation of your family's literacy goals and aspirations. Use images, words, and drawings to depict the reading and writing experiences you want to foster in your home. Learning Outcome: Clarifies family literacy goals and creates a visual reminder of your aspirations.
2. **Literacy Environment Audit:** Conduct a "literacy audit" of your home. Note all the places where reading and writing materials are available and identify areas where you could add more literacy-rich elements. Learning Outcome: This will increase awareness of the home literacy environment and identify areas for improvement.
3. **Family Reading Challenge:** Design a month-long family reading challenge. Set individual and family reading goals, create a tracking system, and plan a celebration for when goals are met. Learning Outcome: Encourages consistent reading habits and family engagement in literacy activities.
4. **Literacy Modeling Journal:** Keep a week-long journal of all the times you model literacy behaviors (reading, writing, discussing books, etc.) for your children. Reflect on opportunities to increase visible literacy activities. Learning Outcome: Enhances awareness of parental modeling and identifies opportunities for improvement.
5. **Create a Family Literacy Action Plan:** Develop a concrete plan for implementing literacy strategies in your family. Include short-term and long-term

goals, specific activities, and methods for overcoming potential obstacles. Learning Outcome: Translates learning into actionable steps and creates a family literacy development roadmap.

Endnotes

Adichie, C. N. (2009). *The danger of a single story* [TED Talk]. TED Conferences. https://www.ted.com/talks/chimamanda_All_the_danger_of_a_single_story

Allington, R. L. (2012). Reading volume and reading achievement. *Reading Today, 29*(3), 7.

Allington, R. L. (2019). *The reading crisis: Why poor readers struggle*. Teachers College Press.

Baron, N. (2021). *How We Read Now: Strategic Choices for Print, Screen, and Audio*. Oxford University Press.

Bishop, R. S. (1990). Mirrors, windows, and sliding glass doors. *Perspectives, 6*(3), ix–xi.

Brooks, R. (2018). *The psychology of success: Understanding and cultivating resilience*. Harvard Education Press.

Cummins, J. (2000). *Language, power, and pedagogy: Bilingual children in the crossfire*. Multilingual Matters.

Dehaene, S. (2009). *Reading in the brain: The science and evolution of a human invention*. Viking.

Duke, N. K. (2020). Reading by third grade: A key predictor of high school graduation. *The Reading Teacher, 74*(3), 239-248. https://ila.onlinelibrary.wiley.com/toc/19362714/2021/74/6

Dweck, C. (2006). *Mindset: The new psychology of success*. Random House.

Epstein, J. L. (1995). School/family/community partnerships. *Phi Delta Kappan, 76*(9), 701-712.

García, O., & Wei, L. (2014). *Translanguaging: Language, bilingualism and education*. Palgrave Macmillan.

Gay, G. (2018). *Culturally responsive teaching: Theory, research, and practice* (3rd ed.). Teachers College Press.

Gopnik, A. (2016). *The gardener and the carpenter: What the new science of child development tells us about the relationship between parents and children*. Farrar, Straus and Giroux.

Guernsey, L. (2021). *Screen time: How electronic media affects children from birth to age five*. Basic Books.

Hart, B., & Risley, T. R. (1995). *Meaningful differences in the everyday experience of young American children*. Paul H. Brookes Publishing.

Jenkins, H. (2009). *Confronting the challenges of participatory culture: Media education for the 21st century*. MIT Press.

Johnston, P. H. (2022). *Opening minds: Using language to change lives*. Stenhouse Publishers.

Justice, L. M. (2019). Early literacy development. In D.C. Phillips (Ed.), *Encyclopedia of educational theory and philosophy*. Sage Publications. https://www.sagepub.com/en-us/nam/encyclopedia-of-educational-theory-and-philosophy/book246289

Kraft, M. A., & Rogers, T. (2015). The underutilized potential of teacher-to-parent communication. *Educational*

Researcher, 44(2), 112-126.
https://journals.sagepub.com/doi/10.3102/0034654314558499

Ladson-Billings, G. (2009). *The dreamkeepers: Successful teachers of African American children* (2nd ed.). Jossey-Bass.

Livingstone, S. (2021). The digital environment. *Current Opinion in Psychology, 39*, 72-77.
https://www.sciencedirect.com/science/article/abs/pii/S2352250X21000296

Moats, L. C. (2020). *Teaching reading is rocket science: What expert teachers of reading should know and be able to do*. American Federation of Teachers.
https://www.aft.org/teaching-reading-rocket-science

Neuman, S. B. (2016). *Giving our children a fighting chance: Poverty, literacy, and the development of information capital*. Teachers College Press.

Nieto, S. (2010). *Language, culture, and teaching: Critical perspectives*. Routledge.

Robinson, K. (2006). *Do schools kill creativity?* [TED Talk]. TED Conferences.
https://www.ted.com/talks/ken_robinson_do_schools_kill_creativity

Shanahan, T. (2018). Why children struggle with reading. *Reading Rockets*.
https://www.readingrockets.org/article/why-children-struggle-reading

Snow, C. E. (2017). Early literacy development and instruction: An overview. In K. A. Renninger & I. E. Sigel (Eds.), *Handbook of child psychology* (pp. 1-27). Wiley.

Toffler, A. (1970). *Future shock*. Random House.

Wolf, M. (2018). *Reader, come home: The reading brain in a digital world*. Harper.

Index

A
Adaptive literacy, 315-216,376
Adichie, Chimamanda Ngozi, 195, 253, 372
Allington, Dr. Richard, 124, 346, 372
Augmented Reality (AR), 107, 217, 230, 294, 302, 330

B
Baron, Dr. Naomi, 308, 372
Bilingual education, 132, 198,
Brooks, Dr. Robert, 155, 171, 173, 372

C
Chen, Dr. Lina, 274
Community resources, 76, 182, 218, 276, 285-287, 291-292, 341
Cook, Dr. John, 224
Cummins, Dr. Jim, 132, 180

D
Data literacy, 230, 315-316, 332, 335
Dehaene, Dr. Stanislas, 313, 372
Digital literacy, 8, 11, 35, 67, 105-107, 118, 190, 201-204, 208, 211-212, 218-221, 225-233, 250-251, 264, 275, 284, 314-319, 332-335, 340, 343, 349
Duke, Dr. Nell, 347, 357, 372
Dweck, Dr. Carol, 152, 251-258, 372

E
Early childhood development, 58, 204, 207
Edwards, Dr. Patricia, 123
Environmental print, 61-67, 84, 86, 88
Epstein, Dr. Joyce L., 55, 115, 373

F
Family literacy, 20, 89, 112, 115, 139, 145, 271, 289-295, 317-320, 331-338, 342-345, 354, 362-371
Fontichiaro, Dr. Kristin, 227

G
Gaming in literacy, 328-333
Gay, Dr. Geneva, 195-196, 373
Gopnik, Dr. Alison, 362, 373
Greene, Robert, 293
Guernsey, Dr. Lisa, 74, 348, 373

H
Harris, Dr. Karen R., 246
Heitner, Devorah, 211, 233
Hobbs, Dr. Renee, 225, 228, 233
Home Literacy Environment, 61-62, 67, 85, 276, 370

I
Information literacy, 11-12, 202-203, 236, 238, 257-258, 265

J
Johnston, Dr. Peter, 350, 357, 373
Justice, Dr. Laura, 342, 373

L

Ladson-Billings, Dr. Gloria, 179, 198, 374
Language development, 5, 25-28, 36, 41-46, 52-57, 62, 132, 181, 205
Learning disabilities, 21, 130-131, 139, 147-150, 155, 166, 175
Lee, Dr. Marcus, 301, 316
Literacy difficulties, 147, 160, 167-170, 173-176
Livingstone, Dr. Sonia, 107, 228, 374

M

Media literacy, 11-12, 202, 229, 250, 257, 262, 322-323
Mitra, Dr. Sugata, 359
Moats, Dr. Louisa, 150, 170, 176, 374
Moje, Dr. Elizabeth Birr, 352
Multilingual, 36, 56, 59, 73, 86, 179, 181-184, 189, 196-199, 279, 284, 286, 317-324, 332-335

N

Neuman, Dr. Susan B., 67, 71, 268, 291, 374
Neumann, 218
Nieto, Dr. Sonia, 183, 198, 374

O

Oatley, Dr. Keith, 253
Ogle, Dr. Donna, 93
Online safety, 12, 106, 202-203, 211, 215

P

Parent-teacher, 26, 81, 126, 135, 137
Parental involvement, 21, 48, 206

R
Reading strategies, 111, 119, 144, 170

S
School-home connections, 114-146
Shaywitz, Dr. Sally, 131, 147, 160, 176
Snow, Dr. Catherine, 54, 91, 269-270, 338, 375

T
Technology in education, 76, 234
Trelease, Jim, 63, 66, 86, 100
Turner, Dr. Kristen Hawley, 105, 201
Twain, Mark, 10

V
Virtual Reality (VR), 74, 237, 302, 331

W
Wolf, Dr. Maryanne, 33, 111, 159, 176, 262, 280, 334, 369, 375
Writing development, 79, 358

www.ingramcontent.com/pod-product-compliance
Lightning Source LLC
LaVergne TN
LVHW041741060526
838201LV00046B/870